JAMES Moore

Law for the Layman

About the Author

George Gordon Coughlin received his B.O.E. and LL.B. degrees from Syracuse University. He was admitted to the New York State Bar in 1922 and has been admitted to practice before five federal courts. Mr. Coughlin is a former president of the Broome County Bar Association, the Federation of Bar Associations of the Sixth Judicial District of New York, and the New York State Bar Association. He is the coauthor of *You and Your Car Insurance*.

Law for the Layman

George Gordon Coughlin

MEMBER, THE NEW YORK STATE BAR

Harper & Row, Publishers, New York
Grand Rapids, Philadelphia, St. Louis, San Francisco
London, Singapore, Sydney, Tokyo, Toronto

The original title of this book is
Your Introduction to Law.

LIBRARY OF CONGRESS CATALOG CARD NUMBER: 75–547

STANDARD BOOK NUMBER: 06–465020–0

91 92 93 OPM 20 19 18 17 16 15 14 13

To Edith

Preface

Everyone in a democracy should familiarize himself with the laws regulating his daily life. Obviously, he cannot know all the law, but he should know the fundamentals for his own protection.

In ancient Greece and Rome, small boys were obliged to commit to memory the laws of their countries. In our country, students must become familiar at least with the basic law of the land, and immigrants are required to learn some of the basic tenets of the law before being naturalized. Both naturalized and native-born citizens would greatly benefit, however, from learning more about the practical workings of our public and private laws, for in a democracy there is a fiction that people are "presumed to know the law." Actually, few do.

Our laws are complex, but our civilization is so interwoven with complexities that the laws cannot be made simple. After forty years of legal practice, I have attempted to clarify some of the law's workings in an effort to help the layman to better understand legal fundamentals and procedures. This book only scratches the surface of the subject. Neither it nor any single volume can state the law as a whole.

My efforts here do not constitute a law-made-easy book or a do-it-yourself book. (Do it yourself—unless you are trained in the law—and you are headed for trouble.) The idea of "every man his own lawyer" is a foolish one, as foolish as expecting every man to be successful as his own surgeon, dentist, or electrical engineer.

The aim of this book is to stimulate the layman's interest in the elementary principles by which we must all live, in the rules which govern our American society. Read this book, then, for self-protection, education, and sharpened awareness of when you need legal advice.

GEORGE G. COUGHLIN

This publication is designed to provide accurate and authoritative information in regard to the subject matter covered. It is sold with the understanding that the publisher is not engaged in rendering legal, accounting or other professional services. If legal advice or other expert assistance is required, the services of a competent professional person should be sought.

—from a Declaration of Principles jointly adopted by a Committee of Publishers and Associations on Bar Co-operation and the American Bar Association's Standing Committee on Unauthorized Practice of Law.

Contents

1
The Legal Profession

The rules that govern our complicated civilization are known as *law*. Law is interpreted and administered by lawyers. Because they are the stewards of the rights and obligations of all citizens, they are public servants and make a unique and fundamentally important contribution to American society.

THE AMERICAN LAWYER: ETHICS AND SERVICE

The standards of the American lawyer are high. He must meet rigid character and educational requirements established by the courts in order to become a member of the legal profession, and in daily practice he must conform to a rigorous code of principles and practice.

Despite the high character of lawyers and despite the great trust which has been placed in them in public office and private life, famous writers and wits from Benjamin Franklin to Mark Twain have delighted in poking fun at the legal profession. Even today it is possible to find many persons who believe that lawyers do not tell the truth, that they are paid to lie. This is not true. A lawyer is sworn to be loyal to his client, but this loyalty does not include the obligation to manufacture false testimony or to permit bribery or perjury. Elihu Root, one of the greatest public servants in American history, stated, "For every detractor, we find a thousand men and women who trust their lawyers implicitly in their most intimate and vital affairs, with the frankness and confidence of personal friendship, and who are justified in their trust."

Complaints against lawyers are said to stem from complaints against the administration of justice. The primary end of law is justice, and every citizen feels he knows what is just. He would like to be able to go to court and tell his story without having to employ a lawyer. But when two or more individuals have a dispute, each one

1

has a different idea of what constitutes justice. Instead of solving their dispute with fists or revolvers, they are compelled by the law to resolve their differences in court; in order to do this, each one needs to hire a lawyer to explain the complicated laws involved in their dispute.

In every profession there are dishonest, unethical practitioners, but the number of unscrupulous lawyers is infinitesimal. There are more than 385,000 lawyers in the United States, and less than 1 percent has been found guilty of crimes or unethical conduct. Most lawyers have great personal integrity and live up to the high standards of ethics imposed upon them by their profession.

The Organized Bar

The term *organized bar* refers to members of bar associations as distinguished from lawyers as individuals. A bar association generally is established for the purpose of advancing the science of law and promoting the administration of justice and upholding the standards of the legal profession.

In 1870 the Association of the Bar of the City of New York was organized. Almost immediately the association came in conflict with the Tweed Ring (which then dominated New York politics), for an investigation it had recommended resulted in the impeachment of two judges and the resignation of a third. This action played an important part in the downfall of the Ring and established public confidence in that bar association.

The American Bar Association was organized in Saratoga Springs, New York, in July 1878. Today, after many struggles and a reorganization, the American Bar Association is a potent force in upholding and defending the Constitution and in promoting the public good. The work of the American Bar Association is broken down into various subjects and is handled by sections. The sections embrace the following fields: administrative law, antitrust law, corporation, banking and business law, criminal law, family law, individual rights and responsibilities, insurance negligence and compensation law, international and comparative law, judicial administration, labor relations law, legal education and admission to the bar, local government law, natural resources law, patent, trademark, and copyright law, public contract law, public utility law, real property, probate and trust law and tax law. Each state has its own bar association, as do large cities and many counties. The Association of the Bar of the City of New York is regarded as a model for all other city or county bar associations.

The organized bar activity polices its own ranks. Bar associations of the United States have successfully resisted pressure, political or otherwise, to go easy on those lawyers against whom disciplinary measures should be taken.

Ethics and Discipline in the Profession

Dean John H. Wigmore, one of America's great legal writers, once said,

> This living spirit of the profession, which limits it yet uplifts it as a livelihood, has been customarily known by the vague term "legal ethics." . . . An apprentice must hope and expect to make full acquaintance with this body of traditions, as his manual of equipment, without which he cannot do his part to keep the law on the level of a profession.*

The term *legal ethics* has been defined as "that branch of moral science which treats of the duties which a member of the legal profession owes to the public, the court, his professional brethren, and his client."†

In his authoritative book, *Legal Ethics,*‡ Mr. Henry S. Drinker examines the four duties of a lawyer. In discussing a lawyer's obligation to the public, Mr. Drinker says that just criticisms of the bar are the unwillingness of lawyers to expose their colleagues' abuses and the reluctance of judges to disbar, suspend, or even publicly reprimand such lawyers. He attributes much of the public suspicion of lawyers to the realization that most of the abuses of which lawyers are guilty could be eliminated if the bar and the courts were constantly alert and willing to do their full duty in this regard. Mr. Drinker cites the Canons of Professional Ethics (now superseded by the Code of Professional Responsibility), which places upon lawyers the obligations (to endeavor) to prevent political considerations from outweighing judicial fitness in the selection of judges, to represent the poor and the indigent, and the duty not to stir up litigation. "Ambulance chasing" (solicitation of automobile ac-

---

* Albert P. Blaustein, *et al.*, *The American Lawyer* (Chicago: University of Chicago Press, 1954), p. 240.

† Francis Rawle, ed., *Bouvier's Law Dictionary* (St. Paul, Minn.: West Publishing Co., 1914).

‡ Henry S. Drinker, *Legal Ethics* (New York: The William Nelson Cromwell Foundation and Columbia University Press, 1953), pp. 59–64.

cident and negligence claims) is an example of stirring up litigation. Undoubtedly, this abuse is prevalent in various communities, and the bar and the courts have from time to time had difficulty in stamping it out.

For years the bible on the subject of ethical conduct in the legal profession was the Canons of Professional Ethics, which had its origin in 1887. In 1964 the American Bar Association began a five-year study to update and modernize the Canons of Professional Ethics. In 1970 a new set of rules known as the Code of Professional Responsibility was established.

A lawyer is prohibited by the Code of Professional Responsibility from:

1. Recommending employment of himself or his partner or associate to a nonlawyer.

2. Accepting employment from a layman to whom he has given unsolicited advice that the layman should obtain counsel or take legal action, except that a lawyer may accept employment of a close friend or relative of client or former client.

3. Holding himself out publicly as a specialist or as one limiting his practice except (1) a lawyer admitted to practice before the United States Patent Office may use the designation "patent attorney" or "trademark attorney," (2) a lawyer actively engaged in admiralty practice may use the designation "admiralty lawyer" on his letterhead or office sign, and (3) a lawyer may permit his name to be listed in a lawyer referral system (explained below) according to his specialized field of law.

4. Accepting employment on behalf of a person who brings a legal action merely for the purpose of harassing or maliciously injuring any person.

5. Assisting a nonlawyer in the unauthorized practice of the law or practicing law in another jurisdiction (namely, a state or foreign country) where to do so would be in violation of the regulations of the profession in that jurisdiction.

6. Sharing legal fees with a nonlawyer or forming a partnership with a nonlawyer if any of the activities of the partnership consist of the practice of law. The reason for the prohibition against the practice of law by or with laymen is the need of the public for integrity and competence of those who are trained and licensed to perform legal services. The public can be better assured of responsibility and competence if the practice of law is confined to those who are subject to the requirements and regulations imposed upon the legal profession.

7. Revealing a confidence or secret of his client or using the confidence or secret of his client to a disadvantage of the client or using a secret or confidence of his client for the advantage of himself or a third person.

8. Accepting employment if the interest of his prospective client will conflict with his own financial or personal interest.

9. Handling a legal matter which he knows he is not competent to

handle without associating with him a lawyer who is competent to handle it.

10. Handling a legal matter without preparation.

11. Knowingly using perjured testimony or false evidence.

12. Knowingly making a false statement of fact.

13. Participating in the creation of evidence if he knows the evidence is false.

14. Counseling or assisting his client in conduct that the lawyer knows to be illegal or fraudulent.

15. Knowingly engaging in illegal conduct.

16. Communicating with a party he knows to be represented by a lawyer unless he has the consent of the other lawyer.

17. Threatening criminal charges solely to obtain an advantage in a civil matter.

18. Stating any matter in court that he has no reasonable basis to believe is relevant to the case or that would not be supported by evidence.

19. Asserting in court his personal knowledge of the facts in the case except where he is testifying as a witness.

20. Engaging in undignified or discourteous conduct which is degrading to a court.

21. Communicating before the trial of a case with the panel from which a jury will be selected.

22. Communicating privately either directly or indirectly during the trial of a case with any member of the jury.

23. Suppressing in a court case any evidence which his client has a legal obligation to reveal or produce.

24. Advising or causing a person to leave the jurisdiction of the court for the purpose of making himself unavailable as a witness.

25. Paying or offering to pay compensation to a witness contingent upon the content of his testimony or the outcome of the case, except that a lawyer may advance expenses reasonably incurred by a witness in attending to testify in court and reasonable compensation to a witness for the loss of time attending or testifying and a reasonable fee for professional service of an expert witness.

26. Giving or lending anything of value to a judge, official, or employee of a court.

27. Using his position in public office to obtain or attempt to obtain any special advantages in legislative matters where such action is not in the public interest or using his public position to influence a court to act in behalf of himself or his client.

28. Mingling his clients' funds with his own.

29. Accepting compensation, commissions, rebates, or other advantages from others without full disclosure to his client and without his client's consent.

Practice and procedure for disciplining lawyers varies from state to state. In almost all jurisdictions, however, anyone may file a complaint concerning a lawyer's misconduct. Most state bar associations and many county associations have grievance committees, which are charged with receiving and investigating complaints, making preliminary findings, and, if they warrant it, referring complaints to the appropriate court. The court rules on the lawyer's conduct and may suspend him from practice or even disbar him. In some states court proceedings are instituted and conducted by the attorney general of the state or by the county attorney.

A lawyer may be suspended from practice or disbarred if his conduct indicates that he cannot be trusted to advise and act for clients and also in those cases where his conduct indicates that he would cast serious reflection on the dignity of the court and on the reputation of the profession if he were allowed to continue to practice.

Bar associations are striving for stricter adherence to the Code of Professional Responsibility. The question is whether greater adherence should be brought about by educational processes or through harsher disciplinary action. Surveys throughout the country indicate that in some areas disciplinary action is more or less futile, for only the most brazen violations are prosecuted and grievance committee members are often too lenient with offenders.

Effective disciplinary action is difficult because most violations are accomplished in secret, making evidence hard to obtain. The difficulty of disciplinary action was increased by differing interpretations of the old Canons of Ethics. Grievance and ethics committees throughout the United States have interpreted the meaning and application of the canons in different ways, although, generally, the interpretations made by the committee of the American Bar Association are considered the most authoritative. It appears, then, that a more widespread understanding of the Code of Professional Responsibility should be attempted by education (advising new members of the ethical standards of the profession) and by publicity (making the public aware of the high standard of the bar).

Legal Aid and Other Services

Legal aid is the organized effort of a bar association and the community to provide the services of lawyers free or for token charges to persons who cannot afford to pay attorneys' fees. The aim of legal aid is that no citizen because of his financial hardship be denied protection and benefits under the law. This goal has been achieved in substantial measure in the large cities, such as New York and Chicago; in smaller cities, however, there is much to be accomplished in providing legal assistance to the indigent. The enlightened attitude of the organized bar has been responsible for the great increase in the number of legal aid offices established.

In determining eligibility for legal aid, family income, health, property ownership, and similar factors are considered. The Legal Aid Society of New York sets up this test: "Could a competent private attorney be found to take the case for whatever fee the case might yield?" If one would take the case, then the society refers the person seeking assistance to a private attorney. A large part of legal aid work is devoted to tasks of counseling, mediation, and drafting papers.

The term *legal aid* does not include the private donation of free service to deserving people by lawyers. Again, organized legal aid should not be confused with the assignment by the court of counsel to represent a needy person in a criminal case. In this situation, the lawyer's compensation is fixed by the court and is paid by the state. In addition, certain communities support the so-called public defender system; the *public defender* is paid by the state to defend indigent persons accused of crimes.

Legal aid should also not be confused with lawyer reference plans through which bar associations bring persons needing legal advice into contact with lawyers who are willing to advise them. The lawyer reference plan is simply a means of helping individuals find lawyers to serve them for modest fees.

THE AMERICAN LAWYER: TRAINING AND SPECIALIZATION

In colonial days so-called attorneys were uneducated minor court officers, such as deputy sheriffs, clerks, and justices, who fostered litigation for petty court fees. Gradually, however, a system of legal training began to develop.

Legal Education in the United States

In the early days of our republic lawyers studied the works of the leading authorities in Europe and England, particularly *Blackstone's Commentaries*. Blackstone's influence is said to have resulted in the establishment of chairs of law at several American universities; yet the main education of lawyers remained for some time in office apprenticeships.

Lawyers of the last century were still reluctant to accept the idea of university training. They clung to the belief that legal education was nothing more than the mastering of a craft, the skills for which had to be passed on from the practitioner to the novice. Supreme Court Justice Joseph Story criticized the narrowness of the legal instruction at that time and pointed to the need for knowledge of the principles of law and broad study liberalized by acquaintance with philosophy and the wisdom of ancient and modern times.

The first university school of law was founded in Harvard in 1815; Yale followed in 1826 with its law school. In 1850 there were fifteen university law schools in the United States and in 1870, thirty-one. Moreover, in 1870, Dean Christopher C. Langdell of Harvard established the case method, a system of teaching law through the study of judicial decisions. Some law schools continued to use the textbook method of teaching for many years, but today the case system is still accepted and used in almost every well-recognized law school in the country.

High Standards of Modern American Law Schools

The American Bar Association in 1921, led by such men as Elihu Root and William Howard Taft, recommended that all law colleges require of students the following conditions for admission to the bar: (1) at least two years of college study before attending law school, (2) at least a three-year course in law school, (3) full-time attendance at law school and instruction by full-time teachers, and (4) examination by public authority (that is, graduation from law school should not automatically determine fitness for admission to the bar).

In 1923 the American Bar Association published its first list of approved law schools. It became apparent, however, that it was impossible to evaluate the qualifications of law schools without personal inspection. In 1927 advisers of the American Bar Association began inspecting law schools and assisting them with their problems. They also began urging the state and local bar associations to adopt the American Bar Association standards for admission to the bar. As a result of these activities law schools in 1952 increased to three the number of years of acceptable college study necessary for admission.

Postadmission Legal Education

A hundred years ago when a lawyer completed his legal education and was admitted to the bar, he assumed that his schooling was
over. The modern lawyer, on the other hand, appreciates the need
for continuing his legal education. Keeping up with current reading
is not sufficient. Various organizations such as the American Law
Institute, the Practicing Law Institute, and state and local bar associations give regular postadmission courses of instruction. Each
year the Practicing Law Institute conducts courses for thousands of
lawyers through Saturday forums, summer sessions, home study programs, and published monographs. In addition, the American Law
Institute supervises postadmission legal education programs on a
national level.

Classification of Lawyers

The four main fields in which lawyers serve are (1) private
practice of the law, (2) government service, (3) direct employment
by private business, and (4) employment by labor unions. More
than 75 percent of the total number of lawyers in the United States
are in the first category, private practice. Unlike English lawyers
who are either *solicitors* (office lawyers) or *barristers* (courtroom
lawyers), all American lawyers are licensed to be both office and
courtroom lawyers.

Private practitioners may be grouped in scores of classifications
of which the following are typical but not coequal: general practitioners, office, trial, patent, tax, corporation, real estate, or estate
lawyers. A lawyer employed by a business firm may be counsel for
the corporation (sometimes designated as "house counsel") or a
member of the law department of the particular firm.

Lawyers serving the government directly may be employed at the
federal, state, or local level.

The so-called labor lawyer may work either for private industry
or for labor unions. In the early days of the labor movement in
this country there was some prejudice against lawyers who represented unions. The stigma has gradually disappeared, and the integrity of the labor lawyer is now recognized. Lawyers may also be
district attorneys, public defenders, law enforcement officers or work
as staff members in the judicial branch of a government, or they
may be judges, legislators, mayors, or governors.

THE AMERICAN LAWYER: PRACTICE

The average person is more familiar with the work of physicians and dentists than with the work of lawyers. An individual usually consults a physician or dentist regularly, but he may consult a lawyer only once in his lifetime.

The Work of the Average Practitioner

What, then, are the everyday activities of the American lawyer? Whether he practices alone, in partnership, or as a member of a law firm, he may perform any or all the following tasks. He may assist clients in the purchase, sale, leasing, and mortgaging of houses, buildings, and other real estate. He may give advice through estate planning, preparing wills, and handling general estate matters. He may also give advice concerning the tax consequences (including income, estate, and gift taxes) of certain proposed transactions and prepare federal and state tax returns. He may advise businessmen about the advantages and disadvantages of the different forms of business organization—selecting the form which would be most advantageous in a particular circumstance. He may continue this sort of activity by organizing partnerships, corporations, and other forms of business and by preparing all the documents needed for purchasing and doing business in various situations. He may provide counsel in labor relations cases, including such matters as union negotiations, union contracts, minimum wages, and labor laws in general. He may handle negotiations for the settlement of controversies; when negotiations fail he may institute legal proceedings to recover damages for wrongful acts or for the enforcement of legal rights or, when representing a person or persons against whom legal proceedings have been started, enter defense in behalf of the person or persons sued. He may advise and defend those accused of crimes. He may attempt to reconcile estranged husbands and wives and, if necessary, institute or defend legal proceedings for divorce, separation, and annulment. He may prepare documents of every conceivable kind for his clients. He may appear before administrative tribunals and legislative bodies.

It is almost impossible to list all the activities and services which lawyers provide, for their functions are almost as varied as the fields of human endeavor. It has been said that the work of the lawyer is (1) to be a wise counselor, (2) to be an advocate, (3) to work toward the improvement of the profession, (4) to answer calls to public office, and (5) to help form public opinion.

Selection of a Lawyer

Too many individuals wait until they are in serious trouble before seeking legal assistance. Individuals should become aware of the legal difficulties which may confront them. For example, one should realize that one should never sign an important document without having it examined by a lawyer, nor should one accept legal advice from those without proper training.

Before engaging a lawyer, one should carefully check his qualifications, experience, and reputation. One's lawyer should be a person of character and integrity, the lawyer in his community that one would most trust.

If the individual has a special type of legal problem, he should consider lawyers experienced in that particular field. If, for example, he wants to have a will drawn, he should choose a lawyer who specializes in the handling of estate matters. He may also want to ask his banker or a reliable merchant or the president of the local bar association for assistance in selecting a lawyer experienced in a particular area of law.

Beware of lawyers who are guilty of unethical practices. For instance, it is unethical for a lawyer to solicit automobile accident cases. A person who will not conform to the rules of his own profession is not to be trusted and, of course, should not be employed or retained.

Most experienced lawyers apply the principles of *preventive law* to many problems and, when feasible, encourage the settlement of controversies out of court, for litigation is costly and time consuming. These lawyers know the real service they can render their clients is keeping them from going to court, even though their fees are smaller when certain types of cases are settled out of court. For example, many lawyers try to reunite estranged couples and to prevent families from being broken up by divorce or annulment. Whenever a lawyer tries to provide a service of this type, he is performing a public service, and in the strictest sense he is fulfilling his obligation to society.

Once an individual has selected a lawyer, he should decide about consulting or retaining (employing) the person. In *consulting* a lawyer an individual simply goes to the lawyer's office for advice.

Consulting an attorney does not obligate him to give the attorney the case. When an individual *retains* a lawyer, however, he does put his problem in the lawyer's hands.

Determination of Lawyers' Fees

When a prospective client consults a lawyer he should expect to pay him a fee for his advice. The fees charged by lawyers are largely determined by the cost of doing business and by the competition. Many individuals are under the false impression that one visit to a lawyer for advice would cost a great deal. Actually, consulting a lawyer costs no more than a consultation with a physician. A lawyer's consultation fee may be $10, $25, or $50, depending on the amount of time spent with the client, the amount of research involved in obtaining the answer to the problem, the lawyer's experience and standing in his profession, and the size of the community in which he practices. It is sensible for the client to ask the lawyer in advance what the consultation fee will be.*

There are several methods of paying a lawyer, if he is retained to handle a particular case. Probably the two most widely used means for paying legal fees are (1) the contingent fee and (2) the flat fee.

In a *contingent fee* arrangement the client and the lawyer agree that the lawyer is willing to handle the case for a percentage—for instance, one-third—of what is obtained in settlement of the case or through litigation. Payment under the contingent fee agreement is conditioned on success; that is, the fee is paid only if the lawyer wins the case. If he fails, the client pays nothing except the out-of-pocket expenses the lawyer has advanced for his client.

The Code of Professional Responsibility has this to say on the subject of contingent fees:

Contingent fee arrangements in civil cases have long been commonly accepted in the United States in proceedings to enforce claims. . . . Because of the human relationships involved and the unique character of the proceedings, contingent fee arrangements in domestic relation cases are

---

* Bar associations in more than 250 communities of the United States have lawyer reference plans so that a person who needs the advice of a lawyer may phone the local bar association, which will refer the prospective client to a local lawyer (knowledgeable in a particular field). The prospective client will be told in advance the lawyer's fee for the conference. The average fee is $10.00 for a half-hour consultation.

rarely justified. . . . Public policy properly condemns contingent fee arrangements in criminal cases.

The fundamental reason for the use of contingent fee contracts is to assist those who have no funds with which to hire lawyers. Under certain circumstances clients prefer contingent fee plans because they do not have to pay fees if the cases are lost; lawyers like them because they are generally rewarded with larger fees when their cases are successful. A contingent fee arrangement is not the only one under which a lawyer will handle a case, as many people seem to believe. A client may reject the contingent fee plan.

If an individual feels that his case is a sure thing, that it will never go to trial (and thereby entail the high trial expenses), he may wish simply to pay the lawyer a *flat fee* for his time and advice. The payment of a flat fee does not depend on the outcome of the case: the client has to pay the fee—win, lose, or draw.

The Code of Professional Responsibility sets forth the following factors as guides for determining the reasonableness of lawyers' fees:

1. The time and labor required, the novelty and difficulty of the questions involved, and the skill requisite to perform the legal service properly
2. The likelihood, if apparent to the client, that the acceptance of the particular employment will preclude other employment by the lawyer
3. The fee customarily charged in the locality for similar legal services
4. The amount involved and the results obtained
5. The time limitations imposed by the client or by the circumstances
6. The nature and length of the professional relationship with the client
7. The experience, reputation, and ability of the lawyer or lawyers performing the services
8. Whether the fee is fixed or contingent

2

The Court System
in the United States

In spite of the complexity of American civilization, our system of jurisprudence continues to settle with justice the many different types of legal disputes that arise out of modern living. And the pronouncements of our highest court are accepted everywhere in this country.

Once a question of law has been deliberately examined and decided in the United States, it is binding on the courts within the jurisdiction; this is the principle of *stare decisis*. Under the American court (or English court) system (and unlike civil and other systems) this doctrine is considered indispensable to the administration of justice. Although it is in general bound by this doctrine along with the lesser courts, the United States Supreme Court, in its wisdom, sometimes tips over a long-established line of decisions and establishes a new principle. Its decisions are binding on all other courts.

TYPES OF COURTS

A *court* is a place where justice is administered. It may consist of a judge and a jury or only a judge and a clerk, or it may be a tribunal including a number of judges. The words *judge* and *court* are sometimes loosely interchanged, but they are not necessarily synonymous.

A *term of court* is the period fixed by law for the holding of court sessions. Although each state legislature has the power to set the schedule, very often the designation of time for holding court sessions is left to the court itself. Terms of court may be regular or special; the latter are held for a special purpose, usually for the hearing of nonjury cases.

Courts of Original and Appellate Jurisdiction

*Jurisdiction** has been defined as the authority of a court to hear and determine a case. A *court of original jurisdiction* is one in which a legal proceeding is first started. A *court of appellate jurisdiction* is one which reviews cases removed by appeal from a lower court.

Courts of Law and Courts of Equity

A *court of law* is one which administers justice according to the principles and the forms of common law. A *court of equity* is one which administers justice according to the rules and principles of equity. (The term *equity* is a survival from ancient English times when litigants felt the harshness and rigidity of the common law and, therefore, appealed to the king's chancellor for special consideration [justice] based on equitable principles.) Many states have abolished the distinction between courts of law and equity.

Courts of Record and Courts Not of Record

A *court of record* was originally defined as one where the acts and judicial proceedings were enrolled permanently on parchment; today a court of record may be defined as a superior court that keeps a permanent record of its proceedings and that may have power to fine or imprison. A *court not of record* is an inferior court that has no power to fine or imprison and that does not record proceedings.

Civil and Criminal Courts

Civil courts are those which are established to decide disputes between persons in their private capacity, whether they be individuals, partnerships, or corporations. Sometimes civil courts decide disputes between private persons and governments or between branches of the government. *Criminal courts* are those established for the determination of and punishment of crimes and misdemeanors.

---

* There is perhaps no word in legal terminology so frequently used in a general and a vague sense as the word "jurisdiction." There are many kinds of jurisdiction, among them territorial, civil, and criminal, plus jurisdiction over the person, jurisdiction over property, and many others.

THE FEDERAL JUDICIAL SYSTEM

The Constitution of the United States provides, "the judicial power of the United States shall be vested in one Supreme Court and in such inferior courts as the Congress may, from time to time, ordain and establish." Judges in federal courts are appointed for life and can be removed only if impeached for gross misconduct by the House of Representatives and convicted by the Senate.

The federal judicial system consists of the following courts:

The Supreme Court of the United States, holding sessions in Washington, D. C., and consisting of nine judges, is the court of final resort. It hears appeals on federal questions from circuit courts or the highest state courts, but it hears only such cases as it deems necessary to the public interest.

Courts of appeal, one for each of ten circuits in the United States, are courts of appellate jurisdiction. Each court of appeal has five or six judges. These courts were formerly called and, hence, are sometimes now referred to as "circuit courts of appeal."

District courts have been set up in each of the fifty states and the District of Columbia; there are eighty-nine in all. Each of these courts, as a rule, has jurisdiction over a state or part of a state.

The *court of claims* is the court in which suits against the government of the United States are heard.

THE STATE JUDICIAL SYSTEMS

Each of the fifty states is to a great extent a law unto itself, because each of the original thirteen colonies insisted that it had the right to run its own internal affairs. Legal authorities differ in their opinions about whether the legislature or the courts should determine the detailed rules governing the conduct of legal actions and proceedings. In certain states the powers to make rules are vested in the legislature; in others the courts, by convention of judges, adopt specific rules for legal procedure.

State judicial systems consist of the following courts:

Courts of original jurisdiction, as indicated above, are those in which a legal action or a proceeding may be started. Courts exercising original jurisdiction may be divided into two groups: those of general or superior jurisdiction and those of limited, inferior, or special jurisdiction.

Courts of general or superior jurisdiction have different names in the various states. In some states they are called circuit courts. In other states they are called district courts, superior courts, or courts of common pleas. In some states, all courts of record are consolidated into one court. (See list of courts by state at the end of this chapter.)

Courts of special, limited, or inferior jurisdiction are not set up uniformly in the state judicial systems. Some states have special courts to handle the estates of deceased persons; these are often called probate courts, orphans' courts, or surrogates' courts. A few states have courts of claims that have jurisdiction over claims against the state, although in the majority of cases states cannot be sued. Almost all states have special courts, such as juvenile courts, courts of crimes, police courts, domestic relations courts, courts of tax appeals, justice courts, municipal courts, and city courts.

MOST SUITS BROUGHT AT STATE LEVEL

When does an aggrieved person bring his suit in a federal court and when does he bring his suit in a state court? In almost all cases a person seeking justice brings his suit in a state court in the state in which he lives.

In order for the suit to be brought in a federal district court, it is necessary to show that the suit would be between citizens of different states or between a citizen and an alien, or that the suit involves a question arising under the laws or Constitution of the United States (called a federal question), and that in civil cases the amount involved is at least $10,000. Federal courts also have jurisdiction over admiralty, maritime, bankruptcy, patent, copyright, postal, internal revenue, and a variety of other matters. When the suit has been brought before a federal court and if after a federal district court has made a final decision a litigant still feels that justice has not been reached, he may appeal to the court of appeals. The decision of the court of appeals is final unless appealed to the Supreme Court.

Sometimes an irate litigant may say that he will carry his case to the United States Supreme Court, and he may desire very strongly to do so. This does not mean, however, that he is entitled to have his case heard there. Many thousands of cases are heard in the United States every year, but only a few hundred get to the Supreme Court. In a few very special cases the Supreme Court will issue what is known as a writ of certiorari to the court below; in this way the case will be brought before it, and it will review the decision of the court of appeals or another lower court.

JURISDICTION OF STATE COURTS

In order for a case to be properly brought in a state court, the court must have (1) jurisdiction of the subject matter of the action and (2) jurisdiction of the parties to the lawsuit. A state court action may involve an injury to a person or to property, a breach of contract, the determination of title to real estate, or a score of other matters.

Generally, jurisdiction is acquired by the court of the state where the claim (called in law the "cause of action") arose. The theory is that all other elements being equal, the place where the cause of action accrues determines jurisdiction, but in practice this is regarded as a platitude with many exceptions.

In bringing suit the first thing to determine is whether an action is local or transitory. A *transitory action* is one which may be brought in any state regardless of where the cause of action arose. Almost everywhere actions for damages, personal injury, property damage, or for breach of contract are regarded as transitory actions. Certain other actions are regulated by state statutes and are called *local actions*. For example, the law of Pennsylvania gave abutting landowners the right to sue a canal company for injuries to property resulting from the overflow of the canal; this was held to be a purely local action. Most actions involving real estate may be brought only in the state in which the real estate is located.

A number of states require litigants in disputes involving trifling amounts to bring their suits in inferior courts. Hence, cases involving less than a specified amount (for instance, $500) may not be brought in a superior court. In most states constitutional and statutory provisions restrict the jurisdiction of lesser courts (such as justice courts, municipal courts, county courts) to certain specified amounts. For example, if a particular city court is limited in jurisdiction to cases involving not more than $1,000 and if a suit is brought in that court for $3,000, the case is dismissed because the court does not have jurisdiction of the subject matter.

An essential requirement in the action is that the court obtain jurisdiction of the parties: Without jurisdiction of the parties, the court is powerless to settle a legal controversy. Broadly speaking, in order for the court to obtain jurisdiction over a defendant in a lawsuit, it is necessary that the defendant be personally present within the state so that he may receive service of a summons or other court process. (See Chapter 3 for proceedings in commencement of actions.) There is, however, a broad class of exceptions that allows state courts jurisdiction in an action against a nonresident if he happens to be within the state or if he voluntarily submits to the jurisdiction of the court. If the nonresident has real or personal property within the state, the court may acquire jurisdiction by issuing an attachment on the property within the state. In most states where the defendant owns real property that is the subject of the action, the court may serve the nonresident defendant by "substituted service" or "service by publication." *(Substituted service* may be by a court order which requires the defendant owning property within the state to be served by mail and also by publication of a notice in the newspapers in the area where his property is situated.) Then, there is a special class of cases concerning nonresident motorists passing through a state, who are generally deemed to have appointed the secretary of state of the state where an accident takes place to be their agent and, thus, receive service of summons in behalf of nonresidents.

CONFLICTS IN COURT JURISDICTION

Fortunately, considering the hundreds of thousands of court cases, there are relatively few cases where there is a conflict of jurisdiction among the courts of several states or between the state and federal courts. There is a basic rule of comity between states which helps eliminate many conflicts among the laws of several states. *(Comity* is the recognition that one state gives to the laws of another; it is not a matter of right, but rather a matter of courtesy and goodwill.) Therefore, the court in one state generally will recognize proceedings of the court of another state, and when the courts of one state have first taken jurisdiction of a controversy, the courts of a second state will usually not interfere.

On the other hand, a federal court will interfere and assert its proper jurisdiction when a state court has acted in a matter given by the Constitution of the United States or the federal statutes to the protection of the federal courts. In other words, state courts cannot invade a field which has been given by federal law to its own courts. For example, the state courts have no jurisdiction in admiralty cases or in matters arising under the patent or copyright laws of the United States nor in bankruptcy matters, interstate commerce, nor matters affecting the property or territory of the United States.

Courts of Original Jurisdiction and Appellate Courts

STATES	APPELLATE COURTS*	COURTS OF ORIGINAL JURISDICTION*
Alabama	Supreme Court, Court of Appeals	Circuit Courts, County Courts
Alaska	Supreme Court	Superior Court
Arizona	Supreme Court, Court of Appeals	Superior Courts
Arkansas	Supreme Court	Circuit Courts, Chancery Courts, County Courts, Common Pleas Courts
California	Supreme Court, District Court of Appeals	Superior Courts, Conciliation Courts, Small Claims Courts
Colorado	Supreme Court	District Courts, Superior Courts, County Courts, Small Claims Courts
Connecticut	Supreme Court	Superior Court, Circuit Courts, Courts of Common Pleas
Delaware	Supreme Court	Court of Chancery, Superior Court, Courts of Common Pleas
Florida	Supreme Court, District Courts of Appeals	Circuit Courts, County Courts Small Claims Courts, Civil Courts of Record
Georgia	Supreme Court, Court of Appeals	Superior Courts, County Courts
Hawaii	Supreme Court	Circuit Courts
Idaho	Supreme Court	District Courts
Illinois	Supreme Court, Appellate Courts	Circuit Courts, Court of Claims County Courts
Indiana	Supreme Court, Court of Appeals	Superior Courts, Circuit Courts
Iowa	Supreme Court	District Courts, Superior Courts
Kansas	Supreme Court	District Courts, County Courts
Kentucky	Court of Appeals	Circuit Courts, Quarterly Courts, County Courts
Louisiana	Supreme Court of Louisiana, Court of Appeals	District Courts
Maine	Supreme Judicial Court of Maine	Superior Courts, State District Courts

* Not including justices of the peace; probate or orphans' courts; police or magistrate's courts; domestic relations, family, children's, or juvenile courts; or city, municipal, or other inferior courts.

Maryland	Court of Appeals of Maryland	Circuit Courts of Counties
Massachusetts	Supreme Judicial Court	Superior Court, Land Court
Michigan	Michigan State Supreme Court	Circuit Courts, Court of Claims
Minnesota	Supreme Court of Minnesota	District Courts of Minnesota, Small Debtors' Courts
Mississippi	Supreme Court	Circuit Courts, Chancery Courts, County Courts
Missouri	Supreme Court of Missouri, Courts of Appeals	Circuit Courts, Courts of Common Pleas
Montana	Supreme Court of Montana	District Courts
Nebraska	Supreme Court of Nebraska	District Court, County Courts
Nevada	Supreme Court of Nevada	District Courts of Nevada
New Hampshire	New Hampshire Supreme Court	Superior Court
New Jersey	Supreme Court	Superior Court, County Court, County District Courts
New Mexico	Supreme Court, Court of Appeals	State District Courts, Juvenile Courts, Small Claims Court
New York	Court of Appeals, Appellate Divisions of the Supreme Court	Supreme Court, County Courts, Court of Claims
North Carolina	Supreme Court, Court of Appeals	Superior Courts, County Courts
North Dakota	Supreme Court	District Courts, County Courts
Ohio	Supreme Court of Ohio, Courts of Appeals	Courts of Common Pleas
Oklahoma	State Supreme Court, Court of Criminal Appeals, Court of Appeals	District Courts, County Courts, Probate Courts
Oregon	Supreme Court of Oregon, Court of Appeals	Circuit Courts, County Courts, District Courts
Pennsylvania	State Supreme Court	State Superior Court, Commonwealth Court, Common Pleas Courts, Court of Quarter Session, Oyer and Terminer
Rhode Island	Supreme Court	District Courts, Superior Courts
South Carolina	Supreme Court	Circuit Courts, County Courts,

South Dakota	Supreme Court	Circuit Courts, County Courts
Tennessee	Supreme Court of Tennessee, Court of Appeals	Chancery Courts, Circuit Courts, Courts of General Sessions, County Courts
Texas	Supreme Court of Texas, Court of Civil Appeals, Court of Criminal Appeals	District Courts, County Courts
Utah	Supreme Court	District Court, Small Claims Courts
Vermont	Supreme Court	County Courts, Court of Chancery
Virginia	Supreme Court of Appeals	Circuit Courts, Corporation Courts
Washington	Supreme Court, Court of Appeals	Superior Courts
West Virginia	Supreme Court of Appeals	Circuit Courts, County Courts
Wisconsin	Supreme Court	Circuit Courts, County Courts
Wyoming	Supreme Court of Wyoming	District Courts

3
Court Procedure:
Legal Wrongs and Remedies

It is a fundamental principle of law that for every wrong (the violation of a right) there is a remedy. The subject of rights and wrongs embraces the entire subject of human relations.

RIGHTS AND REMEDIES

One has to recognize a right before one can have a wrong. A right may exist because of its recognition from time immemorial or a right may be granted by the legislature under a statute. A wrong is committed when a right is violated; it may be committed by the denial of a right or by refusal to perform an obligation which is considered a right.

When new cases (questions in law) arose under recognized principles during the formative period of the common law, it was necessary to find new remedies to fit them. Throughout the centuries of common law both in England and in this country, the maxim "wherever there is a right, there is a remedy" has been an ideal to which the law aspires. It cannot be said that in all ways the law has lived up to this ideal; admittedly, the best the law has done is to *strive* for perfection.

ACTIONS, SUITS, AND SPECIAL PROCEEDINGS

In a court of law an *action* or *suit* is a proceeding by which one party prosecutes another for the enforcement or protection of a right or for the prevention of a wrong. In a *civil action* one sues to enforce a private right or redress a private wrong. Through a *criminal action* an individual or the state sues to redress a public wrong.

Common-Law Forms of Action

Many states have preserved common-law forms of action which are highly technical and labeled with Latin or obscure phrases. Among these are the following:

Action of assumpsit is brought to recover damages for a breach of simple contract.

Action of covenant is brought to recover for a contract under seal.

Action in trespass is a suit to recover for direct injury.

Action on the case is brought for indirect injury.

Action in trover is a suit for interfering with or converting the goods of another.

Action in detinue is brought for the recovery of specific chattels.

Pennsylvania and New Hampshire have retained common-law forms of action, but they are gradually being liberalized by court rules and statutes.

Most states have adopted "codes of civil procedure" or "practice acts" that abolish the distinction between the different common-law forms of action and provide for one single form of civil action.*

Forms of Equity Action

In the early days of the common law in England, the various forms of common-law actions were found to be too inflexible to fit many human demands. Therefore, when the legal maxim "wherever there is a right, there is a remedy" could not otherwise be satisfied, an appeal was made to the king's chancellor who would set up a court of chancery to mete out justice in the case. This court became known as a *court of equity*.

As with a common-law action, the form of an equitable action is often significant. It is important to determine, for example, whether the action is brought in the "law side" or the "equity side" of the court. Many states say that in effect the distinction between actions in law and suits in equity has been abolished but that the substantive rules governing legal actions and equitable actions are preserved.

Actions of a *legal* nature include, among others, action for the recovery of a money judgment, action for breach of contract, and action for damages for personal injuries. Actions of an *equitable* nature include, among others, action for an accounting, action for the specific performance of a contract, action to enforce a trust, and action for an injunction.

---

* Civil or Roman law, rather than the common law, forms the basis of practice in Louisiana.

Commencement of Actions

Procedural matters vary greatly among the states. In most jurisdictions an action is commenced when a summons or other writ is issued or served. Some states follow the federal rule that an action is commenced with the filing of a complaint in the office of the clerk of court; in other states the summons must be served by the sheriff or another officer of the court; in still other states the summons may be served by any person over eighteen years of age. Service of a paper means that the paper is delivered to and left with the person to be notified.

Statutes of Limitations

The commencement time of an action is very often important because most legal actions have to be brought within time limits known as *statutes of limitations.* The time within which legal actions may be brought varies from one to ten years, according to the type of action and the state where the claim arises. Furthermore, in order to decide whether the action is begun within the proper time limits, it is necessary to determine at just what time a cause of action accrued. A *cause of action* is a claim that can be enforced; hence a "good" cause of action is a valid claim. Examples of the operation of statutes of limitations follow:

Sam Bufort was struck by an automobile in the City of Columbus, Ohio, on January 10, 1972. On January 20, 1974, Sam commenced an action in an Ohio court to recover damages for bodily injury. Sam cannot succeed in his lawsuit because in Ohio an action for bodily injury must be commenced within two years from the date of the injury.

In Texas, actions on contracts in writing must be brought within four years from the time of accrual of the cause of action. On July 14, 1972, Robert Wayman brought suit on a contract entered into in Texas for the sale of merchandise; he claimed that on July 15, 1968, the man who agreed to sell him the merchandise failed to deliver the goods and so broke the contract. The action was timely brought and within the statute of limitations.

See the end of this chapter for the various state statutes of limitations.

PLEADINGS

Pleadings are written statements constituting a plaintiff's (the person who instituted the action or suit) cause of action or a defendant's (the person against whom the action or suit is brought) ground of defense. They are allegations in writing of what is claimed on one side or denied on the other. The function of pleadings is to define the issues in the case for the court and for the opposing party (a litigant in an action or a suit); it also gives that party the opportunity to prepare to meet the issues raised at the trial (the judicial hearing held for the purpose of deciding on the issues in a case).

The Federal Rules of Practice expound the concept that it is no longer necessary in pleadings to set forth facts but necessary only to state a claim. The current theory is that the facts may be developed later; all an adversary needs to know is that the claim is being made.

In most jurisdictions there is a trend away from the old common-law forms of pleadings. The codes and practice acts enacted in the various states have abolished certain technicalities of the common-law systems, thus simplifying legal pleadings.

Complaint or Declaration

At common law the plaintiff's first pleading was known as a *declaration*; under the modern codes and practice acts it is variously referred to as a complaint, petition, or statement. A *complaint* begins with the title of the action, identifying the plaintiff and the defendant, designates the court where the action is brought, and tells the story of the claim in legal form. The complaint usually includes the residence of the parties, a statement of the plaintiff's claim of grievance, the basis for the defendant's legal liability, and a request for damages or another remedy.

Plea or Answer

If the defendant desires to contest the claim of the plaintiff, he must file a *plea* or *answer* admitting or denying the various claims set forth in the complaint or declaration. The answer or plea may also state separate, affirmative defenses or a counterclaim (a claim introduced by the defendant in opposition to the plaintiff's claim).

Replication or Reply

The pleading after the answer is the *replication* or *reply*. Its purpose is to give the plaintiff an opportunity to answer the new material, such as a counterclaim, set forth in the defendant's answer.

Demurrer

When the pleading is served in an action and one party does not believe that the pleading is sufficient at law, he is then given an opportunity to make a motion or application to the court to this effect: "It is not necessary to go to trial because even assuming that all my adversary says is true, he still does not have a good case." Such an application is called a *demurrer*, a testing of the sufficiency of the pleading.

Years ago demurrers were very popular. Today demurrers, or motions to dismiss pleadings for insufficiency, are still permissible, but they are less frequently acted upon favorably by the courts. The trend is for the courts to say, in effect, "We are not so much concerned with the technicalities of pleadings as we are with the facts and with finding out where truth and justice lie."

Bill of Particulars

When a party to a lawsuit wants more specific information concerning a claim set forth in his adversary's pleading, he may require his adversary to furnish more specific details in a *bill of particulars*. An example of such an instance follows:

Foley sues Jennings, claiming in his complaint that Jennings ran into and damaged Foley's automobile to the extent of $600. Jennings demands a bill of particulars requiring the make, model, year, and mileage of the automobile, a list of the automobile parts which were damaged in the accident, and, if the automobile was repaired, a copy of the repair bill and any other pertinent information.

PRETRIAL PROCEEDINGS

Although our court calendars are still so clogged with lawsuits that in some metropolitan centers the courts are from three to five years behind in the trial of litigated matters, in recent years great strides have been made in procedural reform and especially in connection with pretrial proceedings.

Pretrial proceedings include the discovery of evidence, the inspection of documents before trial, application to the court for the granting of judgment before trial, and pretrial conferences.

Disclosure Proceedings

Proceedings for the discovery of evidence before trial and the inspection of documents and the like are known as *disclosure* or *discovery proceedings*. Generally, such proceedings take the form of *examinations before trial*, often referred to as EBTs. Lawsuits in which both parties are examined before trial are more apt to be settled out of court or if they go to court their trials are apt to be shorter than those suits in which no pretrial examinations take place.

At first, there was much resistance to reforms in court procedures which permitted unlimited examinations before trial. Such examinations were called "fishing expeditions" and "unfair." Currently, there is the feeling that all facts should be disclosed before trial so that the trial itself will not be (as it might have been in the past) a surprise or a game of wits and strategy.

Summary Judgments

The remedy for deciding a case on affidavits without the necessity of a trial is called *summary judgment*. If the court is satisfied from the affidavits or the documents presented that there is no dispute concerning the facts but simply a question of interpretation of those facts, then judgment may be entered for either party. Here is an example of summary judgment before trial:

The Excelsior Bank sues Fred Applebottom on a $1,000 note. In response to the complaint Applebottom has his lawyer file an answer alleging that the vice-president of the bank made a verbal agreement with Applebottom that he would not have to pay the note for three years after it was due. Instead of waiting until the case was reached for trial, the bank makes an application to the court for summary judgment, saying that the vice-president never made the agreement claimed and that because he had no authority to make the agreement (even if he had made it), it is void. The court upholds the bank, says that there is no reason for delay, and grants summary judgment in favor of the bank against Applebottom.

Pretrial Conferences

Originally, *pretrial conferences* were designed merely as a means whereby the trial judge could shorten trials by having the attorneys in lawsuits narrow the issues and agree on certain facts. However, pretrial conferences have become a means of settling cases without going to trial at all. In these conferences the judge meets with the attorneys for the parties to a lawsuit (and sometimes with the parties themselves) and concentrates with them on reaching a common ground for settlement. An example of the workings of a pretrial settlement conference follows:

Webster sues the Valley Lumber Company for personal injuries resulting from a collision between Webster's automobile and the lumber firm's truck. Webster claims that as a result of a broken hip suffered in the accident, he will not be able to work again for the rest of his life and that he should be paid $50,000 for his injuries.

The lumber company carries liability insurance, and the attorney for the insurance company (defending the lawsuit) claims that the accident was caused by Webster's intoxication and that the lumber company should not pay anything, but, in order to dispose of the litigation, his firm will pay $5,000. A pretrial settlement conference is arranged before the trial judge who confers first with the attorneys for both parties, then separately with each of them, and later with the plaintiff and the plaintiff's attorney. The judge points out to the plaintiff and his attorney that he is satisfied (1) that there was serious doubt as to Webster's sobriety at the time of the collision and (2) that there would be reliable proof in two years' time that Webster will recover completely. As a result of the pretrial settlement conference, the case is settled out of court for $10,000.

TRIAL OF A LAWSUIT

Someone once said that for a litigant to win a lawsuit he must have a good case, a good lawyer, good witnesses, a good judge, and good luck. It is unfortunate to liken justice in our courts to win-or-lose games, but in many respects the analogy holds true. Lawsuits in American courts are not won because of lawyers' brilliance and wit, but because of the hard work, the experience, and the skill of those who participate in the trial.

Trial by Jury and by Judge

The distinguishing feature of the English and American systems of law is the *trial by jury*. When a case is tried in front of a jury, it is up to the jury to decide what the facts in the case are, in other words, to decide who is telling the truth. It has been said that in a jury trial there are two sets of judges: the jurors, who are judges of the facts, and the judge on the bench, who is the judge of the law.

Some persons think that in a jury trial a judge is nothing more than a glorified referee. This is not so. Throughout a jury trial the judge must decide all questions of law, all questions concerning whether or not evidence should be received (in the case), and whether or not there is sufficient evidence to permit the case to be decided by a jury. When a case is tried without a jury before a judge, referee, or commissioner, one of the latter occupies a dual role: he is the presiding officer who must guide the trial and, at the same time, he is the finder of the facts.

Preparation for Trial

Every experienced lawyer knows that most lawsuits are won or lost before they are heard in court. Thus, a good lawyer prepares his case carefully, undertaking exhaustive research and investigation, before he goes into the courtroom. He interviews and takes statements from all available witnesses; he ascertains what witnesses are likely to be called by the other side and finds out all he can about them. He plans his strategy in the handling of the case, decides whether expert witnesses should be called (such as physicians, engineers, chemists, architects, or others who have special knowledge of the subject matter of the suit), reads books and articles on the subject, meets with the witnesses time and time again, and prepares his witnesses for courtroom pitfalls, including the questions which might be asked by opposing lawyers. As a result of thorough preparation, the lawyer knows the strong and weak points of his case and is thus able to serve his client well.

In getting his case ready, the experienced lawyer also prepares a trial memorandum of law to be handed up to the court at the outset of the trial. Although some assume that the judge is the fountainhead of law and endowed with complete knowledge of it, he is, in actual fact, just a lawyer who has been elevated to the bench to preside at trials. As such, he welcomes these memoranda.

Selection of the Jury

The *petit* or *trial jury*, as contrasted with the *grand jury*, serves in the trial of a civil or criminal case. It consists usually of twelve jurors and sometimes of alternate jurors, who replace other jurors in emergencies.

A petit jury (consisting of 6 or 12 jurors, depending on the particular court) is drawn from a large jury panel (varying in size from 25 to 300 or more citizens, depending on the size and activity of the court). The panel is chosen by a jury commissioner or other public officer. In most states the names of the jurors are drawn from the jury panel by lot; then the prospective jurors take their places in the jury box, and the lawyers examine them about their acquaintanceship with the parties, interest in the case, and prejudices or predispositions. In federal courts the judge, not the lawyers, asks questions of the prospective jurors to determine whether or not they will be impartial.

A prospective juror is often perplexed by the questions a lawyer asks in determining if the juror should be selected to serve in the case. Sometimes he is resentful of a lawyer's questions concerning his private affairs. He should realize, however, that the average lawyer is only trying to discover if he has a pet notion or prejudice which might influence his judgment of the case.

If an attorney decides that he does not want a particular juror to sit in the case, he exercises a challenge in an attempt to have the juror excused. Challenges are of two kinds: challenges for cause and peremptory challenges.

A *challenge for cause* may be granted when the court rules that the prospective juror, by reason of blood relationship, pecuniary interest in the outcome of the case, or other prejudice, may not look at the case objectively and, thus, may not make an impartial juror. Challenges for cause are unlimited in number. A *peremptory challenge* is one which may be made without giving any reason for it. Generally in each state lawyers may make only a limited number of peremptory challenges in one case. In New York state, for example, each side may make six peremptory challenges. The *peremptory challenge* (when within the number allowed by lot) is automatically granted, and the court does not have to approve it.

In selecting jurors lawyers are guided by knowledge of and insight into human nature and experience. The appearance and behavior of a prospective juror and the way he answers questions help the lawyer to determine whether or not he would be favorably disposed to the lawyer's side of the case. For example, a lawyer representing a plaintiff who is suing for damages for personal injuries would like to have as jurors kindly, warm-hearted persons who would be sympathetic toward an injured person and willing to give a generous verdict. But a lawyer representing the defendant in a personal injury case would like to have as jurors cold, thrifty individuals who would be apt to bring in a miserly verdict. Although the court is interested in seeing that a fair and impartial jury is selected, each litigant wants a jury which will favor his side of the controversy.

Opening Statement

Lawyers for the parties make *opening statements*, that is, each lawyer outlines to the jury his version of the facts and explains his theory of the case. The opening statement is not an argument; its purpose is to inform the jurors of the nature of the case so they will understand the evidence as it is presented.

Direct Examination and Cross-Examination of Witnesses

A trial should be a search for truth. Under the English and American systems of law, it is believed that the search for truth can best be conducted by opposing attorneys who (1) call as witnesses those people who claim to know something about the particular case and (2) bring out the testimony of the witnesses by questioning them. (In many European countries, only the judge can interrogate the witnesses.)

Briefly, the *direct-examination procedure* in an American court is as follows: Each witness is called before the clerk of the court or the judge and is required to take an oath that the testimony he gives in the courtroom will be the truth. This is known as *swearing a witness*. Each witness is first examined by the lawyer who called him. His testimony is produced by a combination of the lawyer's questions and his answers. In obtaining the testimony the lawyer is not supposed to ask questions that suggest to the witness the response desired. Such leading questions can be objected to by the opposing lawyer (except in unimportant preliminary matters).

Much has been written and said about the skills of the trial advocate and the art of cross-examination. Nevertheless, most trial lawyers agree that there is as much skill required in the direct examination of witnesses as there is in the cross-examination of them. In direct examination, it is especially important, however, that the attorney be adept at getting witnesses to tell their stories naturally and convincingly.

The purpose of *cross-examination* is to test the truth or falsity of the testimony given by an opposing witness. If it is skillfully employed, cross-examination can expose falsehoods and reduce exaggerated statements to their true proportion. However, young lawyers are constantly warned against too much cross-examination, for it can bring out harmful testimony or give the witness an opportunity to reinforce his direct testimony.

People sometimes have the idea that to cross-examine is to "question crossly," to bully or browbeat a witness or to proceed in a rude or offensive tone. This may be because actors playing lawyers in the theater, motion pictures, television, and radio often do these things. Most members of the legal profession regard these as bad tactics. The intelligent cross-examiner is respectful and courteous to the witness; his gentle, casual questions are much more likely than bullying ones to evoke the answers he wishes, and he does not noticeably react when the witness gives damaging answers.

Documentary Evidence

Documents, such as correspondence, deeds, maps, photographs, diagrams, and miscellaneous memoranda and writings, often are important as evidence. Documents to be offered as evidence in a suit are referred to as exhibits for identification. Once they are received in evidence they are exhibits and may be read or shown to the jury. For example:

The attorney for the plaintiff in a lawsuit wishes to introduce in evidence five letters written by the defendant and also the contract entered into by the plaintiff and defendant. First he asks the court stenographer to have the five letters marked "Exhibits *A, B, C, D, E* for identification"; then he asks the court stenographer to have the contract marked "Exhibit *F* for identification." Next he shows the exhibits for identification to an appropriate witness and proves the signature and the mailing of the letters and the delivery of the contract. After that he offers the exhibits in evidence. When the exhibits are received in evidence, the stenographer crosses out the words "for identification," and the letters and contract become Exhibits *A, B, C, D, E, F* in the case.

Objections, Exceptions, and Motions to Strike

The trial of a lawsuit is an inquiry into a dispute to determine where justice lies. Rules of evidence have been developed over the years to determine what testimony would best assist the court and the jury in deciding the truth of the matter in controversy.

Observers in court are often confused by the number of *objections* made by lawyers, but under the rules of evidence objections may be necessary to preserve the rights of a party to a lawsuit. Thus, when one party to a lawsuit offers evidence which is inadmissible under the rules of evidence, the other party must *object* if he wishes to keep such evidence out of the case. Generally, a lawyer who fails to object to evidence waives all claims as to its inadmissibility. An example of proper objection follows:

In a suit brought by Wright against Gillespie to recover damages for breach of contract, Wright is questioned by his lawyer about a conversation he had with his neighbor concerning the subject of the contract. Gillespie's lawyer properly objects on the ground that the conversation is "hearsay and not binding on my client." The court sustains the objection.

Blanket objections on the ground that proposed evidence is "incompetent, immaterial, irrelevant, and improper" are considered outdated. In current practice an objection pinpoints for the court the precise reason why the lawyer feels the proposed evidence is improper.

The purpose of an *exception* is to give the trial court notice that an attorney does not agree to a ruling. Nowadays attorneys rarely take exceptions when it is obvious to the court that a ruling is adverse. In such an instance the attorney is more likely to make his position known to the court by objections or by other means.

A *motion to strike out evidence* may sometimes be granted by the court (1) when evidence was apparently proper when it is received but is subsequently shown to be objectionable, (2) when evidence is admitted with the understanding that it will be ruled on at a later stage of the proceedings, (3) when evidence is admitted subject to later consideration by the court of a motion to strike out, (4) when a witness makes a voluntary statement or testifies without a question being asked of him, or (5) when an answer is not responsive to a question.

Expert Witnesses and the Hypothetical Question

Expert witnesses are permitted by the rules of evidence to give their opinions regarding scientific and technical matters and concerning cause and effect. Such opinions are not permitted from ordinary witnesses. The expert, by reason of his special training and experience, is deemed qualified to assist the court and jury in arriving at a determination of the facts. Medicine, engineering, and the sciences are the most common fields from which experts are required to provide testimony.

A *hypothetical question* is used when the expert witness called is not personally familiar with the facts in the case. The hypothetical question includes all the testimony on a given point. The expert is asked to base his opinion on the assumption that the testimony included in the question is true. Here is an example of an abbreviated hypothetical question:

Dr. Atlas, assume that a man forty-eight years of age who had previously enjoyed excellent health was employed in a factory on a day when the temperature was about 94°F. Assume further that this man was engaged in lifting heavy barrels of sand which weighed from 400 to 500 pounds each and that the barrels were heavier and larger than any he had previously lifted on the job. Assume that he had been doing this work for about 5 hours and that about 3:00 o'clock on the afternoon in question, this man suddenly fell to the floor and died 5 minutes later. Assume further that a post-mortem examination of the man revealed an aorta ruptured about 6 inches from where it entered the heart. Assuming, Doctor, the foregoing statements to be true, what is your opinion concerning whether or not the work of lifting the barrels was a probable cause of the man's death?

Recently, courts in some jurisdictions have held that an expert witness may be asked his opinion directly, instead of having to give it as an answer to a hypothetical question.

Final Argument to the Jury

A party to a lawsuit has the right to have his case fully and fairly argued to the jury. The judge, exercising reasonable discretion, may limit the length of the *final argument* to the jury. This argument is popularly called "summation" or "summing up."

The plaintiff's attorney makes his opening statement first, but sums up last. The theory is that the party having the burden of proof should present the last argument to a jury in order to demonstrate that he has sustained his burden of proof.

Great latitude is given attorneys in summation. They may (although it is not so popular today as in the past) indulge in bursts of oratory or may resort to poetry or flowery language. They are permitted to draw all reasonable inferences from the evidence. They may comment fairly on the testimony of witnesses or argue to the jury that some witnesses should not be believed. In summing up, lawyers are not permitted to go outside of the evidence and discuss facts which have not been proved, nor may they resort to appeals to passion or to prejudice.

The Court's Charge to the Jury

The court's *charge to the jury* advises the jury regarding the law applicable in the case and aids the jury in understanding the case and in reaching a just conclusion and verdict. It is the function of the judge to decide the law applicable to the case; it is the function of the jury to decide the facts after the judge has instructed them concerning the law.

The judge's charge can be divided roughly into four parts: (1) a statement of what the case is about, what each side contends, and, sometimes, even a brief outline of the testimony on both sides; (2) the general rules of law applicable to lawsuits, that is, what tests should be applied by the jury in passing on the weight of testimony, what is meant by "burden of proof," "interested witnesses," "false testimony," "opinion evidence," and so forth; (3) the law that should be applied to the particular case being considered by the jury; and (4) the form the jury verdict should take.

At the conclusion of the court's charge to the jury, any party may object to or except to portions of the court's charge. Any party may also request that additional instructions be given to the jury.

Verdict of the Jury

The ultimate verdict of the jury (or decision of the court) must be based on the evidence. As lawyers and judges constantly remind juries, they must decide a case "not on what the lawyers say, but solely on the evidence presented."

A *verdict* is the answer of the jury concerning the issues in a case. Verdicts are of two kinds—general and special. A *general verdict* is one by which the jury makes an overall decision on the issues in a case. A *special verdict* is one by which the jury answers a request made to it to decide on a particular question of fact; the special verdict leaves the ultimate decision of the case to the judge.

A general verdict in a personal injury accident case might be: "We find a verdict in favor of the plaintiff for xx dollars," or, "We find in favor of the defendant," or "No cause of action" (meaning a verdict in favor of the defendant).

A special verdict might take the form, "We find that Bailey was an employee of Brown at the time of the accident," or "We find that Mary was the common-law wife of Roberts."

APPEALS

In American law an essential right of an aggrieved person in a legal proceeding is review of a court decision by a superior or appellate court. The right to appeal derives from English law. Review by a higher court was obtained by means of a *writ of error*, which directed the judge in the lower court to send the record of the case to the appellate court, where it was examined in order to correct any errors in the proceedings. Most American states have abolished the writ of error, and an appeal proceeding is initiated by the filing of a *notice of appeal*.

The person who appeals to a higher court is called the *appellant* or the *plaintiff in error*. The person in favor of whom the judgment or decree in the lower court was rendered is known as the *appellee, respondent,* or *defendant in error*.

General Appellate Procedure

In some states a case may be completely retried in a higher court, but this is the exception rather than the rule. For the most part an appeal involves (1) the filing of a notice of appeal, (2) the preparation of a record on appeal, which contains a typewritten, mimeographed, or printed record of all the proceedings in the lower court, (3) the preparation and filing of typewritten or printed "briefs" that outline the reasons (points of law) why the decision of the lower court should be reversed and that furnish information to the appellate court and opposing counsel, and (4) the oral presentation of arguments by counsel for both parties before the appellate court, which generally consists of three or nine judges (three judges in many appellate courts and nine in the Supreme Court).

Technicalities of an Appeal

Not every decision or order of a court may be appealed. In some states appeals are permitted only in certain types of cases or certain types of decisions. Some state laws restrict appeals action to final judgments, orders, or decrees and require a litigant who is dissatisfied with orders and decisions of the court at various stages of the case to await the final decision before he may appeal. (The legislature in each state may authorize an appeal from a court decision or public officer or board or commission.)

Sometimes appeals are permissible only to an intermediate appellate court, and the proceedings end there. In other cases the decision of the intermediate appellate court may be appealed to a higher and final appeals court. The decision of the appellate court may determine that the court below committed procedural error or error in the admission of evidence, either of which requires a new trial; or the appellate court may decide the case once and for all by its own decision.

Preserving Rights for an Appeal

Not every alleged error will be reviewed by an appellate court. An appellate court does not have the power to review questions which were not raised nor properly preserved for review in the trial court. The reason for this almost universal rule, which requires the points at issue to be raised in the court below, is to give the opposing party the opportunity to correct the alleged error or to furnish neces-

State Time Limitations in Years for Commencement of Actions

State	TORTS											CONTRACTS		
	Personal Injuries	Property Damage	Wrongful Death	Libel	Slander	Assault and Battery	Malpractice	Malicious Prosecution	False Imprisonment	Trespass or Conversion	Suit or Judgment of Court of Record	Oral	Written Under Seal	Written Not Under Seal
Alabama	2	1	2	1	1	6	2	1	1	6	20	6	10	6
Alaska	2	2	2	2	2	2	2-6	2	2	2	10	6	10	6
Arizona	2	2	2	2	1	2-6	2-6	2	1	2		3-4	6	4-6
Arkansas	3	3	3	1	1	1		5	1	3	10	4-5	5	5
California	1	1-3	1	3	1	1	1-4	1	1	3	10	2	4	4
Colorado	6	6	2	1	1	1	1-2	6	6	6	6	6	6	6
Connecticut	2	1-2	1-3	3	3	3	2	3	3	3	21	3	17	4-6
Delaware	2	2		3	3	3	4	3	3	3		3	20	3-6
Florida	4	3-4	2	2	2	2	2	4	2	3	7-20	3	20	5
Georgia	2	4	2-4	1	1	2		2	2	4	10	4	20	6
Hawaii	2	2	2	2	2	2	2	6	6	6			6	4-6
Idaho	2	3	2	2	2	2	2-10	4	2	3	6	4	5	5
Illinois	2	5	2	1	1	2	2	2	2	5	20	5	10	10
Indiana	2	2	2	2	2	2	2	2	2	6	20	6	10	4-10
Iowa	2	5	2	2	2	2	2	2	2	5	20	5	10	10
Kansas	2	2	2	1	1	2	1	1	1	2	5	3-5	5	4-5
Kentucky	1	5	1	1	1	1	1	1	1	5		4-5	15	4-15
Louisiana	1	1	1	1	1	1	1	1	1		10	3-10	10	3-10
Maine	6	6	2	2	2	2	2	6	2	6	20	6	20	4-6
Maryland	3	3	3	1	1	1	3	3	3	3	12	3	12	3-4

Massachusetts	8	2	2-3	3	3	3	3	3	3	3	20	6	6	20	4-6
Michigan	3	3	3	1	2	2	1	1	2	2	10	2-3	6	6	4-6
Minnesota	6	6	3	2	2	2	2	2	2	2	10	6	6	6	4-6
Mississippi	6	6	6	1	1	6	6	6	2	6	7	6	3	6	6
Missouri	5	5	2	2	2	2	2	2	1	1	10	5	5	10	10
Montana	3	2	3	2	2	2	3	3-5	3	2	10	2	5	8	4-8
Nebraska	4	4	2	1	1	1	1	2	4	4	6	4	4	5	4-5
Nevada	2	3	2	2	2	2	4	2-4	2	3	6	3	4	6	4-6
New Hampshire	6	6	2	6	6	6	6	6	6	6	20	6	6	20	4-6
New Jersey	2	6	2	1	1	2	6	2	2	6	20	6	6	16	4-6
New Mexico	3	4	3	3	3	3	3	3	3	3	7	4	4	6	6
New York	3	3	1	1	1	1	1	3	1	1	20	6	6	6	4-6
North Carolina	3	3	1	2	3	3	3	3	3	3	10	3	3	10	3-4
North Dakota	6	6	2	2	6	6	6	6	6	6	10	6	6	6	4-6
Ohio	2	2	2	1	1	1	1	1	2	4	21	6	6	4-15	4-15
Oklahoma	2	2	2	1	1	1	1	1	2	2	5	3	3	5	5
Oregon	2	6	3	1	1	2	2	2	2	6	10	6	6	6	4-6
Pennsylvania	2	6	1	1	2	2	2	2	2	6	20	4-6	20	20	4-6
Rhode Island	3	6	2	6	1	3	3	3	6	6	20	6	20	20	4-6
South Carolina	6	6	6	2	2	6	6	6	6	6	20	6	20	20	6
South Dakota	3	6	2	2	2	2	2	2	2	6	10	6	20	20	4-6
Tennessee	1	3	2	1	1	1	1	1	1	2	10	3	6	6	4-6
Texas	2	3	2	1 (6 mos.)	2	2	2	2	2	2	10	3	2	4	4
Utah	4	3	2	1	2	4	4	4	3	3	8	6	4	6	6
Vermont•	3	3	2	3	3	3	3	3	6	6	8	6	6	8	4-6
Virginia	2	5	2	2	2	2	2	2	2	5	10	3	3	10	4-5
Washington	5	3	3	2	3	3	3	3	2	3	6	3	3	6	4-6
West Virginia	3	2	3	2	2	2	2	2	2	2	5	5	5	10	4-10
Wisconsin	3	6	3	2	1	3	3	3	1	6	10	6	6	20	6
Wyoming	4	4	2	1	1	1	3	1	1	4	21	8	8	10	10

• Injuries sustained in skiing 1 year; all others, 3 years.

sary proof in the court below. The most common example of the necessity for raising points in the lower court is in the matter of objections or exceptions. By raising an objection, counsel tells the court and his adversary that he does not think the evidence should be considered. Generally speaking, errors concerning the admission of evidence should not be reviewed in the appellate court unless proper objections were made in the trial court. The objection must be timely; it ordinarily must be made during the trial and in time to allow the alleged error to be avoided or corrected. An exception, another form of objection, is used to challenge the correctness of a ruling or decision of the trial court so that the ruling or decision may be corrected by the judge himself. An objection is normally made before the court's ruling or decision, and an exception is made after the court rules.

In most states it is a rule of law that an appropriate exception should be taken to a court ruling in a trial. There is a trend today to relax this rule when the court obviously knows that the person against whom the ruling is made would not be satisfied with it.

Time for Taking and Perfecting an Appeal

The time within which an appeal must be taken to a higher court and perfected is regulated by statute; of course, the appeal should be taken and perfected within the prescribed statutory time (varying from ten to ninety days). In some jurisdictions an appeal must be taken at the term of court in which the decree or order appealed from is entered. There is no relief when a person is late in taking an appeal, and the other party cannot consent to an appeal in order to confer jurisdiction on the appellate court. *Perfecting an appeal* includes filing the notice and filing the record and briefs.

Under some state laws an appeal is taken as a matter of right. In other states the appellant must first apply to the appellate court and obtain permission for the appeal. The theory in such a case is that the appellant must convince the appellate court that there is a unique or novel question of law involved which ought to be reviewed by the appellate court.

4
Contracts

A *contract* is a promise that creates a legal obligation. Every day of our lives we enter into contracts. We do this when we buy a newspaper, a meal, groceries, or an automobile. Most contracts are simple everyday affairs that are forgotten when completed and that cause no trouble. It is the one contract in a thousand that becomes a problem and requires legal attention.

TYPES OF CONTRACTS

An *express contract* is one in which the terms are specifically stated by the parties. In an *implied contract* the terms are not expressly stated but are inferred by law from the acts of the parties and the surrounding circumstances.

A *contract under seal* is a written agreement with a seal attached. In ancient common law the seal was a piece of wax, wafer, or other substance affixed to the written contract. In more recent years a printed scroll, sign, or impression has been used in place of the wax or the word *seal* has been printed or written opposite the signature. Sometimes the initials *L.S.* (for the Latin phrase *locus sigilli*) are used in place of the seal. Nearly half of the states have abolished the distinction between sealed and unsealed writings, except in deeds and bonds. Today, the sealing of a document is no longer essential to its validity.

Void contracts are those that are bad from the start and that create no legal obligation. *Voidable contracts* are those that either party may have set aside by court action. Typical voidable contracts are those entered into by a minor and those brought about by fraud, mistake, or duress. An *executed contract* is one which has been carried out, and an *executory contract* is one which has not been completed.

ESSENTIAL ELEMENTS OF A CONTRACT

A contract need not be in writing to be binding. Only certain types of contracts must be in writing. For an oral or written contract to exist, however, there must be first an offer and then an acceptance of the offer; in some states there must also be "consideration," something given in return for a promise. There must be at least two parties to a contract.

A contract should be complete; it should cover all the important acts to be performed by each party, and nothing should be left for future understanding or agreement. There should be a definite understanding of who is to do what and when and where and how.

There is an old saying, "An agreement to agree is no agreement."

Mr. Black writes to Mr. White, "I will buy your house for $20,000. Just how much I will pay down and how much mortgage I will give you is something we must decide upon at a later date. Also, the time when the purchase will be completed is something that you and I must mutually agree upon." Mr. White writes back saying that they have a deal. There is no contract. They made nothing more than an unenforceable "agreement to agree."

There are many rules governing the subject of offers and acceptances; those discussed in the following sections are among the important ones.

Offer

An *offer* is a promise that something will or will not happen.

Jones says to Smith, "This watch is yours if you will pay me $25 for it." As soon as Smith says yes to Jones, the offer, or promise to turn over the watch, has been accepted, and a contract has been made.

An expression of intention is not an offer. An offer should also be distinguished from preliminary negotiations.

Mr. Harsh writes to Mr. Loomis, "I am planning to sell my house for $20,000. I would really like to get rid of it." Loomis promptly writes an answering letter and says, "I will buy your house at the price stated in your letter." There is no contract, because Mr. Harsh simply expressed a plan or intention.

Definite Offer An offer must be so definite in its terms that the parties can be certain about what is intended. If promises are indefinite concerning the time and the place of performance or in other material respects, they do not constitute valid offers.

Mr. Cohen promises to sell Mr. Levy certain goods, and Mr. Levy promises to buy the goods from him at cost plus "a nice profit." This promise is too indefinite to form a contract.

Mr. Hempel promises Mr. Smith to do a specified piece of work, and

Mr. Smith promises to pay a price "to be mutually agreed upon." Since the only method of settling the price is dependent upon the future agreement of the parties, there is no contract. (An agreement to agree is no agreement.)

On the other hand, an indefinite offer accepted by partial performance may sometimes create a contract.

Howard says to Bill, "I will employ you at $20 a day." This offer is too indefinite because it does not specify the length of time for which Howard will employ Bill. If, however, Bill works one or more days, Howard has created a contractual obligation to pay Bill $20 for each day's work.

Withdrawal of Offer   An offer may be withdrawn at any time before it is accepted. Withdrawal of the offer must be definite and positive.

Mr. Ball makes an offer by mail to Mr. Hall and subsequently by mail revokes the offer. Before receiving the revocation, Mr. Hall mails an acceptance. The revocation is too late.

Offers may be withdrawn if they can be considered to comprise parts of a series of separate contracts.

Mr. Brown offers to sell Mr. Gray five tons of coal a day and offers five tons at once. Mr. Gray accepts the offer. The five tons are furnished daily for a number of days; then Mr. Brown states to Mr. Gray that he revokes the offer. The revocation is good because each sale of five tons a day was a separate contract. If Mr. Brown's original proposal had been to sell to Mr. Gray five tons of coal daily during the period of two months, Mr. Brown could not revoke the contract once it was accepted.

Termination of Offer   For how long is an offer good, and how is an offer terminated? Generally an offer is deemed to be terminated (1) when it has been rejected by the person to whom it was made, (2) by the lapse of the time specified or the lapse of a reasonable time when the offer is silent concerning duration, (3) by the occurrence of a condition laid down in the offer relating to termination or withdrawal, (4) by the death of the person necessary to carry out the contract, (5) by the destruction of the subject matter of the contract, (6) by revocation of the person making the offer.

Acceptance

One party to a contract must accept the offer made by the other party or parties if there is to be a contract. *Acceptance* is the act of assenting by word or by conduct to the offer made.

Conditions of Acceptance   If an offer attaches conditions of acceptance, those conditions must ordinarily be met. If the offer prescribes only the time, place, or manner of acceptance, another method of acceptance which is just as good may be satisfactory.

Mr. Crane writes Mr. Vickers, "I must receive your acceptance by return mail." Mr. Vickers sends a telegram, which arrives even more quickly than the mail would, and the contract is made.

Mr. Gay makes an offer to Mr. Sour and adds, "Send a messenger with an answer to this by 12:00 o'clock." Mr. Sour comes himself before 12:00 o'clock and accepts. There is a contract.

If Mr. Gay had said to Mr. Sour, "You must accept this, if at all, by coming in person to my office at 10:00 o'clock tomorrow morning," Mr. Sour would have had to comply strictly with that method of acceptance.

Means of Acceptance If a person making an offer specifies or authorizes the means by which the acceptance is to be made and the person making the acceptance uses that method, the contract is complete.

Mr. Miller makes an offer to Mr. Gifford by mail stating, "Telegraph your answer." Mr. Gifford promptly telegraphs an acceptance. The telegram never reaches Mr. Miller, but there is a contract as soon as the telegram is released to the telegraph company.

When an offer has been rejected, it ceases to exist. Once the offer has been rejected, the person to whom the offer is made cannot change his mind and later accept the offer. A counteroffer is considered to be a rejection of the original offer.

Mr. Hartwig offers to sell Mr. Gordon the Hartwig farm for $10,000. Mr. Gordon counters, "I will pay you $9,500 for the farm." Hartwig promptly rejects this offer. Then Gordon writes, "Now I will accept your offer to sell for $10,000." Too late! The counteroffer of $9,500 wiped out the offer of $10,000 and, thus, there is no contract.

Hartwig makes the same offer to Gordon and Gordon replies, "Will you take less?" and Hartwig answers, "No." Within 5 days, Gordon accepts Hartwig's $10,000 offer, and the contract is made.

Obviously, an offer terminates at the time specified, but if no time is specified it is said to terminate at the end of a "reasonable time." What is a reasonable time? That depends on the nature of the contract and other circumstances. Thus, a reasonable time is often a matter of common sense.

A newspaper offers a reward for information leading to the arrest and conviction of a murderer. Mr. Citizen, intending to obtain the reward, gives the requested information two months after publication of the offer. There is a contract.

Mr. Adams sends Mr. Boston a telegraphic offer to sell soybean meal which at the time is subject to rapid fluctuations in price. One week later Mr. Boston accepts the offer. Mr. Adams says, "Too late." Undoubtedly Mr. Adams's position would be upheld in court.

Mr. Cook sends Mr. Warter an offer by mail to sell a piece of land. After three days Mr. Warter sends an acceptance. No doubt Mr. Warter's acceptance would be good, and a valid contract would be created.

Consideration

Although the rule has been relaxed in some states, generally a contract must be supported by consideration. Bearing in mind that a contract is essentially a promise, *consideration* is something given in return for a promise. It does not necessarily have to have monetary value. Consideration will support a promise if the condition of the promise is that the person to whom it is made agrees to do something in return or to refrain from doing something.

Mr. Ames promises his nephew that if he will go to college and complete his course he will pay him $10,000. The nephew receives a degree and has a valid contract claim against his uncle.

In the average case the consideration does have a dollars-and-cents value, but this is not necessary.

When one says to the owner of a garage, "I will pay you $150 if you will make my car run properly," the undertaking by the garage owner of the job is sufficient consideration for the promise.

It is not necessary that the person making the promise be benefited by the consideration.

A father promises to pay his son the sum of $500 if the son does not use intoxicating liquor until he reaches the age of 25 years. The forbearance by the son of his legal right to use intoxicating liquors is sufficient consideration.

Written as well as oral promises generally require consideration, but some states have reconsidered consideration; that is, they have changed the rules of the common law in order to provide that the majority of written contracts are presumed to have valid consideration.

WRITTEN CONTRACTS

In 1677 the English Parliament passed a law providing that no suit nor action could be brought on certain contracts unless a note or memorandum thereof in writing was signed by the party to be charged with an obligation. This law became known as the Statute of Frauds, and its purpose was to close the door to numerous fraudulent and perjurious claims that contracts existed when there was nothing in writing to support these claims. During the past three hundred years the Statute of Frauds has been qualified and varied in many ways. For example, partial performance of a contract that would otherwise be unenforceable under the Statute of Frauds makes it enforceable. The Statute of Frauds has been adopted in one form or another in nearly all the states.

The requirement that contracts be in writing applies to

1. conveyances or agreements to convey interests in lands (real estate)
2. the undertaking or guaranty to perform the obligations of another person
3. a contract which by its terms is not to be performed within a specified period of time (generally one year)
4. an agreement to create a trust in land (real estate)
5. a lease of land, except a lease for a specified period (in most states, less than one year; in a few states, three years)
6. a contract for the sale of goods of a specified value (in some states $50 and in other states $500)

ASSIGNMENT OF CONTRACTS

Contracts may be "assigned" or transferred except in the following cases: (1) the transfer is prohibited by the contract, (2) the contract requires personal or special services, or (3) substitution of a new party to the contract would be contrary to the spirit of the contract.

Mr. Briggs, an excellent house painter, in consideration of the sum of $1,300 agrees to paint Mr. Tuttle's house during the month of May. In April Mr. Briggs moves to another state and assigns the contract to another painter. The assignment is not valid.

Mr. Wade contracts to sell his house to Mr. Ware. Mr. Ware assigns the contract to Mr. Smith. The assignment is good.

Lord Bromfield makes a contract with Smithers for Smithers to serve Lord Bromfield as a valet. Smithers signs and delivers to Jones a paper reading, "I assign to Jones my rights under my contract with Lord Bromfield." Jones acquires no right to act as valet to Lord Bromfield. The contract is too personal to assign.

INTERPRETATION OF AGREEMENTS

In court a lawyer may object to testimony, saying, "I object to any attempt to vary the terms of a written contract by parol evidence." In making the objection, the lawyer refers to the rule that written contracts ordinarily speak for themselves, and the parties are not permitted to give verbal testimony to show that a different meaning was intended. There are, however, exceptions to this rule. Parol evidence may be admitted (1) to establish the meaning of ambiguous provisions of the contract or (2) to prove facts rendering the agreement void because of illegality, fraud, duress, mistake, or insufficiency of consideration.

ILLEGAL CONTRACTS

Contracts which have for their purpose or object the violation of law are illegal and will not be enforced.

Cook entered into a written agreement with Phillips to lend him $1,000 at a usurious rate of interest. Because the agreement called for an unlawful act, it was held invalid.

The Excellsior Factory made a contract with the Heart Company for Heart to build stairways and exits which were known by both parties not to be in compliance with the state building codes. The Excellsior Factory agreed to pay $15,000 for the work instead of the $25,000 the job would cost if the stairways were built in compliance with the codes. The executives of the Excellsior Company changed their minds and decided not to go through with the contract. Heart sued. The court held that the contract was illegal and that it would not enforce a contract in violation of laws designed to protect human safety.

A party to an illegal contract cannot ask a court to assist him in carrying out a plan which would be in violation of a statute or an established principle of law. The courts have applied this principle not only to contracts involving the commission of a crime but also to contracts involving a civil wrong or a contract which is contrary to public policy or public morals.

Joe, a professional boxer, made a contract with two managers which violated the state laws regulating the amount of the managers' fees and the duration of the contract. The court held the contract was void and unenforceable.

Hanes agreed to conceal and withhold evidence in the trial of Rudd's son, who was charged with stealing money. In return for the agreement Rudd gave Hanes a 6-months' promissory note for $500. At the end of the 6 months Rudd did not pay. Hanes sued. The court said there could be no recovery because giving the promissory note was part of the plan to do an illegal act.

BREACH OF CONTRACT

A *breach of contract* is the nonperformance of any contractual obligation. A contract may be entirely or partially breached.

The Sloan Automobile Agency agrees to sell Mr. Post an automobile, and Mr. Post agrees to pay $5,000 on delivery. The Sloan Agency tenders the automobile to Mr. Post, but Mr. Post refuses without justification to accept delivery. Mr. Post has committed a breach of contract.

Mr. Green, a tile worker, contracts to point up the brick front of Mr. Wilson's apartment house and to do the work carefully. Mr. Green does a sloppy, unskilled job and, thus, commits a breach of contract.

REMEDIES FOR BREACH OF CONTRACT

When a contract is broken, the person who is damaged may sue for breach of contract; in such a suit ordinary, traditional remedies for breach of contract are (1) recovery of damages in a court of law or (2) specific performance. *Damages* means a sum of money awarded as compensation for injury. Damages may be nominal when the harm caused by the breach is insubstantial. Ordinary damages are called compensatory damages, that is, damages for substantial injury.

The Blanford Automobile Agency sells an automobile for $2,000 to Mr. Rubin, who has already found a purchaser who will pay $2,500 for the car. If the Blanford Agency fails to deliver the machine in accordance with the contract, Mr. Rubin can recover for his expected profit of $500. If Mr. Rubin had no such definite purchaser, he could only recover the difference between the market price of the automobile and the contract price of the automobile.

Sometimes the granting of money damages would be an inadequate remedy for the contract breached, so a court will say to the party who has breached the contract, "You are commanded to carry out the contract that you entered into; if you do not do so, you will be guilty of contempt of court and go to jail." This is called *specific performance*.

Mr. and Mrs. Foster saved for years to buy their dream house. They entered into a written contract with Mr. Ruther to buy his house for $30,000. Then Mr. Ruther changed his mind and said, "I guess I won't sell." A court would say, "Dollars-and-cents damages would be an insufficient remedy. You agreed to sell the house to Mr. and Mrs. Foster, and you must go through with the deal."

FINE PRINT IN CONTRACTS

The United States Supreme Court in recent decisions has held that any waiver of constitutional rights must be "voluntary, intelligently, and knowingly" made and that the waiver clause must be conspicuous in the contract to meet the requirements of the Uniform Commercial Code (see Chapter 10). Although the field of consumer protection has only been scratched in connection with the law of contracts, legal scholars predict that fine print clauses in contracts between parties of unequal economic status and bargaining power are on the way out and will not be enforced by the courts in the future.

5

Intentional Harms
to Person and Property

This chapter concerns a branch of the law of torts. A *tort* is a civil wrong, other than a breach of contract, for which one may have a remedy in the form of an action for damages. In order to be charged with legal responsibility for a tort, one must be at fault, that is, guilty of an intentional wrong or of negligence. This chapter deals with intentional wrongs to persons and property; negligent wrongs are discussed in Chapter 7.

In law neither hostile intent nor harmful design is necessary to constitute an intentional act. A person may be liable for doing something even though he meant it to be nothing more than a good-natured practical joke or though he honestly believed he would not injure anyone. In law a person intends to do something when he has the simple desire to bring about an immediate result.

INTENTIONAL INTERFERENCE WITH PERSONS

Interference with persons includes assault, battery, illegal confinement, false imprisonment, and words or acts causing mental suffering. (Defamation, involving the law of libel and slander, is another type of intentional wrong and is treated in Chapter 6.)

Assault and Battery

An *assault* does not involve physical contact with another person; a *battery* does.

What Constitutes Assault? When one intends to inflict harm on another and puts the other person in fear of injury, one may be liable for assault.

Mr. Litton threatens to strike his neighbor with a club. Bystanders intervene and prevent Litton from striking his neighbor. The mere threat of bodily harm is sufficient to make Litton liable to his neighbor for assault.

Even though the intent is only to scare and not to cause bodily harm, the one threatening the action may be liable for assault if the person threatened believes he will be injured.

Rococco, an expert knife thrower, intending to frighten but not hit, Baldy, his friend, who is standing against a building, throws a knife at him. Baldy fears that he will be injured by the knife. Rococco is technically liable for assault.

Personal hostility is not necessary to make a person liable for assault.

Harry, intending to play a joke on Jim, disguises himself as a thug, accosts Jim on a lonely road, and pointing an unloaded pistol at him says, "Stick 'em up." Harry is liable to Jim for assault.

What Constitutes Battery? Any intentional, harmful, unprivileged contact with another person is a battery and may give rise to legal liability. As in the case of assault, it is not necessary that the battery be inspired by personal hostility or the desire to injure the other person.

Blackie, a practical joker, trips his friend Joe. Blackie's intention was only to throw Joe off balance and embarrass him to the amusement of friends who were standing nearby. Instead, Joe did not recover his balance and was thrown against a picket fence, lacerating and bruising his arm. Blackie is liable to Joe even though Blackie had no hostility toward Joe.

Moreover, the courts have held that well-meaning but unauthorized surgical operations may give rise to a cause of action of battery.

Mr. Ingalls employs Dr. Jones to operate on the septum of his nose. During the course of the nose operation Dr. Jones removes Mr. Ingalls' diseased tonsils. Because the tonsillectomy was unauthorized, in a suit the court awards damages against Dr. Jones.

Injuries Inflicted in Self-Defense If one should inflict injury on another person in self-defense, one would not be liable (1) if he believed that the other person intended to injure him, (2) if the bodily harm was not intended or not likely to cause death or serious bodily injury, and (3) if he believed that the injury about to be done to him could be prevented only by infliction of injury on the other person. As Justice Holmes said, "Reasoned reflection cannot be demanded in the face of an uplifted revolver."

Butchman, known to be a desperate character, has threatened to shoot Senko on sight, and Senko knows it. Butchman comes into the room where Senko is standing and reaches into his pocket. Senko mistakenly believes that Butchman is about to shoot him and knocks Butchman down. Senko is not liable to Butchman.

The law does not permit infliction of injury as a punishment or in retaliation for a past aggression or as a warning.

Harvey strikes Dewey with a cane. Dewey disarms Harvey. Dewey is not then privileged to inflict a beating upon Harvey.

Little Joe throws a snowball at Mr. Brown, hitting Mr. Brown in the eye and causing severe pain. Mr. Brown is not privileged to inflict a beating on Joe, either as punishment or as a warning against similar misconduct in the future.

The question of whether excessive force may be used in self-defense frequently arises. The answer is that the person attacked may use only reasonable means to stop the attack.

Edson attempts to slap Taft's face. Taft can prevent Edson from doing so by pushing him away or leaving the room or locking the door or even confining himself, but Taft is not privileged to beat and inflict serious injuries on Edson.

A person is privileged to knock another down if the latter threatens him with violence. But the one attacked is not privileged to knock his attacker down if he knows that to do so may kill him.

Jones threatens to slap McDonald's face. Although he knows that Jones is suffering from heart disease and that the slightest shock to Jones may prove fatal, McDonald picks up a cane and strikes Jones several times. McDonald has abused his privilege of self-defense; he had no right to use such violent means to resist Jones's threat of slight harm.

Defense of Land as Self-Defense   Bodily harm may be inflicted on another in order to prevent intrusion on one's land or property. In other words, defense of land may be a form of self-defense.

During a family automobile tour in the country, the Shavers stop to admire Mr. Lint's apple orchard and to gather fruit. Mr. Lint may use such reasonable force as is necessary to expel the Shavers from his farm.

However, as in defense against personal harm, a possessor of land or property is not privileged to expel an intruder if he knows that the intruder's condition or surrounding circumstances are such that expulsion would be likely to cause death or serious bodily harm.

Beatrice comes to the railroad station to take a train. She finds that it has already departed. The stationmaster permits Beatrice to remain in the station until late at night. At closing time he forces her to leave, ejecting her into a violent sleet and ice storm. She goes out in search of a hotel and catches pneumonia. The stationmaster may be liable to Beatrice.

Owners of land and property are privileged to use mechanical devices to protect their land and property. For example, a property owner may close off his lawn with a barbed-wire fence to prevent neighbors from taking a shortcut across it. The property owner is not liable if the neighbor uses a shortcut without the landowner's permission and scratches himself on the barbed-wire fence. On the other hand, a landowner may not charge his fence with electric voltage strong enough to electrocute an animal or a person. The use of electrically charged fences to confine or exclude animals is generally permissible providing the voltage is mild.

Illegal Confinement

Illegal confinement is a broad term including any confinement by physical barriers or by force or by threats of physical force. Illegal confinement may be committed by any person whether or not he claims to have legal authority. A person may be liable to another if he causes the other to be illegally confined.

Just before the lunch hour, Mr. Grant sends his clerk into a cold-storage vault to take inventory. Then he locks the door of the vault during the lunch hour. Mr. Grant is liable for the illegal confinement of his clerk.

Some authorities call any illegal confinement "false imprisonment," but the modern and more easily understood viewpoint interprets false imprisonment as one phase of the general subject of illegal confinement. Usually *false arrest* is committed by someone who asserts he has the legal authority to arrest or to imprison. In false imprisonment it makes no difference whether or not the illegal act is inspired by malice or by personal hostility. The first of the two examples which follow illustrates false arrest; the second, false imprisonment.

Mr. Jameson, a private citizen, obtains a policeman's uniform and badge. He accosts Mr. Dickerman saying, "I arrest you." Dickerman, believing Jameson to be a policeman, submits to the arrest. Jameson is liable for illegal confinement of Dickerman.

Sharp exhibits to Montgomery an invalid warrant for Montgomery's arrest. Montgomery, after inspecting the warrant, concludes it must be valid and submits to the arrest. Sharp takes Montgomery into custody (and is liable for false imprisonment).

False arrest and false imprisonment should be distinguished from *malicious prosecution*, the groundless institution of criminal proceedings. A person may be guilty of false arrest even though there was a formal compliance with the requirements of law, such as swearing out a valid warrant for arrest. Liability in malicious prosecution depends on proof of malice and an absence of probable cause for conviction as well as a termination of the proceeding in favor of the person who is criminally prosecuted.

Words or Acts Causing Mental or Emotional Distress

Emotional distress may be brought about in many ways. The victim of an intended physical injury almost always suffers at least temporary emotional or mental stress. Emotional or mental distress may simply be the desired result of one person's action or attack on another.

There is a growing tendency for the courts to recognize liability for inflicting intentional mental or emotional disturbances, even though unaccompanied by physical injury. In the past New York courts have held that mental or emotional injuries, standing alone, were so nebulous that it would be against public policy to permit money recoveries; this "type of injury could be feigned without detection and to permit recovery would result in a flood of litigation." Pennsylvania has held that to allow such claims "would open a Pandora's box." In 1962, however, the New York Court of Appeals in a four-to-three decision overruled a sixty-year-old doctrine and now allows recovery for emotional or mental injuries even though there is no physical contact, if the injured person was within the "zone of danger" of physical injury. California has gone one step further by allowing a dollars-and-cents recovery for the emotional stress which a mother suffered in witnessing an injury to her child.

Intended Emotional Distress   No matter how evil the intention of the one causing the emotional or mental disturbance, there is in most states no legal liability simply for causing a person mental or emotional distress unless it is accompanied by physical injury.

Miss Simpson, as a joke, tells her friend that an ordinary dance to which she is invited is a fancy dress dance. The friend goes to the dance in a masquerade costume. Realizing the situation at the dance, the friend is humiliated. Miss Simpson is not liable.

Mr. Corey tells Mr. Ditmore, his enemy, that his neighbors believe him to be guilty of gross immoral conduct. Mr. Ditmore so worries over this that he becomes ill. Mr. Corey is not liable to Mr. Ditmore.

Emotional Distress Resulting from Illegal Acts   One who commits an illegal act may be liable for damages resulting from mental or emotional distress incident to other damages which are recoverable. This is an exception to the broad rule that an act that simply causes emotional distress results in no legal liability. The reasoning for the exception seems to be based on situations in which the wrongdoer's crime or flagrant violation of human or property rights results in mental or emotional damage for which he should be held responsible.

A hotelkeeper breaks into a room occupied by his two guests, Mr. Seltzer and his wife, and accuses them (wrongly) of not being married and orders them to leave the hotel. The hotelkeeper is not only liable for the invasion of the Seltzers' privacy and breach of his obligation to them as a hotelkeeper but is also liable for the humiliation and emotional suffering caused the Seltzers by his unlawful acts.

Emotional Distress and Common Carriers Common carriers, such as railroads, are obligated to provide the public with comfortable, safe, and courteous service. A special rule makes common carriers liable to the public for offenses resulting from the insulting conduct of employees. Common instances that created the need for this special rule are the case of a conductor who wrongfully accuses a passenger of not paying his fare, the case of a passenger who has paid his fare but who is ejected from the train or otherwise treated as though he had not paid, the case of a trainman who uses insulting language to one who is slow in leaving the train, and so on.

INTENTIONAL INTERFERENCE WITH PROPERTY

Interference with persons discussed in the preceding section differs from intentional interference with property, which is concerned with trespass and conversion.

Trespass

The rules of trespass come down to us from the common law and are extremely complicated. Trespass, in its broadest sense, is any injury to person or property; in this chapter trespass is treated in its strict or technical sense as an unlawful entry on land or real property.

Trespass is a technical invasion of property (real estate) rights. One who intentionally and without consent enters on the land of another is liable to the owner as a trespasser regardless of whether any harm has been done. The same technical trespass may apply if the person throws or places on land anything that does not belong there.

Lewis intentionally throws a pail of water against his neighbor's house. Lewis is a trespasser.

Egbert drives a stray horse from his pasture into the pasture of his neighbor. Egbert is a trespasser.

Wilcox erects a dam across a stream thereby causing the water to back up and flood Smithfield's land. Wilcox is a trespasser.

An intrusion is not restricted to the surface of the earth but may be anything above or below the land in question.

Biggs erects a house on the border of Lounsberry's land. The eaves of the roof overhang Lounsberry's land. Biggs is a trespasser.

Hinkleman strings a telephone wire across the corner of Harrison's land. This is a trespass.*

Damage Resulting from Trespass   Technical trespass may not be of serious consequence in the ordinary case, but it becomes important when damages result to the owner of the land.

Lowey, without permission, decides to do a little amateur welding in McCabe's blacksmith shop. In order to do so he lights a fire in the forge, but before leaving he takes precautions to make sure that the fire is out. However, a high wind brings the fire to life again, and the fire burns down the shop. Lowey is liable to McCabe for the loss of his shop.

Trespass by Mistake   One who intentionally enters the land of another under the mistaken belief that he is entitled to the possession or ownership of the land or that he has consent or privilege to enter the land may be liable as a trespasser.

The X Mining Company, having mistaken the location of its boundary, takes coal from Mr. Abbott's land. The mining company is liable to Abbott although the mistake was reasonable.

Mr. Cady employs a surveyor of recognized ability to survey his land. The survey shows that he owns a particular strip of land. He tills the land and prepares it for cultivation. It turns out that the survey is wrong and that the land belongs to his neighbor, Mr. Christian. Cady is liable to Christian for trespassing.

Accidental Trespass   The situation in the case of a completely accidental and nonintentional trespass on land is different from the intentional, though mistaken, trespass. It does not result in legal liability.

Mr. Felter is driving his automobile along the street when he suddenly has a heart attack. He loses control of the automobile and it runs up on Mr. Goodman's property, damaging his lawn. Mr. Felter is not liable to Mr. Goodman.

Conversion

The subject of trespass is real property; here we will discuss the subject of conversion, personal property. *Conversion* may be com-

* For liability of landowner for injuries sustained by trespasser, see Chapter 7.

mitted (1) by intentionally taking property from its owner, (2) by intentionally destroying or altering property, (3) by using property without permission, (4) by disposing of property without permission by sale, lease, or in other ways, or (5) by refusing to surrender another's property on demand.

Intentionally Taking Another's Property Personal property may be improperly taken from the possession of another by open or obvious means or may be taken by fraudulent schemes or devices.

While his neighbor Amboy is on vacation, Bird walks over to Amboy's garage and "borrows" his lawnmower. Bird has no legal right to do this and is liable for the conversion of Amboy's lawnmower.

Beck, representing himself as a garage man, goes to the King home and tells Mrs. King that her husband has authorized him to take the King automobile to have it repaired. Through this fraudulent device Beck secures the automobile for a day's pleasure and later returns it to the King garage. Beck is liable for conversion of the automobile.

Destruction or Alteration of Property One who is legally entitled to possession of property but who does not own it has no right to alter or destroy it; if he does so, he commits the legal wrong of conversion. The rule is clear in the destruction of property, but sometimes disputes arise when the form of the property is altered, rather than destroyed, for its identity may be lost when altered. Examples of acts altering property are sawing logs into lumber, making of grapes into wine, and manufacture of cloth into clothing.

Using Property without Owner's Permission When a person lawfully comes into possession but not ownership of property, he has no right to use it without the permission of the owner. If he does so, he may be liable for conversion.

Before Morgan goes to Florida for a month, he stores his automobile in Brennan's garage. Every Sunday Brennan uses the car to take his family for a ride. Brennan is liable to Morgan for conversion of the automobile.

Groves sends his tuxedo to Cleener to be pressed and cleaned. Cleener wears the suit to a social event. Groves finds out and recovers damages from Cleener for converting the suit to his own use.

Disposing of Property without Owner's Permission A person who is legally entitled to possession but not ownership of property may be guilty of conversion if he delivers it to another with the intention of transferring an interest in it. Conversion results when the sale, lease, gift, or other transfer of property is made without permission of the owner.

Jane loans her emerald ring to Margaret for an indefinite period. Margaret keeps it for several years. She finally treats it as her own and one day in a generous mood makes a gift of the ring to Helen. Margaret is liable for converting the ring to her own use.

Scott borrows money from Belcher who pledges negotiable bonds as security for the loan. Before the loan is due Belcher sells the bonds. Belcher is liable for conversion for the improper sale of the bonds.

Refusal to Surrender Property on Owner's Demand   When one in possession of property refuses to surrender it to the owner he is liable for conversion. If the demand for the surrender of the property is unreasonable or if the delivery is held up because of doubt about the proper claimant, there is no liability for conversion.

Johnson, who has stored his furniture at the Excellent Warehouse, demands delivery of the furniture at midnight. Excellent tells Johnson that it will not deliver the furniture at midnight but that the furniture will be available to Johnson at a reasonable hour in the morning. Excellent Warehouse is not liable to Johnson for conversion.

Manhouser ships goods to Bush. Bush presents to the railroad company a bill of lading for the goods and demands immediate delivery. The railroad informs Bush that the goods will be delivered as soon as it is satisfied that he is really Bush. Bush becomes angry and sues the railroad for conversion. The railroad is not liable, and Bush loses the suit.

6
Defamation of Character

Character may be defamed in law in two ways: by libel or by slander. *Libel* consists of the publication of defamatory matter in the form of written or printed words or pictures, caricatures, statues, and so forth in letters, circulars, petitions, newspapers, or books. A libel may be published by broadcasting or telecasting, by means of radio or television, if the speaker or the actor reads or follows a prepared script or written notes. *Slander* consists of the publication of defamatory matter by spoken words, gestures, and so on.

DETERMINING A DEFAMATION OF CHARACTER

When is a communication defamatory? It is defamatory when it tends to harm the reputation of another, to lower his esteem in his community, to cause persons to stop associating or dealing with him, or to expose a person to scorn, ridicule, or contempt. One can defame another by questioning his personal morality or integrity or by branding him with a loathsome disease which would cause people to shun him. Examples of defamatory statements or acts follow:

A newspaper publishes a statement that a certain department store is conducting dishonest business or is in financial distress.

Miss Smith states that Miss Jones, while posing as a dressmaker, is really the mistress of a prominent citizen.

Mr. Roberts draws and circulates a caricatured figure labeled "murderer." The figure is easily recognized as Mr. Edwards.

A tells his friends that *X*, the neighborhood druggist, consorts with dope peddlers.

A woman tells her friends that a certain market sells contaminated meat.

Although decency and courtesy require us to speak well of the dead, there is no legal liability to the estate of a deceased person for defaming the deceased's reputation. One who falsely and without justification publishes defamatory material about a corporation or a partnership is liable to the firm.

The Jones Newspaper Company publishes an article charging that a life insurance company has fraudulently issued stock. The newspaper has defamed the life insurance company and would be liable in a suit for damages.

The Smith Newspaper Company publishes a statement that a law firm is composed of shysters who are devoid of honesty and fair dealing. The firm and the individual members of the firm have been defamed and may sue separately for damages.

DETERMINING PUBLICATION OF DEFAMATION

What constitutes publication of defamatory matter? In law, *publication* of defamatory matter is the communicating of the defamation, intentionally or carelessly, to a person other than the one defamed. Thus, three people must be involved to establish publication. Examples of an unpublished and a published defamation follow:

Harry and Joe are in the woods on a hunting trip. Harry accused Joe of murder. There is no one else in the vicinity to hear the accusation. Harry has not published a slander.

McDonald, during his lunch hour, tells his fellow employee that his neighbor Wilson, a teller in the bank, has been caught dipping into the till and that the bank is going to turn him over to the authorities. McDonald has published a slander.

TYPES OF DEFAMATORY COMMUNICATION

The general types of defamatory communication are statements of fact and expressions of opinion.

Statements of Fact

Statements of fact which amount to defamation consist of accusing a person of a particular act and, thus, exposing that person to scorn, ridicule, or contempt or jeopardizing his business or financial reputation. The example immediately above and the one below illustrate this point.

Cooley writes a letter to his friends accusing Spencer, an amateur golfer, of accepting money for playing in exhibition matches. A number of persons understand that by so accepting money for playing golf Spencer has forfeited his amateur standing. In making the alleged statements of fact, Cooley has defamed Spencer.

Expressions of Opinion

Defamation may consist of opinions expressed with reference to facts either known or undisclosed. Defamation consists of implying that another has been guilty of reprehensible conduct. If you call a person a thief or a murderer, you imply that he has stolen or murdered. As a result, the majority of newspapers are very careful in characterizing the conduct of others.

Harwood writes an article for a newspaper in which he refers to Cahill as a traitor and a "second Benedict Arnold." Harwood has defamed Cahill.

RULES FOR LIBEL AND SLANDER

Entirely without logic and owing to historical background, there are basic differences in the rules for determining when libel and slander are actionable per se. *Actionable per se* means that the publication of the libel or slander makes the publisher liable for defamation even though no special harm results. This is another way of saying that the person defamed does not have to prove damage; it is presumed.

When Libel Is Actionable Per Se

Almost any published libel is actionable per se, regardless of whether special harm has been caused. The person defamed may recover nominal damages and thus be vindicated. Common forms of libel which are actionable per se are those which accuse persons of crimes, immoral conduct, improper conduct in business or profession, dishonesty, and so on.

A newspaper publishes a false article stating that Harmon has "jumped his board bill." The newspaper is liable to Harmon without any proof of special harm to Harmon.

Margaret, a beneficiary of an estate, writes her sister that their cousin, Herbert, the executor of the estate, has been spending estate funds for his own personal gain and has been investing some of the estate funds in his own personal business. Margaret has published a libel which is actionable per se.

Cuphbert circulates a memo to his business associates warning them not to use the services of Boothbay, a certified public accountant, because "he is drunk half the time, runs around with notorious women, and is not to be trusted." When Boothbay sues Cuphbert for libel he does not have to prove special damages.

Robert writes his brother that he is disgusted with Dr. Cuttem, a surgeon, because "he is money crazy, more of a businessman than a doctor, and operates on people at the slightest excuse, whether or not they need surgery." Dr. Cuttem has a libel claim against Robert.

When Slander Is Actionable Per Se

Through the years the courts have handed down rules distinguishing slander from libel and providing for the special treatment of it. How absurd it is to have a law making people responsible for all libel but responsible for slander in only four situations. The need for reform is obvious when a person may be sued for writing a post card saying that someone is dishonest, but he may go scot free for saying the same thing to an audience of a thousand persons.

Slander (generally the spoken word) which results in no special harm is actionable per se only in the following four cases:

1. When one who falsely and without justification publishes a slander to suggest that another has been guilty of a criminal offense which would be (a) chargeable by indictment and (b) punishable by death or imprisonment, he is liable for slander without proof of special damage.

McGillacuddy falsely states to McDonald, "Gunther has served time in state prison." Gunther may sue McGillacuddy for slander and recover nominal damages even though he cannot show any special harm resulting from the slander.

Donovan says to Wilbur, "Gunther is the type of man who would commit murder at the slightest provocation." Donovan has not charged Gunther with the crime and is not liable for slander.

2. When one who falsely and without justification publishes a slander which suggests that another has an existing loathsome disease he is liable, even though there is no proof of special harm.

Jones tells Smith that Brown has venereal disease. Jones is liable to Brown without proof of damages.

3. When one accuses another of improper conduct of a business or profession, he is liable without proof of special harm.

Fisher accuses Smith, a bricklayer, of being a hypocrite. He has not committed slander per se.

Fisher accuses lawyer Jones of being ignorant and incompetent and says that he neglects his clients, spending his time in gambling and drinking. He has committed slander per se.

Cutts calls Vincent, a dry-goods store operator, insolvent. He is liable for slander per se.

4. When one imputes unchastity to a woman, he is liable for slander without proof of special harm.

Herman tells Stanley that Julia is unfaithful to her husband. Herman is liable for damages to Julia.

Proving Special Damages

When slander does not come within the four categories enumerated above, it is necessary to prove special harm. The special harm must be a specific money or material loss which the injured person can show, such as losing his job.

A priest falsely and without justification says that a merchant had been excommunicated from his church. The merchant loses a large number of customers and can prove that his loss stems from the priest's words. The priest is liable to the merchant.

Mary falsely and without justification tells Helen that Beatrice is a vulgar gossip. Helen, though previously a very good friend of Beatrice, stops speaking to her. Mary is not liable to Beatrice without proof of resulting special harm.

Republication of Slander or Libel

One who repeats or republishes defamatory matter is just as liable as if he had originated it.

Sarah tells Mary that their neighbor, Mrs. Blackstone, is a kleptomaniac and has been found guilty of shoplifting. Mary repeats this to her bridge club. Mary is guilty of republishing a slander.

Each time an article is republished a fresh wrong is committed. Thus, a newspaper is liable if without justification it republishes false and defamatory statements, even though it names the author and the paper in which the statements first appeared.

A newspaper syndicate supplies a defamatory article to each newspaper using its service. Each paper that prints the article has published a libel and may be sued.

The Centerville *Herald* prints a libelous article and says that the article has been copied from the Boston *Times*. The fact that it originated elsewhere is no excuse: Reprinting it is libel.

The fact that a mistake has been innocently made or that the person republishing the libel or slander did not intend defamation is no excuse.

DEFENSES TO ACTIONS FOR LIBEL OR SLANDER

There are several defenses to actions for libel and slander; among them are truth, consent, and privilege.

Truth

Truth is always a defense to libel or slander.

Bertram moves to Syracuse, New York, and there opens a real estate brokerage office. Harold, an old acquaintance, recognizes Bertram and writes a letter to a friend saying that Bertram is a proven crook and cannot be trusted. It turns out that Bertram was previously convicted of embezzlement under a different name and had a bad reputation in Nevada, his home state. Harold was justified in libeling Bertram because the statements he made about him were true.

A mistaken belief in the truth of the matter published, although honest and reasonable, is not a defense.

Miss Bonam applied for a teaching position at a private school for girls. The headmistress, in processing Miss Bonam's application, received a report from a reliable investigation agency that Miss Bonam had been discharged from another school for immoral conduct. The headmistress prepared a detailed report to a committee of the school trustees stating that in her opinion Miss Bonam was unfit to hold the teaching position. The report of the investigation agency turned out to be untrue. Although the headmistress of the school acted in good faith in making her report to the committee, she is legally responsible for libeling Miss Bonam.

Consent

A good defense is the *consent* of the person who claims to have been defamed to the publication of the defamatory matter.

A school teacher is summarily discharged by the school board. The teacher demands that the reason for his dismissal be made public, and the president of the school board publishes the reason. The reason turns out to be defamatory, but because the teacher consented to the publication he does not have a case.

Privilege of Those Performing Public Functions

Certain public officials and others charged with the performance of public functions are said to be *privileged,* or free from liability for libel or slander. Judges or judicial officers in the performance of their duties; lawyers, witnesses and jurors, during the course of judicial proceedings; and members of Congress or of state legislatures in the performance of their legislative functions are privileged and cannot be held responsible for libel or slander.

Senator Kleghorn, from the floor of the state senate, charged that Governor Broomfield was a dishonest grafter and was stealing from the public treasury. The governor challenged the senator to repeat such slander outside the walls of the senate. The senator declined and confined his defamatory remarks to the privileged legislative halls.

Circuit Judge Buffim in sentencing Harry S. for the crime of treason, called him a "Judas Iscariot" and "a traitor to his flag and his country"; these judicial pronouncements were broadcast over the radio and appeared in the press. It later turned out that Harry S. was convicted on perjured testimony, and he was subsequently freed. Thereafter he sued Judge Buffim for slander. The judge was not liable, because his remarks as a judicial officer are privileged.

Husband and Wife

A husband or wife is absolutely privileged to publish to his or her spouse false and defamatory matter concerning a third person. This exception to the rule undoubtedly came from the old common-law concept that a husband and his wife were, in law, one person. Today the rule has a practical application: When one spouse tells the other some scandalous slander about a neighbor, the scandal, up to that point at least, has not been broadcast.

Fair Comment

The interests of society require that matters of public interest should be the subject of frank and open comment, criticism, and discussion without fear of liability for libel or slander; hence, the law says that *fair comment* is a matter of right. The question occasionally arises, "Is the comment fair and reasonable?" Sometimes comment or criticism goes beyond the bounds of fairness and becomes a matter of personal malice or spite.

A comment is said to be fair when it is (1) based on facts, (2) truly stated, (3) free from charges of improper or dishonorable motives on the part of the person whose conduct is criticized, and (4) an honest expression of opinion or belief.

Mere exaggerations, irony, wit, or sarcasm will not render the comment defamatory.

A congressman voted against the Lend-Lease Bill in the House of Representatives in February 1941. As a result, a newspaper in an editorial charged that the congressman was giving aid to the agents of Hitler and Mussolini and asked the congressman if he wanted to be classed as a Quisling. The congressman brought suit for libel. The court held that the editorial was fair comment and hence free from liability.

But, when comment or criticism is motivated by malice, the privilege of fair comment is lost.

A newspaper critic refers to a college lecturer as illiterate, uncultivated, coarse, and vulgar. The critic also says that the professor is sensational, absurd, foolish, and a literary freak. In a libel suit the court holds that the critic went beyond the limits of fair comment and indulged in a personal attack that exposed the professor to public contempt, shame, and ridicule. The court held the newspaper to be responsible.

The defense of fair comment should not be confused with the privilege of making a fair and true report of legislative, judicial, or legal proceedings. A defendant in a libel suit may show by way of defense that he was just reporting a public proceeding or divulging to the public (by way of newspaper report, for example) matters that are on file in a public office and open to inspection by the public.

The Supreme Court in recent years has changed the basic law of libel by protecting freedom of the press under the First Amendment of the Constitution. In the decision of *New York Times* v. *Sullivan* (1964), the Court held that a public official may not recover damages for libel against a newspaper unless the public official can prove that the defamatory statement was published with malice: that is, with knowledge that the statement was false or with reckless disregard of whether it was false or not. Later the Supreme Court extended the protection of the *New York Times* rule by holding that news media are protected in making otherwise libelous statements against private individuals where the defamatory statements involve issues of "public or general concern."

A radio station in reporting on a crackdown on pornographers referred to a magazine as "obscene" and said that the publisher was engaged in the "smut literature racket." The Court rejected the publisher's suit for libel saying that the radio station was discussing "an issue of public concern."

DAMAGES FOR LIBEL OR SLANDER

As indicated before, the victim of a libel or slander that is actionable without proof of special harm may recover at least nominal damages. Nominal damages usually are a trivial sum, such as six cents. But a person who has been the victim of libel or slander may also recover compensatory damages for the value of the loss suffered. The injured person may also show special harm resulting from the libelous publication.

Cato falsely and without justification writes a letter to Raedes's employer telling him that Raedes is a radical labor agitator and a bad influence on other employees. As a result, Raedes is discharged and may recover damages from Cato for the injury to his reputation and may also recover for the loss of his employment.

Hapgood falsely and without justification, in the presence of another, charges Lemon, a merchant, with using false weights and measures, as a result of which Lemon's business drops off noticeably. Lemon may recover from Hapgood damages for loss of reputation and loss of business.

Facts which tend to restrict or limit the amount of damages are sometimes called "matters in mitigation of damages." Such facts include (1) publication, (2) bad reputation of the plaintiff, and (3) proof that the defendant acted with proper motives and a belief in the truth of what he said. These three factors have reduced damages, but they do not limit or restrict basic liability for libel or slander. Proof of proper motives or belief in the truth of the slander or the libel would not prevent a verdict in favor of the person libeled or slandered, but it could be a factor considered by the jury in determining the amount of the damages. In determining the amount of an award for general damages the jury should consider the character of the plaintiff and his standing in the community together with the effect the language used may have had on his reputation.

7
Negligence

Negligence is a branch of the law of torts. *Tort* is a term applied to a miscellaneous group of private or civil wrongs, excluding breach of contract, for which courts provide remedies in the form of actions for damages. A negligent act is a careless or reckless one rather than an intentional harm. It is the omission of a duty that should have been performed or the performance of an act that should not have been done. A person is negligent when he fails to use the care that a reasonable person would use in the same circumstances. The criterion is: How would a reasonable person act?

FACTORS AFFECTING NEGLIGENCE CLAIMS

In a negligence claim a person must generally prove (1) that the person against whom the claim is made had a duty and was negligent and (2) that he himself was not guilty of even the slightest negligence contributing to the accident.

Duty

A person suing another for negligence must prove that a duty actually devolved on the second person. Duty may be imposed by statute, by court decisions, or by circumstances peculiar to the situation. A duty may also be assumed; that is, one may offer to perform a particular act and then may perform it negligently.

Contributory Negligence

Contributory negligence is the want of ordinary care which contributes to an accident. Contributory negligence may result from the failure of the person claiming damages to use the care which a reasonable person would have used to avoid danger, or it may result from his voluntarily exposing himself to danger. The latter, sometimes called "assumption of risk," will defeat a recovery in a negligence action.

The rule of contributory negligence is: If the claimant (one who seeks damages) is guilty of *any* negligence which contributes to his own injury, he has no claim.

Fredericks is injured in an accident in which he himself is 10 percent to blame. Even though his own negligence contributes only slightly to the accident, he is not permitted to recover for his injuries.

The rule of contributory negligence has been criticized for its harshness, for it may absolutely bar recovery for damage against the person most to blame.

Comparative Negligence

Some states (Arkansas, Colorado, Connecticut, Florida, Georgia, Hawaii, Idaho, Maine, Massachusetts, Minnesota, Mississippi, Nebraska, Nevada, New Hampshire, New Jersey, North Dakota, Oklahoma, Oregon, Rhode Island, South Dakota, Texas, Utah, Vermont, Washington, Wisconsin, and Wyoming), and in certain cases the federal courts apply the rule of *comparative negligence*, through which an injured person is not barred from recovering damages when he is guilty of contributory negligence. The amount of damages recovered, however, is reduced in proportion to the amount of the negligence of the claimant. The determination of the extent of the claimant's negligence is left to the court and jury.

Egan is injured in the Stone Company's store. The case is submitted to a jury in Wisconsin, which has the rule of comparative negligence. The jury finds that the Stone Company was negligent, that the amount of the damages suffered by Egan was $10,000, and that Egan's own negligence contributed to his injury in the proportion of 25 percent. Therefore, judgment is rendered in favor of Egan against the Stone Company for 75 percent of the total injury, or $7,500.

Doctrine of Last Clear Chance

A person who has negligently exposed himself to injury may nevertheless recover from a negligent wrongdoer if the latter was aware of the claimant's helplessness and could have, had he chosen to, avoided injuring him. This *doctrine of last clear chance* is based on the principle that even when the plaintiff is negligent, the defendant should be charged with liability if by exercising care he might have avoided the consequences of the plaintiff's negligence. The following is a classic illustration:

Caspar, knowing that the motor in his ancient automobile often sputters and stalls, drives onto a railroad crossing where his automobile stalls in front of an approaching train. If the railroad engineer has ample opportunity to discover Caspar's stalled automobile and yet fails to use reasonable caution in stopping the train before it hits the automobile, Caspar, or his surviving relatives, may recover damages against the railroad under the doctrine of last clear chance.

NEGLIGENCE CLAIMS IN AUTOMOBILE ACCIDENTS

Public streets are for everyone's use, but in using public property one must conduct himself in a manner which will not cause injury to others. Thus, one who drives an automobile on public streets must do so in a reasonable manner and with that degree of care which a prudent person would use under the circumstances.

There are certain statutes governing the use of automobiles on the streets, such as laws fixing the speed limit and laws requiring vehicles to be in good mechanical condition (to have passed state inspection). A violation of one of these statutes may be the proximate cause of an injury and hence actionable negligence. Common sense and good judgment are necessary in obeying these regulations, too. For instance, although the speed limit may be thirty miles per hour in a certain area, one cannot always drive at that speed in that locality without fear of negligence, for the street at a particular moment may be so crowded or so icy that twenty miles per hour might be a reckless and excessive rate of speed.

Pedestrians also have certain duties in the use of the streets. A pedestrian jaywalking (crossing against traffic lights or between intersections) or failing to heed a siren timely blown or in rural areas walking on the wrong side of the road or failing to look for approaching vehicles may be just as responsible as the driver of the automobile that hit him. Moreover, the pedestrian's negligence may prevent him from recovering for his injuries.

Automobile Accident Claims

Who is at fault in an automobile accident is usually a question of fact depending upon particular conditions and circumstances at the time and place of the accident. As traffic has increasingly jammed our highways, so also have lawsuits arising out of automobile negligence actions jammed the court calendars in our metropolitan areas. In these court cases the injured persons (the plaintiffs) sue car owners and drivers (the defendants); 90 percent of these car owners and drivers are insured by liability insurance companies which furnish legal counsel to defend suits.

Automobile Liability Insurance

Although there are a number of other kinds of automobile insurance with special benefits (such as medical payments, collision, and comprehensive insurance), the basic type of automobile insurance of concern is liability insurance. *Automobile liability insurance* protects the insured against the claims of others. In a liability policy the insurance company agrees to pay for all damages which the owner of the car may become legally obliged to pay, as a result of ownership, maintenance, or use of the automobile. This type of insurance is based on *legal liability*.

Determining Legal Liability

The rule of contributory negligence in auto accident cases applies in twenty-five of the fifty states: Alabama, Alaska, Arizona, California, Delaware, Illinois, Indiana, Iowa, Kansas, Kentucky, Louisiana, Maryland, Michigan, Mississippi, Missouri, Montana, New Mexico, New York, North Carolina, Ohio, Pennsylvania, South Carolina, Tennessee, Virginia, and West Virginia. In order for a claimant in these states to have a good claim, he must be prepared to prove (1) that the person against whom the claim is made was negligent and (2) that he himself was not guilty of any negligence which contributed to the accident.

If the *driver* (rather than the owner) of the automobile is negligent, is the car owner still responsible (legally liable)? And under such circumstances, can the injured person collect from the insurance company? The legislatures in some states have passed special laws making the car owner responsible in such cases for the driver's negligence, but in most states the owner of a motor vehicle is liable only for his own negligence and not for the driver's. In the absence of a special law passed by the legislature, the car owner when not present in the car at the time of the accident is liable for injuries sustained by others *only if* the car is being driven by his agent or employee.

In California, Florida, Idaho, Iowa, Michigan, Minnesota, Nevada, New York, and Rhode Island, the car owner is liable for the operation of an automobile if it is driven with the permission or consent of the owner.

Saber of Binghamton, New York, lends his automobile to a neighbor. The neighbor runs into a pedestrian who makes a claim against Saber. Saber is held responsible by reason of Section 59 of the Vehicle and Traffic Law of the State of New York, which makes the owner liable for the operation of a vehicle when it is being used "with the permission, either express or implied, of such owner."

In Connecticut, Massachusetts, New Jersey, Oregon, Tennessee, and West Virginia, the law imposes liability on the owner and presumes that at the time of the accident the automobile was being driven by an authorized agent or someone who had the owner's consent. This presumption is called a "rebuttable presumption," that is, the owner can show that the presumption is contrary to the facts.

The *family purpose doctrine* exists in eighteen states (Alaska, Arizona, Colorado, Connecticut, Georgia, Kentucky, Michigan, Nebraska, Nevada, New Jersey, New Mexico, North Carolina, North Dakota, Oregon, South Carolina, Tennessee, Washington, and West Virginia). This doctrine makes the head of the family liable for the negligence of a member of the family while driving the family car. The rule is said to be necessary because not all family members may be financially responsible.

Mr. Rathbun of Detroit, Michigan, owns a Buick which his son, Robert, drives to a high school dance. Owing to his own negligence, Robert is involved in an accident, and his high school classmates make claims against Mr. Rathbun. These claims are sustained under the family purpose doctrine, even though the son was not driving the car on his father's business. Mr. Rathbun's insurance company has to pay the claim because of Mr. Rathbun's legal liability.

Types of Automobile Accident Claims and Means of Settlement

Automobile accident claims may be treated under various headings, such as claims for personal injuries, death claims, and property damage claims and in a different type of classification, claims of passengers and pedestrians.

Personal Injury Claims   There is no absolute yardstick for measuring the dollars-and-cents value of human suffering, of personal injuries. A *personal injury claim* is worth only the amount for which it can be settled or the amount the jury will award.

In a personal injury case insurance adjusters will usually pay an amount based on the following factors: (1) special damages, that is, out-of-pocket expenses, such as doctors', nurses', and hospital fees and lost earnings; (2) an amount for the person's pain and suffering; and (3) an amount to compensate for permanent injury and disability.

Bodecker is struck by a car and suffers a broken leg. He makes what the doctors call an uneventful recovery with no permanent disability. He is laid up for 6 weeks and then returns to work. His medical bills and loss of income total $1,750. The insurance company values the claim at $3,000 and pays it.

Loss of Consortium In legal actions brought by a husband against a third person for causing injury to his wife, he can recover for loss of "consortium," that is, his wife's services and companionship. Until 1950, only the husband could recover for loss of consortium. Now, due to women's emancipation laws, the rule is changed in nineteen states. Today consortium is defined by the courts to include not only "loss of support or services" but also "such elements as love, companionship, affection, society, sexual relations, solace and more."

Mr. M was completely paralyzed from his waist down as a result of an elevator accident. His wife brought a suit for loss of consortium against the elevator company for negligence based on her claim that her husband would spend the rest of his life as an invalid. The New York Court of Appeals overruled its previous law and recognized a cause of action for consortium in the wife "thereby terminating an unjust discrimination under New York law."

Death Claims In most states the amount which can be recovered for "wrongful death" resulting from an automobile accident is limited to the pecuniary loss to the family. Thus, the relatives of the deceased are limited to proving a dollars-and-cents loss, mental anguish, or loss of the companionship of the decedent. In a few states recovery in death cases is not limited to pecuniary loss, and Alabama allows punitive damages.

Kansas and Tennessee allow damages for mental anguish, loss of companionship, and so forth. Irrespective of the earnings of the decedent or the relationship of the survivors to the decedent, sixteen states limit the amount of damages that can be recovered in *death claims* (wrongful death actions), as in the table on page 74.

Property Damage Claims When an owner claims damages to his car, is he responsible for the negligence of the driver? The answer is that generally the owner *as a claimant* is chargeable with the negligence of the driver (1) if the driver is the employee of the owner, (2) if the owner is in the car and has the right to control it, (3) if the owner knows that the driver is reckless, unskilled, intoxi-

STATE	MAXIMUM RECOVERY	
Colorado	$45,000	(if decedent left neither spouse, minor child, nor dependent parent; otherwise not limited)
Kansas	50,000	
Maine	10,000	(for death of minor child)
Missouri	50,000	
New Hampshire	30,000	(unless decedent left a widow, widower, child or children, father or mother, or relative dependent on decedent, in which case there is no limitation)
South Carolina	5,000	(in action against a county based on defective highway)
	8,000	(in action against state highway department based on defective highway, or negligent operation of a vehicle in construction or repair of highway)
	4,000	(in action against a municipal corporation based on negligent operation of a motor vehicle)
Virginia	75,000	(plus certain expenses)
West Virginia	100,000	

cated, or otherwise unfit to drive, or (4) if the owner permits the use of his car with the knowledge that it is unsafe or defective.

In some states the absentee owner rule permits the owner to recover damages although the driver is partially to blame for the accident, providing (1) the owner was not in the car at the time of the accident and (2) the driver was not the owner's agent or employee.

In New York Parker loans his car to Beeman; Beeman collides with a car owned and driven by Nutley. The accident was caused by the joint negligence of Beeman and Nutley. Because Parker was not in the automobile at the time of the accident, he is not responsible for Beeman's negligence. He sues Nutley and recovers for damages to his automobile.

The average insurance adjuster does not like to settle an automobile property damage claim for more than the amount of the auto repair bill, but the owner of an automobile may legally recover for the difference between the market value of the automobile immediately before and immediately after the accident, where that depreciation represents the true damage to the automobile. Again, most insurance companies discourage claims for loss of use of the vehicle during the time it is being repaired, but the loss of use of the automobile during repair can be an element of damage; if the owner insists, he can recover in court the rental value of the car pending its repair.

Passenger's Claims In the twenty-six states listed below *passenger's claims* come under "guest statutes," which prevent a guest passenger from recovering for injuries unless his host is guilty of willful and wanton misconduct, gross negligence, or intoxication. (In Georgia only gross negligence need be proved.)

Alabama	Iowa	Oregon
Arkansas	Kansas	South Carolina
California	Michigan	South Dakota
Colorado	Montana	Texas
Delaware	Nebraska	Utah
Georgia	Nevada	Vermont
Idaho	New Mexico	Washington
Illinois	North Dakota	Wyoming
Indiana	Ohio	

Some regard the guest statutes as harsh, because in a large number of cases they prevent guest passengers from recovering for their injuries. Those favoring the guest statutes claim that they prevent collusion between car owners and their passengers who are often friends and relatives and who attempt to frame cases against insurance companies. Nineteen states entirely ignore guest statutes and support the common-law rule of ordinary negligence.

Pedestrian's Claims Although a right-of-way is never absolute, it often has an important bearing on the claims of pedestrians injured in highway accidents. In over forty states, pedestrians have the right-of-way on crosswalks or at intersections in the absence of traffic lights. Generally motor vehicles have the right-of-way between intersections of streets and on highways. In effect, the law says that crosswalks are for pedestrians, and in the middle of the block automobiles have the right-of-way. The following is an actual court case:

A pedestrian was seriously injured while crossing the street three feet north of the center of the crosswalk. The court said it was the duty of the pedestrian to maintain such a lookout as was reasonably necessary to enable her to yield the right-of-way to the automobile. The pedestrian did not do so and was guilty of negligence that contributed to her injuries and defeated a recovery in court.

NO-FAULT AUTO INSURANCE

The discussion in the preceding pages about automobile negligence claims is based on the so-called fault system that has come to us through the centuries from ancient Anglo-Saxon law. If we do wrong to someone, we are at fault and hence have to pay damages. If we drive an auto carelessly and injure someone, we are legally liable and have to pay the person injured or the owner of property damaged by our carelessness (negligence). Automobiles are such an important part of our lives and the risk of injury and damage to others is so great that we have to insure against legal liability based on fault. Hence auto liability insurance is carried by nearly every automobile owner.

In the past sometimes the determination of legal liability in auto accidents required going to court with long delays. Our court calendars have become clogged with auto accident cases. Delays and legal technicalities caused public dissatisfaction, resulting in a proposed no-fault system of insurance. Politicians, lawyers, insurance companies, and legislators have debated the merits and weaknesses of no-fault proposals.

No-fault insurance has caught public imagination. To many it seems the answer to public dissatisfaction. Its opponents say we will regret its adoption by many states and that auto accident victims will be the losers. Fourteen states (Colorado, Connecticut, Delaware, Florida, Georgia, Hawaii, Kansas, Maryland, Massachusetts, Michigan, Nevada, New Jersey, New York, Oregon, and Utah) have adopted no-fault plans.

Under the fault system that exists in the remaining thirty-six states, if you are injured in an auto accident, you may recover damages from the person or persons who are legally to blame for the accident. Then liability insurance companies for those people pay you. Of course, if you were to blame for the accident, you cannot collect from anybody. If no-fault insurance applies, then you can collect your medical bills and lost wages (economic loss) from your own insurance company, no matter who is to blame for the accident.

Like other professions and all specialized fields of activity, the insurance industry has its own vernacular, which can make simple explanations sound complicated. For example, insurance people refer to no-fault payments as "first-party benefits" because (according to insurance explanations) they are paid directly to the injured person by his own insurance company. These first-party benefits may only be 80 percent of lost earnings and are reduced by workmen's compensation and social security disability benefits paid to the injured person.

Each of the no-fault laws of the fourteen states is different. Someday they may be uniform. Each state puts a different limit on the amount which your insurance company pays you. Some states put the limit at $5,000, some states at $2,000, and New York state (requiring the largest amount) at $50,000.

Under no-fault you cannot sue the other party for damages resulting from the accident unless your medical expenses exceed a specified amount (varying from $400 to $1,000, depending on the law of your particular state) or unless you sustain a fractured bone, permanent injury, or disfigurement. Each state law is different from the others. The lack of uniformity in state laws on no-fault may lead Congress to pass a federal no-fault plan. Check with your insurance agent and ask him to explain the no-fault requirements of your state if it has such a law.

Example of No-Fault Plan in One State

The Insurance Department of New York state explains the benefits and outlines the highlights of the New York plan, adopted February 1, 1974. It brings about:

1. Prompt payment of economic losses to persons injured in auto accidents, regardless of fault, be they motorists, passengers, or pedestrians
2. Elimination of most lawsuits for bodily injury arising out of auto accidents in New York state, thereby easing the burden on our courts
3. Insurance premium savings for New York motorists

An automobile owner automatically will receive basic no-fault auto insurance from his insurance company in the form of a special endorsement to be attached to his present policy. Supplemental benefits also may be bought.

In the event of an accident, the insurance company that issued a policy on a particular car will pay no-fault benefits to *injured occupants* of that car and to *pedestrians* injured by that car.

The Basic Benefits New York law requires that each registered motor vehicle (other than a motorcycle) be insured for up to $50,000 per person in economic losses to an injured driver and passengers of that vehicle, and to pedestrians injured by it, because of an accident in New York state. The benefits may be less than the injured person's actual economic loss, as is explained below. For example, only 80 percent of lost earnings is paid, and benefits would be reduced by a deductible, if there is one, and by workmen's compensation and social security disability benefits, if any. Within the overall limit, the basic no-fault benefits are as follows:

1. All reasonable and necessary medical and rehabilitation expenses

2. Lost earnings up to $1,000 a month for three years, less 20 percent because the benefit payments, unlike earnings, will not be taxable

3. Up to $25 a day for a year for other reasonable and necessary expenses incurred because of an accident, such as the cost of hiring a housekeeper to perform the services of an injured housewife.

About Property Damage The new no-fault law has no effect on present property damage coverages or financial requirements. Claims for damages to your vehicle still will be covered by your own collision or comprehensive insurance policy, if you have one. As in the past, if another motorist is at fault in an accident, you may file a claim against him for property damage. Therefore, each car owner still must buy property damage liability insurance to protect himself against being sued.

The Right to Sue Under no-fault, you, as an accident victim, retain the right to sue a negligent driver for personal injury losses in certain cases:

1. For your medical expenses and other economic losses to the extent they exceed the no-fault benefit levels required by law

2. For "pain and suffering," if you suffer serious injury, which includes a permanent injury, significant disfigurement, a serious fracture, or an injury needing medical treatment with a total value of more than $500.

3. For injury resulting in death.

As previously noted, you retain the right to sue a negligent driver for property damage.

For Bodily Injury Protection Because accident victims will retain the right to sue a negligent driver for personal injury losses in certain cases, and for property damage in all cases, you, as an auto owner, still may be sued in certain cases. Therefore, you still are required to carry minimum liability insurance (bodily injury limits of $10,000 per person and $20,000 per accident and a property damage limit of $5,000). As in the past, you have the choice of buying higher liability insurance limits.

Out-of-State Protection Most other states and the Canadian provinces require that visiting motorists, including New York auto owners, meet certain minimum insurance requirements. Depending on the state or province, that may be some form of basic no-fault insurance or minimum amounts of the traditional liability insurance, or both.

Rapid Benefit Payment Your losses will be paid as they are incurred: as medical bills are received and earnings would be paid.

The insurance company is required to make payment within 30 days after you supply proof of loss. If the company fails to do so, it must pay 2 percent interest per month on the unpaid amounts and reasonable legal fees if it was necessary for you to retain a lawyer in order to collect a valid claim.

NEGLIGENCE CLAIMS AGAINST OWNERS OR TENANTS OF REAL ESTATE

A person who maintains, controls, and operates a building must do so in such a way as not to cause injury to those lawfully within the premises. If a defective condition exists—such as torn door mats, worn staircases or stair railings, accumulations of refuse, weak ceilings or roofs, or damaged flooring—and a person is injured thereby, the owner of or person in control of or managing the building is liable. One who constructs a building must likewise do so in such a manner as not to injure other persons.

A landlord relinquishes control of those parts of the premises he *lets* (leases, rents) but may be required by statute to keep them in repair. Those portions of the premises which are used by all or most of the tenants, such as hallways, vestibules, or plumbing or heating equipment, are under the control of the landlord.

There are distinctions among the various people who use certain premises. To *invitees* (those who are in the building at the express or implied invitation of the landlord or tenants) the landlord owes care and good judgment in maintaining and managing the property. Another class of persons that the landlord permits to enter the premises is *licensees*, and it consists of people who are lawfully in the building on their own business. Still another class of persons that enters the building is *trespassers*; such persons enter the premises without permission of any kind.

Rule Concerning Trespassers

In cases of negligence to trespassers, the general rule is that the owner or tenant of real estate is not liable for harm to trespassers even if his property is in an unsafe condition. This is because our economic system is based on private ownership, and the courts have considered it a sound policy to allow a person to use his own land in his own way without the burden of watching for and protecting those who come on the land without permission.

In order to catch foxes and other small animals, Bly places traps on a tract of woodland which he owns. A trespasser on the land catches his foot in one of the animal traps and is injured. Bly is not liable to the trespasser even though he could have posted signs in the woods warning trespassers of the danger of the traps.

There are three main exceptions to the rule that a landowner is not liable to a trespasser. These exceptions involve discovery or knowledge of the trespassing and "attractive nuisance."

Discovery of Trespasser   If the presence of the trespasser is discovered and the landowner (or tenant) has an opportunity to avoid injury to the trespasser and fails to do so, he may be liable for injuries sustained by the trespasser.

Joe Carlisle, while trespassing upon the right-of-way of the XYZ Railroad Company, walks through a deep cut only wide enough to permit the passage of a single train. The engineer of an approaching freight train sees Joe but thinks that Joe has enough space to get out of the way of the train. The engineer misjudges the space, and Joe is struck down. The railroad company is liable because, even though he was a trespasser, the engineer knew of Joe's presence and should have stopped the train (used reasonable care) before it hit him.

Knowledge of Frequent Trespassing   When the land owner (or tenant) knows that trespassers frequently intrude upon a particular part of his property, he is required to exercise reasonable care in avoiding injury to trespassers.

The RST Railroad Company knows that many inhabitants of Collarville constantly use a part of the railroad right-of-way as a shortcut to their homes. The path they have worn is so close to where the tracks curve sharply that it is dangerous to use while trains are passing. Aridale is walking along the path when an electric locomotive of the railroad company zooms around the curve at high speed in the same direction. Aridale is hit and seriously injured. The railroad company is liable to Aridale for damages.

Attractive Nuisance   The courts in about two-thirds of the states have adopted the rule that a landowner is liable for bodily harm to trespassing children if they are injured by some structure or artificial condition maintained on land, *providing* the landowner knows that (1) the place is one where children are likely to tresspass, (2) the condition or object is attractive to children, (3) the children are attracted to the object, and (4) the owner fails to use reasonable care and the children are not contributorily negligent. The following is an illustration of this doctrine of attractive nuisance:

The Florida and Mexico Railroad Company maintains a turntable at a point on its unfenced land close to a highway which young children constantly cross. The railroad knows the children are in the habit of playing on the turntable, but a simple locking device, which would make it difficult for the children to set the turntable in motion, is never installed. One day the children set the turntable in motion, and one of them is caught in it and seriously hurt. The railroad company is liable for the injury to the child.

The courts of a number of leading industrial states have rejected the doctrine of attractive nuisance as a piece of sentimental humanitarianism that places undue burden on landowners and industry. On the other hand, in those jurisdictions which have refused to recognize the doctrine, resistance to it is lessening and the courts sometimes establish legal liability in favor of a child trespasser.

Rule Concerning Licensees

A landlord ordinarily is not liable to a licensee. The distinction between liability to licensees and trespassers is that to the licensee the landlord owes no duty of active care, whereas to the trespasser he owes only the duty of not intentionally inflicting injury on him. A landowner or tenant is liable for injuries caused to licensees *only* if (1) he knows his land is dangerous and that it involves an unreasonable risk to licensees or (2) he invites or permits licensees to use the land without first having taken reasonable care to make the condition safe or without warning the licensees of the danger.

A landowner or anyone in possession of land, such as a tenant, would be liable for injuries to a social guest only if he is aware that a dangerous condition imperils his guest. If, in the example given below, John had not known the dangerous condition of the bridge, he would not be liable to Jim because his duty is only to warn of known dangers. But a landowner owes his guest no absolute duty to prepare a safe place for his coming, nor to inspect his land to uncover possible dangers.

John invites his friend Jim to have dinner with him at his country place. John knows that a bridge in his driveway over which Jim must pass is dangerous but that the condition is not apparent. John has not warned Jim. The bridge gives way under Jim's car causing him serious harm. John is liable to Jim.

Rule Concerning Business Visitors

The basic distinction between the landowner's (or tenant's) duty to a social guest and to a business visitor is that the landowner (or tenant) must take reasonable care to discover dangerous conditions on the premises and either make them safe or warn his business visitor of the dangerous conditions; to the social guest or the licensee, the landowner is responsible *only* for disclosing to his guest dangerous defects which happen to be known to him.

Since in our country the business guest receives greater protection than the social guest, there seems to be a fundamental obligation which the possessor of land owes to one from whom he expects to derive a profit or economic benefit. The courts are very liberal in defining a business visitor and have held that customers, those who attend a free lecture or meeting or who enter a place of amusement on a pass, those who go into a store to use a telephone or into a bank to change a bill or go with the owner of an automobile to get his car at a parking lot or garage are all business visitors. Once a building is open to the public, anyone who has a legitimate reason for entering the premises is regarded as a business visitor. A business visitor does not actually have to engage in a commercial transaction, such as making a purchase in a store. But, theoretically, anyone who comes into a store merely to loaf or to get out of the rain, is not a business visitor; to be a business visitor he must be on a legitimate errand in the store.

Although the rule concerning business visitors is liberal, there are limitations. There is no liability for harm resulting from dangerous conditions about which the owner or tenant does not know or which an inspection would not uncover. But if he knows of or creates the dangerous condition, liability may ensue.

Jane enters a supermarket and bruises her leg and ruins her stockings on a crate of produce which the department head has been slow in cleaning up. Jane is a business visitor, and the store is liable for the failure to use reasonable care in providing a safe passageway for her.

Drummer, a guest at the Valley Hotel, is injured when he turns a corner in a slippery corridor where the cleaning people are mopping up. He may recover from the hotel because its employees failed to warn him of the slippery floor.

NEW TRENDS REGARDING TRESPASSERS, LICENSEES, AND INVITEES

We have stated the rules of liability of a property owner to trespassers, licensees, and invitees, that are accepted by most American courts. However, there is a trend on the part of some courts to depart from those classifications as being ill-suited to an industrial, urban society. These later interpretations hold that the label or classification of an entrant on another's property is not important. The test, they say, should be (1) Did the owner of the property know of the dangerous condition? and (2) Did he take steps to correct it?

Liability of Landlords under Leases to Persons Injured on the Property

Generally speaking, a landlord is not liable for bodily injuries sustained by his tenant or others owing to a dangerous condition which develops after the tenant takes possession. The four conditions which are exceptions to this rule are discussed below.

Preexisting Conditions or Covenant to Repair   The landlord is subject to liability for bodily injuries caused to his tenant or others if a condition of disrepair existed before the tenant took possession or if the landlord agreed by covenant in the lease or otherwise to keep the premises in repair.

Carter leases an apartment to Smith, with the agreement that he will keep it in good repair if Smith notifies him of such need. Smith does notify Carter that the dining room ceiling needs repairing. One night the ceiling falls and injures guests of the Smiths. If he had ample time to make the repairs, Carter is liable.

Inherent Defect in Leased Premises   A landlord who conceals from his tenant a condition involving risk of bodily harm to persons coming onto the land is subject to the liability for whatever harm results.

In leasing a dwelling to Simkins, Roberts conceals the fact that termites have weakened supporting floor beams of the house. Simkins, on taking possession, gives a housewarming during which the floor gives way, throwing everybody into the cellar. Roberts is liable to Simkins and his guests.

Use of Premises by Large Number of Persons   A landlord who leases real property for use by a large number of persons may be subject to liability for bodily injuries caused by a dangerous condition existing when the tenant took possession if the landlord knows of this condition and realizes that there might be unreasonable risk to patrons of the tenant.

The Island Amusement Company leases its baseball park to the Eagle Baseball Club for the season. The lease contains a covenant by the tenant to make necessary repairs. Two months after the Eagle Club takes possession, a section of the bleachers collapses, injuring a spectator. The collapse was caused by rotted supports, which a reasonable inspection would have disclosed to either owner or lessee. The Island Amusement Company is liable to the spectator, in spite of the baseball club's covenant to repair the premises.

Retention of Control of Part of Premises A landlord who leases part of a building and retains in his possession another part which the tenants are entitled to use is liable to his tenants or others for injury caused by a dangerous condition in the part of the premises in his control.

Scrooge leases apartments in a six-family apartment house. A tread on one of the steps of the common stairway of the apartment house is loose and needs repairing. One of the tenants while descending the stairway catches her foot on the broken tread, falls and breaks her ankle. The landlord is liable to the woman for failure to repair the stairway.

NEGLIGENCE CLAIMS AGAINST PERSONS SUPPLYING PROPERTY FOR USE OF OTHERS

A manufacturer or seller of merchandise is required to conduct his business so as not to injure consumers. This applies to articles for human consumption as well as to other products.

Manufacturers

A manufacturer who fails to exercise reasonable care in the manufacture of merchandise may be subject to liability for bodily harm resulting from his negligence.

The Royal Motor Co. incorporates in its automobile defective wheels made by the Disc Wheel Co. Desmond buys one of the cars through an independent distributor. While he is driving it, a wheel collapses, and the car swerves and hits and injures Applebaum. Desmond and Applebaum can recover damages from the Royal Motor Co., the Disc Wheel Co., and the distributor.

Sellers of Merchandise

The American courts have almost entirely broken away from the old rule of *caveat emptor* ("let the buyer beware"), by which the seller of merchandise assumed no responsibility for defects in the merchandise. Today it is the seller's well-established duty to make sure that the merchandise cannot harm the buyer. Moreover, the liability of a seller to a buyer for negligence is largely superseded by the strict liability for breach of warranty. Nowadays most storekeepers practically guarantee to the buyer the quality and safe condition of goods.

The provisions of the Uniform Commercial Code (see Chapter 20) supersede to a great extent the rules of negligence concerning claims made directly by a buyer against a seller. In every sale of merchandise there is an implied warranty made by the seller to the buyer that the goods are of merchantable quality and suitable to the purpose for which sold.

Mrs. Stevens buys from a hardware store an insecticide bomb and places it on the shelf in her kitchen. It explodes, and Mrs. Stevens is injured. The hardware store that sold Mrs. Stevens the insecticide bomb is liable for her injuries, even though it had no knowledge of the defective condition of the bomb. If Mrs. Stevens sues, the hardware store must in turn seek recourse from the manufacturer of the bomb.

Strict Liability

The legal doctrine of strict liability is rapidly expanding. It means that an injured person may recover against the manufacturer or seller of an inherently dangerous or defective product even though the manufacturer was not negligent and even though the injured person had no dealings or legal relationship with either the manufacturer or the seller. The courts of certain states, including New York, California, Connecticut, North Carolina, Texas, New Jersey, and Wisconsin, have been liberal in recognizing the rule of strict liability as a means of providing greater consumer protection in our complex marketplace. Examples of products to which strict liability applies are foodstuffs, items intended for bodily use such as cosmetics, automobiles, building supplies, and drugs.

This rule applies even though the seller has used all possible care in the preparation and sale of the product; the injured party in making a claim does not have to prove that the seller was negligent.

An electric hot water heater exploded and substantially destroyed a house. The trial court held that several components of the heater were defective and malfunctioned, and it held the manufacturer liable for damage to the house.

Formerly people using dynamite or other explosives for blasting were immune from damage claims of neighboring property owners provided that rocks or other material were not cast upon the damaged premises. In 1893 a court said, "Public policy is promoted by building up of towns and cities and improvement of property. Any unnecessary restraint on freedom of action of a property owner hinders this." Most states have changed this rule and hold a blaster absolutely responsible for vibration damage caused to neighboring property even though the blaster is not negligent.

In 1969 the New York Court of Appeals overturned the 1893 rule and granted an award of damages to a garage owner whose property was wrecked by a dynamite blast about 125 feet away. This is part of the modern concept of absolute liability without proof of negligence.

Nuisance

Nuisance is a term which has been involved in much legal confusion. There are two types: A *public nuisance* is one of a miscellaneous group of minor criminal offenses that obstruct or cause inconvenience or damage to the public. A *private nuisance* is unreasonable interference with the interests of an individual in the use or enjoyment of land. Such nuisance requires substantial harm, as distinguished from a trespass, which may consist of a mere technicality. A nuisance may be intentional or negligent, or it may result from an unusually hazardous activity for which the law imposes strict liability. The term is vague and has been applied indiscriminately to such inconveniences as a foul smell coming from a manufacturing plant and a cockroach found in food. A nuisance used to be considered an independent tort or legal wrong, but today there is no liability for nuisance unless an individual's rights have been intentionally invaded or one has been negligent or has been engaged in an unusually hazardous activity.

8
Wills

A *will* is a written instrument by means of which a person makes provision for the disposal of his property to take effect upon his death. A will has no legal effect on property mentioned in the will until the death of the testator.

Unless he is a lawyer, no one should draw his own will. The old saying, "A man who acts as his own lawyer has a fool for a client" is certainly true for the person who attempts to draw his own will. When an individual becomes aware of the complicated problems connected with settling the estates of deceased persons, he usually realizes the need for a will.

NECESSITY FOR MAKING A WILL

Unless a person is positive that he is going to die a pauper, he should make a will. The one to consult in drawing a will is not the person in the stationery store who sells printed forms for wills nor an accountant nor a banker, nor a so-called estate planner, but a lawyer.

Too many persons assume that "the law takes care of things without a will." The laws of the states do provide for distribution of an individual's property on his death, but not always in the manner he would have preferred. (See the discussion of descent and distribution, pp. 101–107.) In one state the decedent's wife may receive one-third of his estate and his one-year-old baby may get two-thirds if he dies without leaving a will. According to the laws of another state a man who dies without a will and leaves most of his property in real estate may actually leave his widow only one-third of the life use of the real estate. In still another state a man may die *intestate* (without a will), and his widow may be shocked to find that outside of $5,000 she will receive only one-half his property and his parents, though wealthy, will receive the other half.

Too often, married persons believe that they can avoid the necessity for making a will by having all property jointly held. However, there are reasons, among them tax pitfalls, why jointly owned property does not adequately solve estate problems.

MAKING A VALID WILL

The privileges of making a will, or "speaking after death," is extended by law to persons who have reached the age of maturity and who are of sound mind: The person making the will must understand the nature and purpose of the will and the nature and extent of the property bequeathed. All wills except nuncupative wills must be written. *All* property owned by a *testator* (a man who makes a will) or a *testatrix* (a woman who makes a will) regardless of its nature or location may be disposed of in a will.

Types of Wills

A *holographic will* is one that the testator writes, dates, and signs entirely by hand. Twenty-three states (Alaska, Arizona, Arkansas, California, Idaho, Kentucky, Louisiana, Maryland (if written by anyone serving with the armed services), Mississippi, Montana, Nevada, New York (if written by a soldier, sailor, or mariner), North Carolina, North Dakota, Oklahoma, Pennsylvania, South Dakota, Tennessee, Texas, Utah, Virginia, West Virginia, and Wyoming) recognize holographic wills as valid.

A *nuncupative will* is one declared orally by the testator in his last illness or in contemplation of death and is generally limited to soldiers in actual service or seamen at sea. It is not required to be in writing nor to be formally attested. Most states limit nuncupative wills to a small amount of personal property varying from $50 to $500 in value. Where recognized, the oral will must be reduced to writing within a very short time (from three to thirty days) after it is spoken and must also be very quickly admitted to probate. A nuncupative will is so restricted in scope that it is not practical and should not be attempted. See a lawyer and have a will drawn in the proper way.

Although joint, mutual, and reciprocal wills are discussed by legal writers, these types of wills are used infrequently and are only of passing interest. A *joint will* is a single testamentary instrument containing the wills of two or more persons and jointly executed by them. *Mutual wills* are the separate wills of two or more persons that are reciprocal in their provisions and are generally executed in accordance with an agreement between these persons to dispose of their property to each other or to third persons in a particular manner. (The agreements relating to mutual wills and the execution of mutual wills themselves are full of technical pitfalls and for that reason are seldom resorted to.) *Reciprocal wills* are those in which each of two or more testators makes a testamentary disposition in favor of the other or others.

Essentials of a Valid Will

The requisites of a valid will are that it be an instrument in writing (except in the case of a nuncupative will), that it be executed as prescribed by the statute of the particular state, that it be intended as a will by the person making it, that it dispose of the person's property (to take effect) after his death, and that it be revocable during the lifetime of the maker.

The test of whether or not a particular instrument disposing of property is a will (as distinguished from a deed, mortgage, contract, bond, bill of sale, or trust instrument) is whether the person making the instrument intended it to take effect upon his death and to be revocable until that time. The validity of a will is generally determined by the law of the state of the testator's last domicile (the place which he intended to be his permanent residence). When real estate is disposed of by a will, its validity is determined by the law of the place where the real estate is located.

Form and Content of a Will   It is usually not necessary that any particular form or particular words be used in making a will; the form is not so important as the intent of the testator. The will must be worded with sufficient clarity to enable the court to determine from the will itself just what the testator intended.

Execution of a Will   A will must be executed with all the formalities relating to signatures, witnesses, and the like required by the laws of the state. The purpose of the statutory requirements for the execution of wills is to guard against mistake, undue influence, fraud, or deception.

Generally, it is essential to the validity of a will that it be signed by the testator. The use of a mark by the testator sometimes will suffice. Some state statutes require no more than that the will be in writing and be signed. In such cases it does not matter where the testator's signature is placed; it may be in the margin or at the top of the page, if it is clearly intended to be the signature to the will. Other state statutes require that the signature be at the end of the will; so strict is the rule in these states that if the signature is in the middle or at the side or any place but the physical end (bottom) of the will, the will may be held invalid.

The attestation and subscription by witnesses, where required, must be in accordance with the requirements of the statute. Some states require two witnesses, others three. Some states require that the execution be notarized. The witnesses should be disinterested persons, not beneficiaries.

Witnesses should attest and sign at the request of the testator, who should make it known that the instrument to be executed by him is his last will and testament. Making it known that this instrument is a will is called "publication" and is required by many states. Most states require the testator to sign the will in the presence of the witnesses and the witnesses to sign in the presence of the testator and of each other. The witnesses may also sign a certificate known as an "attestation clause," declaring the truth of the facts and circumstances attending the execution of the will. Such a certificate is useful and customary, but it is not essential to the validity of the will.

Legatees and Devisees A gift of personal property in a will is called a *legacy* or *bequest*. The person who receives such a gift is called a *legatee*. A gift of real estate in a will is called a *devise*. The person who receives a gift of real estate is called a *devisee*.

Disinheritance of Husband or Wife and Relatives A testator may disinherit his relatives and in a very few states his wife; a testatrix may likewise disinherit her relatives, but rarely her husband. There is a popular notion that in order to disinherit a child or other close relative, the maker of a will must give the child one dollar or a token gift. This is not literally true. The requirement of the law is that the testator know or is aware of who are the natural objects of his bounty. In drawing a will, some lawyers feel that it is wise to mention the relatives who are disinherited and, sometimes, to give a tactful reason for disinheritance (in the belief that tact is required, because otherwise the disinherited relative may become indignant and contest the will).

Some states still use the common-law rights of dower and curtesy (see pp. 102–103) and provide that even though a husband or wife be disinherited he or she may still have these rights. Such rights, however, are often vague and unsatisfactory. In most states the surviving spouse, if dissatisfied with the provisions of the will, may within a short time after it is probated file a notice of election to take the same share to which he or she would be entitled under law if his or her spouse had died without leaving a will.

In most states children may also be disinherited. Most states provide that children who are born after the making of a will but before the death of the testator inherit as though there were no will—unless it appears that the testator intended otherwise.

Age Requirements The states are nearly evenly divided on the age requirements for making a will. Twenty-two states require a person making a will to be over twenty-one years of age. Most other states set eighteen as the legal age limit; in Georgia, it is fourteen; in Louisiana, sixteen.

Factors Invalidating a Will

A will is invalid when the person making the will was incompetent to do so, when fraud or undue influence was exercised upon the testator, or when the formal statutory requirements for execution were not fulfilled. A person is incompetent to make a will when he or she is under the lawful age or suffering from a mental disability both of which may prevent him from understanding the nature and purpose of a will and from comprehending generally the nature and extent of his property and from recollecting his relationship with the natural objects of his bounty. The mental capacity of testators has been questioned in numerous cases. Despite this, no particular degree of mental capacity has been established. The existence of mental capacity or incapacity must be determined from the facts and circumstances in each case.

Fraud, mistake, or undue influence is a ground of objection to the validity of a will. In order to invalidate a will fraud must be such as to induce the testator to make a disposition of his property that he would not otherwise have made, and he must actually be deceived. Mistakes that will defeat the intention of a testator, such as errors concerning what the will contains, are invalidating. Undue influence is a common ground for avoiding a will. The improper influence must so overpower and subjugate the mind of the testator that it destroys his free will and makes him express the will of another rather than his own. The courts have said that it is impossible to define with precision what constitutes undue influence. Mere influence over a testator is not sufficient to invalidate a will. It has been said that the essential elements of proof of undue influence are

(1) a susceptible testator (such as an aging, ill, or infirm person),
(2) another's opportunity and effort to exert improper influence,
(3) an effort for an improper purpose, (4) the fact that the improper influence was exercised or attempted, and (5) the result showing the effect of the unlawful influence.

In most states when a beneficiary in a will is also witness to a will, the bequest or devise to the witness becomes invalidated. The witness forfeits the provision in the will for his benefit, unless he is a blood relative; then he may still take the share which would be his under law if there were no will. In a few states the voiding of a devise or bequest is extended to a spouse if he or she is an attesting witness. Some states insist that the bequest to the subscribing witness be void unless there are two (or in some places three) competent additional witnesses by which the will can be proved.

Proving a Will or Probate

The mere existence of a will may mean nothing, for it may not be a valid will. It may have basic defects, which prevent it from ever being used as a will.

The term *probate*, as applied to wills, means the proof and establishment of the validity of a will. Whenever the executor (or the beneficiaries) wishes to establish the validity of a will, he institutes in a proper court a *probate proceeding*—an application to establish a document as the authoritative, final, and official will of the deceased person.

The *probate of a will* is a judicial proceeding in which the heirs (those persons who would inherit the decedent's property if there were no will) receive notice that the will has been filed in court and that the court will be asked to establish it as the valid will of the decedent. The heirs are required at this time either to consent to or to oppose the probate. They are given this opportunity to be heard, to say whether they have any objections to the probate, and to show cause in court why the will should not be admitted to probate. Only heirs or next of kin or beneficiaries under a prior will may oppose the probate proceeding. If the probate is not contested, the judge of the probate court will hear the testimony of the witnesses to the will concerning its proper execution; then if the will complies with the statutory requirements it will be admitted to probate. If the will and the probate proceedings are contested, the court conducts a hearing and decides whether or not there are valid legal objections to the will. Public criticism of the leisurely pace of present estate administration may have influenced the legal profession in supporting the Uniform Probate Code, now in effect in nine states, which simplifies and streamlines probate procedure.

Interpreting and Construing Wills

Often the meaning of a will, the intention of a testator, is cloudy or ambiguous. Sometimes there are questions concerning the identification of property and persons. Whenever he desires, an interested party may ask the probate court to *construe* and *interpret* a will. In a construction proceeding it is the court's duty first to examine the will and then, if possible, to determine its meaning. (The court must be careful not to remake or rewrite the will according to its idea of equity and justice.) In some cases the court also takes evidence to aid in construction of a will. By applying the rules of construction and taking evidence the court seeks to uncover and interpret the intention of the testator and, if it is not contrary to an established law or to public policy, to give the intention effect.

Revoking a Will

A will may be revoked (1) by an act of the testator or (2) by operation of law. In order to revoke a will the testator must have the same mental capacity as is required to make a will; he must be mentally competent. (A person may make a will while he is in full possession of his mental faculties and thereafter suffer a mental incapacity that prevents him from making a valid revocation of his will.) A testator may revoke his will (1) by a subsequent writing which may be a later will or a codicil, (2) by an instrument other than a will containing an express declaration of absolute revocation, or (3) by mutilation, cancellation, or destruction of the will. In many states a will cannot be revoked by a subsequent written instrument unless it is executed with the same formalities as a will. Mutilation, cancellation, or destruction may be by tearing, cutting, burning, obliterating, or by other physical destruction and may be done under the direction of the testator, with his consent, or in his presence.

In some states certain changes in the condition or circumstances of the testator may work a revocation of his will by implication of law. In other jurisdictions the doctrine of implied revocation has been abolished. Examples of revocation by operation of law, where permitted, are marriage and the birth of children.

State laws differ greatly on the question of whether a marriage revokes a will. Some states provide that if a testator remarries and has issue (children) of the marriage, the will is revoked unless a provision is made for the new mate and children. In other states a will is not revoked by a subsequent marriage; still other states provide by statute that a will is revoked by marriage, unless the will expressly states that it was made in contemplation of the marriage.

GIFT OF PART OF A HUMAN BODY AFTER DEATH

In recent years over twenty-five states have adopted the Uniform Anatomical Gift Act, which permits a person by will, card, or other document to give, upon his death, all or part of his body to some hospital, physician, or research or educational institution.

Sarah Smith has always been interested in problems of blind people. She goes to a lawyer, who puts in her will a clause which reads: "Immediately upon my death, I give both of my eyes to Empress Hospital for the Blind." She tells her family, executor, friends, and the hospital what she has done. She carries in her purse a card which reads, "I have given my eyes to the Empress Hospital for the Blind. Please notify the hospital of my death." The card is signed by Sarah, with two witnesses to her signature.

TRUSTS

A will may give one's property outright to a specified legatee or devisee, or it may set up a trust and give the income from the trust fund to a specified beneficiary during his life or until he reaches a certain age. Under a *trust* legal title to property is given to a person (called the *trustee*) who is directed to administer the trust (manage and control the property) for the benefit of another party (beneficiary) called the *cestui que trust*. A trust created in a will is called a *testamentary trust*. A trust created by a person during his lifetime is called a *living trust*.

A beneficiary of a trust may have a vested or contingent interest in a trust. An interest is *vested* when it is fixed, certain, absolute, and not subject to defeat by a future uncertain event. An interest is *contingent* when it depends on the happening of an event which may or may not take place. One who receives income from a trust is called an *income beneficiary* and, if circumstances warrant, may be called the *life beneficiary*. One who receives the property after the termination of the trust is called a *remainderman*.

Duration of a Trust

"The rule against perpetuities" originated in English common law several hundred years ago. It was founded on a public policy that disapproved of tying up property for an unreasonable length of time. As a result of this rule no trust was good unless it ended twenty-one years after the life of a person who was alive at the time of the creation of the trust. The life of that person was referred to as a "life in being" when the trust was created.

The common-law rule against perpetuities in this country is limited by most states to "lives in being at the time of the creation of the trust" plus twenty-one years. The "lives in being" rule means that John Jones may provide in his will that at the time of his death his property shall be put in trust, that the income shall be paid to his wife during her lifetime, that on her death it may be paid to John Jones's daughter, and on the daughter's death the principal of the trust shall be paid to the daughter's children. The duration of the trust is then measured by the lives of John Jones's wife and his daughter. The trust terminates legally on the death of his daughter. If, however, John Jones should provide that the trust should continue during the life of his daughter's grandchildren and those grandchildren were not "in being" at the time of John Jones' death, the trust would be invalid because it would violate the rule against perpetuities.

Accumulation of Trust Income

When a minor is a beneficiary to a trust, the income from the trust, instead of being paid to him, may be accumulated until he reaches the age of twenty-one. On the other hand, no accumulation is permitted for an adult beneficiary. The income generally must be paid to the adult beneficiary at once.

Furthermore, the trust may provide that the income be paid to a beneficiary until the happening of a certain condition. Thus, a trust may be terminated according to the desires of the person setting up the trust upon the remarriage of a widow, the marriage of a beneficiary, or a similar condition.

9

Estates of Deceased Persons

A decedent's estate must be managed by someone, whether or not the decedent leaves a will. When the decedent leaves a will he names this person, the *executor*, in the will. The executor must carry out all the responsibilities of the administration of an estate, enumerated below, and, in addition, he must scrupulously carry out the terms of the will. When the deceased does not leave a will the estate is managed by an *administrator*, who may be the surviving spouse or another person appointed by the court. An *administrator with the will annexed* is a person appointed by the court to administer an estate when the executor dies or fails to qualify. The entire property left by a decedent is called the *gross estate*. The balance of the estate remaining after making provision for taxes, administration expenses, and legacies is called the *residuary estate*.

DUTIES AND RIGHTS OF EXECUTOR OR ADMINISTRATOR

An executor or administrator is known in law as "the legal representative of an estate." Most rights, duties, and privileges of a legal representative of an estate apply with equal force to an executor and to an administrator.

The legal representative must be honest, diligent, and vigilant in administering the affairs of the estate. He is not an insurer of the assets of the estate and will not in all cases be liable for loss that may result from his acts. He is, however, required to use that intelligence and that degree of care and diligence in the management of the estate that a reasonably prudent businessman would employ in the management of his own affairs.

· Among the powers of the legal representative of an estate are the following:

1. He may take the assets of the estate into his possession. (Legal possession may not mean physical possession, but rather actual control over the assets.)

2. He may sell and liquidate personal property and convert the assets of the estate into cash.

3. He may pay debts and funeral and administration expenses.

4. He may distribute the estate to the beneficiaries.

Taking Possession of Assets

The legal representative not only takes the assets into his possession but he must also obtain full information regarding the assets. He must examine all the belongings of the decedent, his account books, safety deposit box, and other books and papers. He must inspect every scrap of paper found in the possession of the decedent. Moreover, he must investigate assets carefully to determine their value, for claims which appear to be uncollectible may prove to be collectible, and stocks and bonds that seem to have little or no value may turn out to be of considerable value.

A good example of the requirement that the executor shall reduce assets to his possession is the simple matter of bank accounts and cash belonging to the decedent. The legal representative of the estate must open a bank account in the name of the estate and must transfer the decedent's bank accounts to his own name, as executor or administrator. He is not always required to put the estate monies into an interest-bearing bank account. Because he may be called on to make frequent payments in the administration of the estate, a checking account may be the most practical type of account.

The problems of taking possession of assets are many. The legal representative should have the ownership of the decedent's stocks and bonds transferred to the name of the estate. He should collect the proceeds of life insurance and other types of insurance policies. If the decedent was a member of a partnership firm, he may have to have the interest of the deceased partner determined according to law and proceed with liquidation of the partner's interest. If the decedent owned real property, the legal representative may under certain circumstances be permitted to manage or sell the real estate. He should set aside certain property authorized by law as a "set-off" to the heirs and then make an inventory of all assets in the estate.

The cardinal sin of a legal representative is the commingling of estate funds with his own individual funds. In reducing estate monies to his possession, the legal representative must keep the funds and the property received separate from his own personal funds and property. No investment should be made nor funds deposited with any bank or corporation in the individual name of the legal representative. He must make sure that all funds are deposited in his name as executor or as administrator.

Keeping Records

It is important for the legal representative to keep proper accounts of the disposition of the funds and the property of the estate. He must keep a record of all receipts and disbursements in order to be prepared to make a final account of his stewardship. The keeping of books and records is so important that in the case of sizeable estates the legal representative may employ a bookkeeper or an accountant to keep books for him. Although a small estate cannot be taxed with this expense, it is necessary in a small estate, too, that proper books of account and records be kept.

Sale of Assets and Payment of Claims

In order that he may be able to pay creditors and distribute the estate to beneficiaries, the executor or administrator may have to sell the assets of the estate. Converting the assets into cash is one of his primary duties. Generally, in order to satisfy the decedent's debts, resort is had first to personal property and then to real estate. Very often it is necessary to get authority from the probate court in order to sell real estate.

In complying with his duty to ascertain and pay the debts of the decedent, the legal representative may sometimes have a notice published in a newspaper directing creditors to present their claims. Even if all creditors do not present their claims, the legal representative cannot ignore knowledge of just debts owed by the deceased to other persons. It is his duty to treat all persons interested in the estate fairly and to give all persons the information necessary so that they may present their claims in the proper manner. After claims are presented, the legal representative must investigate them and satisfy himself that they are valid. If he doubts the validity of a claim, he will have to present the matter to the probate court, which will determine whether a particular claim should be accepted or rejected.

Many interesting questions are raised in connection with claims for actual or alleged services rendered to the decedent. It seems to be human nature for persons who have performed services for others (often close relatives) to demand payment after the death of the one for whom the services were rendered. While the decedent was alive there may have been no thought in anyone's mind that services were being performed for compensation; sometimes they seemed to be willingly performed for loved ones. This assumption does not prevent the presentation of a claim after the person's death. If the legal representative thinks that the decedent had no intention of paying for such services, it is his duty to contest the claim.

Inheritance and Estate Taxes

Today, an important aspect of estate administration is the filing of estate tax returns. There are two basic kinds of inheritance and estate taxes: (1) taxes imposed by the state in which the decedent was domiciled and (2) taxes imposed by the federal government. In some instances taxes are imposed by states, other than the state of domicile, in which the decedent owned property.

State and federal income tax returns are relatively simple documents compared with inheritance and estate tax returns. Estate tax returns contain many details, such as schedules of real estate, stocks and bonds, mortgages, notes, contracts, cash and insurance, jointly owned property, and miscellaneous property; they may also contain schedules regarding transfers made in contemplation of death, schedules concerning powers of appointment (involving a right or control which the decedent had over property owned by others), schedules of property previously taxed, schedules of funeral and administration expenses, charitable, public, and similar gifts and bequests, debts of the decedent, and schedules concerning the beneficiaries.

In an estate tax proceeding, the appraisal of the assets is the basis for the tax on the property. The valuation of the assets of an estate is frequently difficult. For example, although there is generally no problem in valuing the stock of publicly owned corporations, which are traded on recognized stock exchanges, it is often a problem to evaluate the stock of family-owned corporations when there are no records of recent sales of the stock.

A federal estate tax return does not have to be filed unless the value of the estate exceeds $60,000. The United States Revenue Code requires that, within 60 days after his appointment, the legal representative file a preliminary notice setting forth rough estimates of the assets of the estate. The federal estate tax return must be filed within 9 months after the date of the decedent's death, and the federal tax becomes due within that period.

The legal representative of an estate may employ agents and others to assist him with the administrative work of the estate and may employ attorneys to advise him about his rights and duties. Those employed by the legal representative for this purpose are entitled to compensation from estate funds. Whenever the legal representative feels that a charge for legal services is not proper, he may ask the probate court to determine the amount to be allowed to the representative for counsel fees.

Distribution to Beneficiaries

After all the foregoing steps have been taken and after all inheritance and estate taxes have been paid, the legal representative is ready to distribute the assets of the estate to the beneficiaries. Although some states set a goal of distribution within 6 or 7 months from the time of the appointment of the executor or administrator, such a goal is in most instances unrealistic. When a federal estate tax return is required, the Internal Revenue Service usually takes a minimum of 1 year to audit it. This year added to the 9 months allowed for preparation of the tax return means that estates of more than $60,000 are very difficult to distribute before 25 months after the decedent's death. If a legal representative does not distribute the estate, a beneficiary may institute a court proceeding to compel the payment of legacies.

Commission of Legal Representatives

The compensation of a legal representative is generally based on the size of the estate; it is fixed by law in each state and varies from state to state. The compensation is awarded by the court and is known as a *commission*. Rates of commission range from 1½ to 5 percent. The higher rates of commission are awarded on estates that are relatively small.

Judicial Approval of Legal Representative's Accounts

After he has completed his duties, the legal representative should file with the probate court an account setting forth all assets that he has received, all debts and administration expenses that he has paid, and showing the balance on hand for distribution to the beneficiaries.

The accounting is the final act of the legal representative; it discharges his responsibility to the estate. In this proceeding, he accounts for his acts in administering the affairs of the estate, and the court directs the manner in which the assets remaining in the legal representative's control are to be distributed. Additional questions, such as contested creditors' claims and also matters of interpreting and construing a will, which have been saved for submission to the probate court during the accounting proceeding, may be finally determined. Occasionally, when the legal representative has been lax in distributing the estate, the beneficiaries may compel an accounting and distribution of the estate.

Settlement of Estate without Accounting

When there are no disputes between the parties, an estate may be settled by written agreement instead of by an accounting proceeding. In such a case, the executor sets forth in the agreement what he has accomplished: the assets that have been collected; the debts, inheritance taxes, and administration expenses that have been paid; the amount on hand for distribution; and the share to which each distributee is entitled. Then the consenting parties acknowledge receipt of their respective distributive shares and release and discharge the legal representative from all legal liability and responsibility for his acts.

INHERITANCE WITHOUT A WILL

When a decedent leaves a valid will *he* directs the disposal of his property; *he* determines which of his relatives and friends shall be his beneficiaries. When, on the other hand, an individual dies *intestate* (leaving property without having directed its disposition by will), his property is disposed of under the inheritance laws of the state in which he resided, that is, by the rules of descent and distribution and in some cases by dower and curtesy.

When a person dies intestate his wife or her husband or children or nearest relative applies to the court for the appointment of an administrator to manage the estate. Once the administrator has been appointed, the management of the estate proceeds under the direction of the court in a manner similar to an estate disposed of by will.

Descent and Distribution

The right to inherit property when there is no will is governed by the laws of descent and distribution in each of the fifty states. *Descent* refers to the handing down of real property (real estate) by inheritance on the death of an owner who dies intestate. *Distribution* means the allocation to heirs of the personal property of an individual who dies intestate after the payment of debts and charges against the estate.

These laws of descent and distribution are diverse and difficult to reconcile, for they represent the varying views of the lawmakers in the fifty states concerning how property should be inherited by blood relatives when the decedent does not leave a will. The National Conference of Commissioners on Uniform State Laws has been successful in promoting uniformity among the laws of the states on more than thirty subjects, but has been unable to accomplish the same for the laws of descent and distribution.

Dower and Curtesy

Strictly speaking, the rules of dower and curtesy are not part of the law of descent and distribution; yet if they were not discussed here it would be difficult to understand the disposition of estates made by those states which retain the common-law rules of descent and distribution and also the rights of dower and curtesy. Such a state may disinherit a spouse from any interest in real estate on the death of the other spouse, except for rights of dower and curtesy.

Dower is the interest that a wife has in her husband's real estate, effective on the death of her husband. Frequently, dower is a life interest in one-third of the real estate owned by the husband at the time of his death; that is, the widow has the right to the use or the right to the income from one-third of her husband's real estate (at the time of his death) for as long as she lives.

More than half the states have abolished the right to dower, but it has been retained in others, among them Alabama, Alaska, Arkansas, Delaware, Florida, Hawaii, Kentucky, Maryland, Massachusetts, Michigan, Montana, New Jersey, North Carolina, Ohio, Rhode Island, South Carolina, Tennessee, Vermont, West Virginia, and Wisconsin. In the states of New Jersey and Oregon, the widow has the life use of one-half of her husband's interest in real property. In Alabama the widow is entitled to one-half of her husband's interest in real estate when he leaves no lineal descendants (children or grandchildren); when he does, the widow receives one-third of the real estate.

Curtesy is the interest which a husband has in his wife's real estate effective on the death of his wife and provided a child has been born to the marriage. The right of curtesy is not used in Louisiana and Texas, and many states have abolished it. It has been retained in Alabama, Arkansas, Hawaii, Massachusetts, New Jersey, Rhode Island, Tennessee, Vermont, and Virginia. The states of Kentucky, Illinois, Maryland, New Hampshire, North Carolina, Ohio, and Wisconsin give a husband, in place of the curtesy right, the same right of dower as a wife. Massachusetts law limits curtesy to the husband's use for life of one-third of all land owned by his deceased wife, other than wild land not used in connection with a farm or dwelling. In Wisconsin, the husband's right of curtesy amounts to an absolute interest (as distinguished from a life use) in one-third of the lands owned by his wife at the time of her death and not disposed of by her will.

Rules of Descent and Distribution

Disparity among the American states' laws of inheritance is almost as great as the differences among the states' climates, soils, and terrains. The rules for descent and distribution concern the six major areas covered in the ensuing paragraphs.

Real and Personal Property   The modern trend among the states has been to eliminate the distinction in the treatment of inheritance rules for real and personal property. Once the term *heirs* referred to those who inherited real property, and *next of kin* referred to those who inherited personal property; in many states the terms are now used interchangeably to cover persons entitled to take both real and personal property. Missouri is typical of those states that have modernized laws of descent and distribution and have thus eliminated a distinction between real property and personal property. Tennessee, on the other hand, has one set of involved rules for the descent of real property (involving distinctions within distinctions concerning whether the real property was acquired from a parent or another ancestor by gift, devise, or descent) and another set of rules for the distribution of personal property (eliminating the requirement concerning whether or not the property was acquired from a parent or an ancestor).

The states of Alabama, Delaware, Kentucky, New Hampshire, New Jersey, North Carolina, Tennessee, Virginia, and Wisconsin have retained the distinctions for inheritance of real and personal property. Arkansas, Indiana, Iowa, Minnesota, Montana, Ohio, Oregon, Rhode Island, South Carolina, Texas, Utah, and Vermont have maintained limited distinctions, such as those concerning dower, homestead, and other rights of spouses.

Community Property States   Community property is that owned by a husband and wife in marital partnership. Arizona, California, Idaho, Louisiana, Nevada, New Mexico, Texas, and Washington are community property states. In these states, all property except property owned by either the husband or wife before the marriage or thereafter acquired by gift, devise, or descent, becomes *community property*.

Under some community property systems and despite the provisions of a will, on the death of a husband or wife one-half of all the community property passes to the surviving spouse; the other half is subject to disposition by will. Thus, the surviving spouse automatically inherits one-half of the community property whether or not there is a will. The surviving spouse may or may not benefit further under the provisions of the will disposing of the other half of the property. The following examples illustrate the lack of uniformity even in community property states:

In the state of Washington the rule is that either spouse may dispose of one-half of the community property by will and the remaining half automatically goes to the surviving spouse.

Nevada and New Mexico have one rule for the death of the wife and another rule for the death of a husband. When the wife dies, the entire community property vests in the husband without the necessity of estate administration. When the husband dies, one-half of the community property vests in the wife and the other half is subject to disposition by the husband's will.

In Texas when either party dies, all the community property goes to the survivor, if there is no surviving child (or children); if there is a child or children or grandchild or grandchildren, the surviving spouse takes one-half and the children and/or grandchildren inherit the other half.

Surviving Spouse and Blood Relatives   The prevailing principle in many states is that the surviving spouse shares the inheritance with the children. Other heirs and next of kin take possession of property in the following order: (1) children and descendants of deceased children, (2) parents or surviving parent, (3) brothers, sisters, or issue of deceased brothers or sisters, (4) other next of kin of equal degree. The following examples show how the pattern of inheritance varies.

In Colorado the estate of a person who dies without a will descends to the surviving husband or wife, provided there are no children. When there are children, one-half goes to the surviving husband or wife and the other half goes to the children or descendants of children. If there is neither surviving spouse nor children, then the property goes (1) to the parents, (2) to the brothers and sisters and descendants of brothers and sisters, (3) to grandparents, uncles, aunts, and their descendants, (4) to the "nearest lineal ancestors and their descendants."

In Georgia a widow is not given the same treatment as a widower. The husband is the sole heir of his wife unless she leaves children or descendants of children; if she does, he and the children share and share alike. (The descendants of the children take the share of their deceased parents.) When the wife is the heir and there are surviving children or issue of deceased children, she takes a child's share unless the shares exceed five in number; when there are five or more shares, she takes one-fifth of the estate.

In Hawaii a surviving spouse takes nothing by inheritance if the decedent left children or grandchildren but acquires only the right of dower or curtesy.

In Alaska, if the decedent leaves issue (children or grandchildren), the surviving spouse takes one-half of the estate. If the decedent leaves no issue, the surviving spouse takes the entire estate.

It is also worthwhile to compare the treatment of widows, children, and other relatives by the rules of descent and distribution in Connecticut, New Mexico, and New York:

In Connecticut the surviving spouse takes $50,000 plus one-half of the estate, and the child or children take the other half. If issue of the deceased are not issue of the surviving spouse, then the estate is divided equally between the issue and the surviving spouse. If there is no child nor descendants of a child but there is a surviving parent (or parents) of the deceased, the widow takes $50,000 plus three-fourths of the remainder of the estate. If there is neither child nor descendant of a child nor parent, the widow takes the entire estate.

Under the laws of New Mexico, a surviving husband or wife gets one-fourth of the estate, and the remainder goes to a child or children. If there are no children, the law gives the whole estate to the surviving husband or wife and excludes parents or other collateral relatives.

Under New York law a surviving spouse takes one-third of the estate if the decedent leaves descendants, but when the decedent leaves only one child (or representatives of a predeceased child), the surviving spouse takes one-half. If the deceased leaves no children nor grandchildren but leaves a parent, the surviving husband or wife takes $25,000 and one-half of the estate. If the deceased leaves no parents, the surviving husband or wife takes all the estate.

Relatives of Half Blood and of Whole Blood   There are different rules among the states concerning whether collateral relatives of the half blood (such as a half-brother) share equally with collateral relatives of the whole blood. Most states provide that there is no distinction and that relatives of the half blood receive the same treatment as relatives of the whole blood. The other states (at this writing Florida, Georgia, Kentucky, Maryland, Massachusetts, Mississippi, Missouri, North Dakota, South Dakota, Texas, Virginia, Washington, and Wyoming) limit the inheritance of relatives of the half blood so that either (1) they take half as much as collateral relatives of the whole blood, or (2) relatives of the whole blood receive inheritances in preference to relatives of the half blood.

Illegitimate Children   Most of the states provide that illegitimate children inherit property from their mothers but not from their fathers. California, Florida, Idaho, Minnesota, Montana, Nebraska, Nevada, New Mexico, North Dakota, Oklahoma, Oregon, South Dakota, Utah, Vermont, Washington, and Wisconsin laws make an illegitimate child an heir of the natural father if the latter has acknowledged paternity in writing. Some states require that the writing be witnessed, and other states require that the paternity be formally acknowledged before a notary public. Kansas and Utah require that (in order for an illegitimate child to be an heir of the putative father) the paternity simply be recognized and acknowledged by the father, without specifying the way in which such recognition or acknowledgment should be made. Alabama has a law permitting a father to make his bastard child legitimate by a written declaration made before two witnesses and filed in the probate office in the county of his residence.

Colorado, Maine, Missouri, New York, Pennsylvania, Rhode Island, South Carolina, Texas, Virginia, Washington, West Virginia, and Wyoming provide that if the parents of an illegitimate child marry each other, the child inherits from both parents as though legitimate. To intermarriage, Arizona, Connecticut, Illinois, Mississippi, Ohio, and Washington add the requirement of written recognition of the child by the father. Indiana, New York, Oregon, and Wisconsin also grant inheritance to a child from his father when he has been adjudged in court to be the father of the child. Iowa grants inheritance from the father when paternity has been proved. Oregon, the most liberal state in this matter, treats illegitimates the same as legitimates under inheritance law.

Escheat   If after the lapse of a certain time no heirs claim the estate of a deceased person, it passes to and becomes the property of the state (or another unit of government). This is the doctrine of *escheat*. It exists in all fifty states, but the time limit in which after-discovered heirs may bring proceedings in order to recover escheated property varies from three to seven years. Certain states have provided interesting variations of the doctrine of escheat:

North Carolina provides that when there are no heirs, the estate escheats to the University of North Carolina.

Illinois directs that escheated property goes to the county where the decedent died.

South Carolina provides that the property goes to the township in which the decedent lived.

Pennsylvania, South Dakota, Tennessee, Utah, and Wisconsin earmark escheated property for common school funds.

10
Commercial Paper

Commercial paper is a broad term which includes drafts (bills of exchange), promissory notes, checks, and other negotiable instruments for the payment of money. To be *negotiable* commercial paper must be transferable by indorsement or delivery without the consent of the debtor and must make the person to whom the instrument is indorsed or transferred the complete owner of the commercial paper. Negotiability is not, however, essential to its validity. Nonnegotiable commercial paper may be considered a valid contract.

LAWS GOVERNING COMMERCIAL PAPER

The use of instruments of credit was known among the early Romans. Following the Renaissance, the use of commercial paper grew with the expansion of international trade. But the legal remedies of the courts of that time were inadequate to settle the merchants' disputes arising in international trade. Thus, the merchants settled their own disputes through informal tribunals which they themselves convened. The mercantile customs which grew out of these tribunals eventually gained legal sanction and became known as the *Law Merchant*.

Credit and negotiable instruments are widely used in modern business and their use is governed mainly by two laws. The first is the *Uniform Negotiable Instruments Law* (a codification of the Law Merchant and a replacement of it), which was prepared in 1896 by the Commissioners on Uniform State Laws. It was adopted by a few states in 1897 and eventually by all the states. In recent years, however, most states have repealed the Negotiable Instruments Law and have substituted the second important contemporary law affecting commercial paper, the *Uniform Commercial Code*. The latter is a law sponsored jointly by the American Law Institute and the National Conference of Commissioners on Uniform State Laws. It covers the law of commercial paper and also nearly every phase of business activity, including sales and banking and commercial transactions.

NATURE OF NEGOTIABILITY

Commercial paper is a form of contract. *Negotiability* is that characteristic of certain commercial paper that permits it to be transferred by indorsement or delivery. Ordinarily a contract is transferred by a written instrument of assignment, but the owner of a negotiable instrument simply needs to write his name on it. If it is payable to bearer, the person who is in possession of commercial paper, he needs only to hand it to the new owner.

Importance of Negotiability

It is very important to determine whether a particular paper is negotiable because the law gives negotiable paper special treatment and in doing so protects "innocent holders" (also referred to as "bona fide holders" or "holders in good faith," see pp. 115–117 ff.). Negotiable bills, checks, and notes represent money and are intended to pass from hand to hand as money. Paper, if negotiable, may be transferred without notice to the debtor. The person to whom a nonnegotiable instrument or contract is transferred takes it subject to all the original agreements, understandings, and defenses available between the original parties to the instrument; but a transferee of negotiable paper takes it free from all previous agreements, understandings, and defenses. The consideration for a negotiable instrument is presumed, while the consideration for nonnegotiable paper must ordinarily be proved.

Tests of Negotiability

All five of the following tests for negotiability must be met:

1. The instrument must be in writing and signed by the maker or *drawer* (the person who originally signs a bill of exchange). It may be handwritten, typed, stamped, printed, and so on. The signature must be intended and must be a name, initials, mark, or trade or assumed name; it, too, may be handwritten, typed, printed, mimeographed, and so on.

2. The instrument must contain an unconditional promise or order to pay a certain sum of money. A promise or order for payment should be distinguished from a mere request or acknowledgment of a debt. For example:

Leslie borrows $100 from Fisher and signs a paper as follows: "I hereby acknowledge receipt of the sum of $100, which sum I have borrowed of you and must be accountable for." The paper signed by Leslie is not a negotiable instrument and may not be transferred by indorsement or delivery.

If the instrument is conditional, then it is not negotiable:

Gray gives to Brown his promissory note: "I promise to pay to you the sum of $200 payable on September 1, this year, provided you make your summer camp at Black Lake available to me." The instrument is conditional and hence is not negotiable.

3. The instrument must be payable on demand or at a fixed or determinable time in the future. An instrument is payable on demand if it says so in those words or equivalent words, such as "on presentation" or "on sight," or if a person takes or indorses it after it is due.

A bill or note or other instrument in order to be negotiable must be due and payable at a time which is either definite or is morally certain to occur. Such certainty must exist at the time the instrument is made.

John Tucker receives a sizeable inheritance and feels a moral obligation to support his Aunt Marie. John signs a promissory note reading, "I promise to pay to my Aunt Marie Tucker the sum of $10,000 at such time as she may need same for her support." The fact that the note was payable on the happening of an uncertain event (that she should need financial support) prevents the note from being negotiable.

Charlie borrows $3,500 from his Uncle Herbert, to help defray the expense of his college education. Charlie gives his uncle his promissory note, which reads, in part, as follows: "I promise to pay to Herbert Brown the sum of $3,500, payable at the rate of $100 per month with interest at the rate of 5 percent per annum, the first payment to be made one month after I obtain a permanent position after graduating from engineering school." This note, though enforceable between the parties, is not a negotiable instrument because the time of payment is uncertain.

And, even though an uncertain event on which a note or bill is payable occurs, the instrument is not thereby made negotiable.

4. The instrument must be payable to order or to bearer. The requirement of the Uniform Commercial Code that a note be "payable to order" means that the draft or note or other commercial paper must be payable *to the order* of a designated person, not just *to the person*. Otherwise, the instrument must be payable to bearer or its equivalent (cash, petty cash, and so on).

Look carefully at a check and read the words, "pay to the order of"; these words make the check negotiable. Making a check payable to "cash" is the same as making it payable to bearer.

5. In the case of a draft, the *drawee* (the person upon whom the draft is drawn and who becomes liable as soon as he accepts the bill of exchange) must be named or otherwise indicated with certainty. If the drawee is not definitely identifiable, the instrument is not negotiable even though valid.

Rowe draws a draft which reads: "To whoever may be my employer six months after date: pay to the order of Jonathan Jones the sum of $50, and charge to my account." The bill of exchange, not containing a definite drawee, is not negotiable.

COMMON TYPES OF NEGOTIABLE INSTRUMENTS

Negotiable instruments or commercial papers are either orders or promises to pay money. There are many different types of negotiable instruments; common among them are promissory notes, bills of exchange, bank drafts, checks, paper money, bonds, trade acceptances, and municipal warrants.

There are, in addition, certain quasi-negotiable documents which do not call for the payment of money and, thus, are technically not negotiable instruments, but which have other qualities of negotiability under the Uniform Commercial Code. These quasi-negotiable documents are stock certificates, bills of lading, and warehouse receipts.

Promissory Notes and Similar Negotiable Instruments

A *promissory note* is a written promise by one person to pay to another or to bearer a fixed sum of money on demand or at a specified time. Promissory notes are most common in the extension of bank credit.

A *certificate of deposit* is similar to a promissory note. It contains an unconditional promise to pay the amount of the certificate on demand to bearer or to the order of the holder. The purpose of a certificate of deposit, unlike that of a promissory note, is to permit a depositor of a certain sum of money in a bank to dispose of his right to the sum by mere transfer of the certificate.

Bonds, like promissory notes, contain a promise for the payment of a certain sum of money. There are many kinds of bonds, among them government and municipal bonds and corporate, industrial, and commercial bonds. *Corporate bonds*, which represent simply the obligation to pay a sum of money and which are not secured by mortgages, are commonly known as "debentures."

Municipal warrants which counties and municipalities issue in anticipation of revenue to be derived from taxation usually contain promises to pay money and, therefore, are negotiable instruments and have the characteristics of promissory notes.

Drafts

A *draft* is an order in writing addressed by one person to another requiring the addressee to pay on demand or at a specified time a

$ 1050.00   Seattle, Washington
                                     April 6, 1974

On demand I promise to pay to the order
of Saturday Diner, Inc., one thousand and
fifty dollars (value received).

                              Samuel S. Depler

Promissory Note*

certain sum of money to the order of the person named or to bearer.
Because it is the most common type of draft, checks are discussed
separately on page 113. Another frequently used type of draft is
a *trade acceptance:* a draft or bill of exchange drawn by the seller
of goods on the purchaser for a fixed sum of money that represents
the purchase price of the goods. Still another common type of draft
is a *bank acceptance,* which is drawn on and accepted by a bank as
drawee. An *accommodation paper* is a draft or note to which the
drawer, maker, or other party has put his name without consideration for the purpose of lending his credit to the paper.

$ 600.00   Philadelphia, Pa., July 1, 1974
One month after sight pay to the order of Charles Jewski
the sum of six hundred and no/100 Dollars (value received)
and charge the same to account of
To Hartley Jones   Seldon Brown
   New Orleans, La.,

Draft†

* A promissory note may also be drawn for a specific date: two months after
date; on the 16th day of May, 1974; or on or before the 123d day of 1974. It may
be made for person, firm, or bearer.

† It may also be drawn to person or order or to the person or bearer.

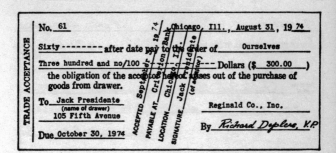

Trade Acceptance

Checks

Besides currency (paper money) bank *checks* are the type of negotiable instruments most often used. As defined by the Uniform Commercial Code, "a check is a draft drawn on a bank and payable on demand." Thus, the provisions of law relating to a draft apply equally to a check.

Types of Checks A *bank draft* is a check drawn by a bank on another bank. And, of course, a garden variety check is a bill of exchange drawn by an individual on a bank and payable on demand.

A *certified check* is issued by a bank, which guarantees that the drawer's signature is genuine and that the amount for which the check is drawn has been set aside for payment from the drawer's account. When a bank's authorized representative puts the bank's stamp, "certified," on a check and signs it, the bank becomes liable for its payment. The maker of a check can stop payment on it any time before it is cashed. Once the check is certified, however, the maker can no longer stop payment.

Danger of Delay in Cashing Checks The Negotiable Instruments Law provides that drafts payable on demand (checks) must be presented for payment within a reasonable time. In those states which have adopted the Uniform Commercial Code, a reasonable time is presumed to be thirty days with respect to the liability of the drawer and seven days after his indorsement with respect to the liability of an indorser. From this reference to time it follows that there are two precautions which apply to the sensible handling of

INDIAN STAR NATIONAL TULSA BANK
Park North at 117th Street, Tulsa, N. Y.

207   9-8
                                                                      000

February 10, 19 74

Pay to the
order of _Table Top Linen Laundry Service_ $ 6 00/100

———————————— Six and 07/100 ————————————— Dollars

Priscilla Brochaser

Check

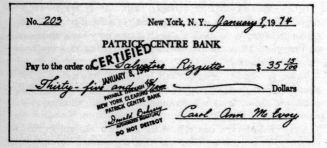

No. 203   New York, N. Y. _January 8, 19 74_

PATRICK CENTRE BANK

~~CERTIFIED~~

Pay to the order of _Salvatore Rizzutto_ $ 35 15/100

Thirty-five and 15/100 ————————————— Dollars

JANUARY 8, 1974
PAYABLE THROUGH
NEW YORK CLEARING HOUSE
PATRICK CENTRE BANK

Donald Bakery
AUTHORIZED SIGNATURE
DO NOT DESTROY

Carol Ann McEvoy

Certified Check

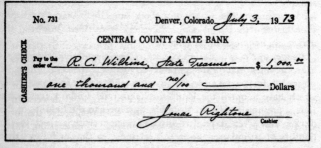

No. 731   Denver, Colorado _July 3, 19 73_

CENTRAL COUNTY STATE BANK

Pay to the
order of _R. C. Wilkins, State Treasurer_ $ 1,000.00

one thousand and no/100 ————————————— Dollars

Jonas Rightone
Cashier

Cashier's Check

checks: it may be unwise to delay cashing a check, and it may be dangerous to accept a "stale" check.

Delay in presenting a check for payment will discharge the maker of the check from liability *only* if he is injured by the delay.

Greely has on deposit in the Excelsior Bank the sum of $525. He gives Kasker a check for $500, which Kasker puts in his desk drawer and fails to present for payment until two months later. In the meantime, the bank fails. Kasker goes to Greely and asks him to make good on the check. Greely is not responsible for the check because he has been injured by Kasker's delay in not presenting the check for payment. (If Kasker had promptly presented the check for payment, instead of waiting two months, the check would have been paid, and Greely would have been $500 better off. But Kasker's failure to promptly present the check relieved Greely from liability for the check.)

Unavoidable delay in presenting a check for payment will discharge an indorser from liability for a check, whether or not the indorser is injured by the delay.

On September 21, Hunter gives Lord a check for $300 drawn by Hunter on a bank in Rushville, 15 miles away. Lord takes the check immediately to his bank, the Dominion Bank, and deposits it in his account for collection. The Dominion Bank forwards the check to the bank in Rushville where it was drawn, but the check is lost. The Dominion Bank does not make any inquiry about the check for more than 10 days. Finally, inquiry discloses that a clerk of the bank had misdirected it, and it had been misfiled. As soon as the check is found, it is again routed to the bank in Rushville, but, in the meantime, Hunter has left the country without leaving sufficient funds to meet the check. During the time between September 21 and October 1, Hunter had an adequate balance in the Rushville bank, and the check could have been paid. The court holds that the Dominion Bank did not use the diligence required by law, and Lord is discharged from his liability as an indorser on the check.

RIGHTS OF HOLDERS OF COMMERCIAL PAPER

The major characteristic of a negotiable instrument is that it circulates freely, that it may be taken or be held for what it appears to be, without concern. A "holder" is anyone legally in possession of commercial paper. A *holder in due course* is a bona fide holder for value of commercial paper without notice of any legal defects. In order for one to be a holder in due course, he must receive the instrument (1) in good faith, (2) for valuable consideration, (3) without notice that the instrument is due and payable, and (4) without notice of any defect in title of the person who transfers the instrument and without notice of any defects in the instrument itself. A holder in due course holds an instrument free from any defenses which would exist between the original parties to the instrument, such as illegal consideration or fraud or mistake connected with the note.

Good Faith

It is necessary that a holder in due course take the commercial paper in good faith; that is, he should have no knowledge that there is something wrong with the instrument.

A promissory note is given by *A* to *B*, who loses it. *C* finds it, forges *B's* signature, and sells the instrument to *D*, who buys the instrument without knowledge of the forgery. *D* acts innocently and in good faith.

Transfer for Valuable Consideration

In order to make one a holder in due course, the transfer of the instrument must be for consideration sufficient to support a simple contract. It is not necessary that one give money for the instrument. He may give merchandise or credit or perform a service in return for the commercial paper.

Transfer before Maturity

In order for a holder in due course to acquire good title, he must obtain the instrument without notice that it has matured. The reason for this rule is the suspicion that something is wrong with commercial paper that remains unpaid after it has become due.

Calhoun gives Langhorne a promissory note for $500 due and payable December 1, 1974. On February 1, 1975, Langhorne transfers the note to Baker. Because the note had already matured, Baker is not a holder in due course; if there is something wrong with the note, Calhoun has a good defense when Baker demands payment.

Before buying an instrument which has reached maturity the person should ask, "Isn't there something wrong with this instrument? Why was it not paid when it came due?"

Notice of Defenses or Defects in the Instrument

In order for a transferee of a draft or note to be a holder in due course, he must have no notice of any defect of title, of illegality, or of fraud or other defects in the instrument. The instrument must be complete and regular on its face and must have no blank spaces.

If the instrument says it is due "—— after date," there is something missing, and the incompleteness of the instrument prevents the transferee from being a holder in good faith. Even leaving the name of the person to whom the instrument is payable blank casts some doubt on the instrument.

In addition, in order to be a holder in due course, it is necessary that at the time the holder gets the instrument he have no notice (1) of any infirmity in the instrument or (2) of any defect in the title of the transferor. Written notice is not necessary, but actual knowledge of the claimed defenses to a note or knowledge of circumstances to put the transferee on notice may be sufficient to prevent the transferee from becoming a holder in due course.

Barlow borrows $500 from Landers. Ingraham, who is in the habit of buying promissory notes, has heard some talk that Barlow claims that Landers exacted an exorbitant discount before entering into the transaction. Hearing this talk has put Ingraham on notice to look into the matter further, but he purchases the note without investigation. He does not become a holder in due course.

Barnes, treasurer of the River Lumber Company, makes out a promissory note on this company, payable to himself. He takes the note to a bank which discounts it and becomes the owner. Stockholders of the company protest that the note was issued without proper corporate authority and that the treasurer had no right to make the note payable to himself; they can successfully claim that the bank is not a holder in due course.

TRANSFER OF COMMERCIAL PAPER

If negotiable paper is payable to bearer, it may be transferred simply by delivery. If negotiable paper is payable to the order of a designated person, it may be transferred only by the indorsement of that person, completed by delivery.

Indorsement of Commercial Paper

An *indorsement* is a written signature on the back of a piece of commercial paper. Generally, it is the signature of the payee of a note or bill of exchange or of a third person, evidencing the transfer of the note. Indorsement is to be distinguished from *assignment,* which is generally made by a separate instrument. An indorsement is (1) a transfer of title to the instrument indorsed and (2) a conditional promise to pay the same.

The indorsement must be written on the instrument itself or on a paper attached to it. The signature of the indorser, without additional words, is sufficient indorsement. An indorsement may be special or in blank, restrictive or qualified, or conditional.

A *special indorsement* specifies the person to whom the instrument is payable, and the indorsement of that person, the *indorsee*, is necessary to further the negotiation of the instrument. This is usually done by saying "pay to the order of" and inserting the indorsee's name. An *indorsement in blank* does not specify an indorsee, and an instrument so indorsed is payable to bearer and may be transferred by delivery. The last indorsee simply signs his name to the back of the instrument.

A *restrictive indorsement* (1) prohibits the further negotiation of the instrument, (2) establishes the indorsee as the agent of the indorser, or (3) vests title in the indorsee in trust for the use of another person. The effect of a restrictive indorsement is to allow the instrument to be used by the indorser without the indorsee parting with title to it. A *qualified indorsement* establishes the indorser as a mere link in the chain of title without attaching any liability to the indorsement. The indorser has no liability for nonpayment of the paper, but he guarantees its validity and his title to it. An indorser may make a qualified indorsement by adding to his signature the words, "without recourse."

A *conditional indorsement*, as the term implies, is an indorsement of a note to become payable on the completion of a condition, providing a specified event happens. Conditional indorsements are not favored in the commercial world and, thus, are rare.

Liability of Indorsers

When a person writes his name on the back of commercial paper, he becomes known as an "indorser." Some indorsers assume that they are responsible only for payment of the instrument (such as a check, promissory note, or bill of exchange). Others assume that they are simply transferring title. Neither assumption is wholly correct. The liabilities and responsibilities of indorsers are considerable and are based on technical rules which have been codified in the Uniform Commercial Code. These rules are so strictly interpreted that if those seeking to impose liability on indorsers do not follow them explicitly, the indorsers are sometimes excused from legal liability. On the other hand, indorsers also have rights and privileges which are protected if the other parties to commercial papers do not live up to their obligations.

Liability to Holder of Commercial Paper   When he indorses commercial paper, an indorser creates a new and independent contract—

one separate from the original contract of the maker or the signer of the original paper. By signing his name and transferring the commercial paper to the new owner, the indorser warrants the following:

1. He has good title to it or is authorized to receive payment from one who has good title.
2. The transfer is rightful.
3. All signatures are genuine.
4. The instrument has not been materially altered.
5. No defense of any party is good against him.
6. He has no knowledge of any insolvency proceedings instituted with respect to the maker or acceptor or drawer of an unaccepted instrument.

Indorsers are liable in the order in which they indorse an instrument. For example:

A gives his promissory note to *B*, payable in six months. One month after the note is given, *B* needs the money and indorses and sells the note to *C*. *C* indorses and sells the note to *D*, and *D* indorses and sells the note to *E*, who is the owner and holder of the note when it becomes due. At that time *A*, the maker of the note, is bankrupt. Then *E* may collect from *D*, *D* may collect from *C*, and *C* may collect from *B*, making *B* the ultimate loser.

Presentment for Payment In order to hold an indorser liable, the commercial paper must be presented for payment. Presentment for payment is not necessary in order to charge the person primarily liable on the instrument, but it is necessary in order to make the indorser liable.

Presentment for payment must be made on the day when the commercial paper falls due (1) by the holder or by a person authorized to receive payment in his behalf, (2) at a reasonable hour on a business day, (3) at the place of payment specified in the instrument or, if no place of payment is specified, at the address or usual place of business or residence of the person required to make payment, and (4) to the person primarily liable on the instrument. In making presentment for payment, the instrument must be exhibited to the person from whom payment is demanded; when it is paid, it must be delivered to the person paying it.

Montgomery signs a promissory note payable to Smith. Smith sells and indorses the promissory note to Jones. Jones sells and indorses the promissory note to Brown. Brown goes to Montgomery and makes a formal presentment and demand for payment of the note. Montgomery says, "I am sorry, but I do not have the money." Brown sends a written notice to Jones that the note has not been paid. Brown has sufficiently complied with the Uniform Negotiable Instruments Act in making the presentment for payment and giving notice of dishonor, and Jones thereupon becomes obligated to pay the note.

Long signs a promissory note saying, "I promise to pay to the order of Meco on September 1, 1975, the sum of $1,000." If payment is not made on the date the note is due, Meco may sue for payment. (No presentment for payment was necessary between the two parties to the note.)

An exception to this rule arises, however, in the case of a forged prior indorsement—when the name of the maker or drawer of the instrument has been forged. The reason for this exception is that the indorser has warranted the instrument to be genuine and the holder of the note may rely on such warranty.

If in the example above facts were changed so that, in the first instance, someone had forged Montgomery's name, it would not be necessary for Brown to present the note for payment or give Jones notice of the nonpayment and dishonor of the note. After all, Jones had warranted that the note was genuine, and Brown is entitled to rely on that fact.

11

Labor and Management

Labor and management have frequently appealed to the government to assist in the settlement of their disputes. In the beginning of the industrial era, representatives of industry were able to obtain injunctions from the courts to halt strikes, picketing, and boycotts. Later in the era, legislation was enacted to regulate the use of injunctions and the various activities of labor and management.

LABOR LEGISLATION

The most important federal laws dealing with employer-employee relations during the last fifty years are the Norris-LaGuardia Act, the National Labor Relations Act, the Taft-Hartley Law (Labor-Management Relations Act), and the Labor Reform Act.

Norris-LaGuardia Act

In 1932, Congress enacted the Norris-LaGuardia Act, which prohibited federal courts from granting injunctions in so many types of disputes that in practice it did away with the use of injunctions in about 99 percent of the cases. This act also prevented the enforcement of "yellow dog" contracts (under which an employee binds himself not to join a union).

National Labor Relations Act

The National Labor Relations Act of 1935 (popularly known as the Wagner Act) might be said to be the real beginning of government intervention in labor relations. This act gave employees the right to form labor organizations and to bargain collectively through representatives of their own choosing. It declared that interferences by employers with the employees' right of self-organization constituted unfair labor practices, and it provided stiff penalties for such violations. The NLRA also created the National Labor Relations Board with power to enforce the provisions of the act, including the curtailing of employer influence through a company-dominated union and the prevention of employer discrimination against employees for union activities.

Taft-Hartley Law

The wave of strikes that followed World War II prompted Congress to curb the power of the labor unions. The Taft-Hartley Law (Labor-Management Relations Act) was the result. Management described its enactment, in 1947, as an attempt to control the extreme power which was vested in the National Labor Relations Board. Unions, on the other hand, called it a "slave-labor law" and an attempt to undermine collective bargaining.

The provisions of the Taft-Hartley Law were many. The most important concerned (1) the establishment of a general counsel (which has authority to issue complaints), (2) the banning of the closed shop (through which only union members could be hired) but the sanctioning of the union shop (which requires an employee to join the union within a certain period of time after he is hired), (3) the prohibition of unfair labor practices by both labor and management (outlawing coercion, discrimination, and refusal to bargain by either one and illegal strikes or boycotts by labor), (4) the guarantee of free speech to employers in carrying their views to employees, (5) the institution of a sixty-day cooling-off period before work stoppage at the end of a collective bargaining contract, and (6) the creation of special procedures for dealing with strikes that threaten the safety of the nation. Other provisions barred Communists from holding union offices, forced unions to file financial reports, and placed unions for supervisory personnel outside the protection of the act.

Labor Reform Act

In September 1959 Congress enacted the Labor Reform Act, which made certain changes in the control of labor and management and set up a system to protect union members from the alleged corrupt influences of union leaders. The law established a bill of rights for union members, assuring them equal rights in the union. It attempted to help union members bring unscrupulous practices of union officials to light and established stringent restrictions on secondary boycotts and organizational picketing.

LEGAL CASES ARISING OUT OF LABOR-MANAGEMENT DISPUTES

Labor legislation has for the most part sought to soften the effects of the unrestricted interplay of labor-management pressures. The National Labor Relations Act has accomplished much of this; later legislation has sought mainly to clarify and improve the provisions of this act. Following are discussions of the types of legal cases which evolve most frequently out of the National Labor Relations Act and from labor-management controversies.

Employers Subject to National Labor Relations Act

The so-called commerce clause of the Constitution, which gives Congress the power to "regulate commerce of foreign nations and among the several states," is broad enough to permit Congress to pass labor legislation governing more than 80 percent of the businesses in the United States. If a business is engaged in *interstate commerce* (trade, traffic, commerce, transportation, or communication among states, the District of Columbia, or foreign countries), it is subject to the National Labor Relations Act. The test of whether a business flows through interstate commerce is not what percentage of business flows through interstate channels, but whether *any* does. For example:

A department store pointed out to an appeals court that its out-of-state mail-order sales of $20,000 represented only .0024 of its total annual sales. The appeals court said that the "application of the Act does not depend upon the magnitude of the business nor the comparative amount of interstate sales." The department store was held to be engaged in interstate commerce and subject to the National Labor Relations Act.

The activities of transportation and communication companies, (including truckers and railroads, telephone companies, radio stations, magazines, newspapers, the motion picture industry), and building and construction, production, manufacturing, warehousing, storage, public utilities, banking and insurance concerns are all regulated by the National Labor Relations Act.

The National Labor Relations Board has declined to take jurisdiction in labor disputes involving a few classifications that it views as "local business." These disputes are handled by the state labor-relations boards. Some of the jurisdictional yardsticks applied by the National Labor Relations Board to determine its regulation of business follow:

It will assert jurisdiction over intrastate or interstate retailers having one or more stores if their gross yearly volume of business is $500,000 or more or over local retail power, gas, and water public utilities companies, if their gross yearly volume is $250,000 or more.

The National Labor Relations Board will assert jurisdiction over a newspaper if it carries nationally syndicated columns, subscribes to a national news service, publishes advertisements of nationally sold products, and has a gross volume of business of at least $200,000.

Employees Subject to National Labor Relations Act

Under the National Labor Relations Act the term *"employees"* includes all those earning wages or salaries or commissions, except agricultural laborers, domestic servants, individuals employed by parents or spouses, independent contractors, and railroad employees. Supervisors, foremen, and executives are also excluded from the protection of the act.

This question often arises: Who is an "independent contractor"? If an employer has the right to control the manner or method by which the work is done, the workman on the job is regarded as an employee. If the workman can do the work whenever he pleases and is accountable only for the final result, he is quite likely to be held an independent contractor. For example:

The Kelly brothers formed a partnership, bought two trucks, and worked out a deal with a cinderblock company to haul blocks at one-half a cent a mile within a given area. They bought their own vehicles, tires, gas, and paid all the vehicle maintenance bills. They were not on the cinderblock company's payroll, and the company did not pay any social security or unemployment taxes for them. The Kelly brothers were held to be independent contractors, not employees subject to the National Labor Relations Act.

The method by which he is compensated is not a deciding factor in determining whether or not a person is an employee. A person may be paid a commission or even a percentage of the profits instead of a salary and may still be held to be an employee. So broad has been the coverage of the National Labor Relations Act that insurance agents, newsboys, seasonal and part-time workers, and persons laid off have been held to be employees under the act.

Company Unions

Labor legislation prohibits an employer from installing or promoting a company-dominated union, known as a "company union," in his organization.

An employer calls in a few "trusted" employees and suggests to them it would be nice if they would form their own union; if they would do so, he would have a room in the plant set aside for the offices of the union and have the company lawyer show the employees how to draw up a set of by-laws for the organization. The union which is subsequently formed becomes an illegal company dominated union.

Sometimes an effort is made to convert employees' social organizations into company unions. Sometimes bona fide unions charge that social organizations such as employees' clubs are "company unions" in disguise. The true test in such cases is whether the employees' club is a purely social organization, without the purpose or power to deal with management in questions relating to wages and working conditions, or whether it is a disguised movement to keep out an external union.

Company unions are often formed to combat nationally affiliated unions. The National Labor Relations Board orders such unions disbanded and orders the employer to stop interfering with the rights of employees in the selection of their own bargaining representative. There are, however, unions which are not affiliated with national labor organizations and which should not be confused with the prohibited company union. These organizations are truly independent of employer influence and faithfully represent employee-members in their dealings with management.

Discrimination in Regard to Employment

The National Labor Relations Act protects the employees' right to "engage in concerted activities for the purpose of collective bargaining or for their mutual aid or protection." Employees may form a union, they may strike, they may petition for a change in working conditions, they may engage in many concerted activities, which are protected under the law.

An employer may not refuse to hire an employee because he is a union member, nor may he discharge an employee for his union activities or because he is related to a union member. If he does either of these things, he is guilty of unfair labor practice.

Howard Rufkin, an employee, posted a notice on the bulletin board of the Solid Bookend Company, saying, "All employees interested in joining the Amalgamated Bookenders' Union will meet at Union Hall, Thursday at 7 o'clock." The next day he was dismissed by the company.

The National Labor Relations Board brought against the Solid Bookend Company a proceeding charging it with unfair labor practice. The company defended the dismissal, claiming that Rufkin had refused to obey orders and that the quality of his work was poor (and that was why he had been fired). The National Labor Relations Board held that the real reason for Rufkin's dismissal was his union activity and ordered him reinstated with back pay.

The law labels as unfair labor practice an employer's discharge of or other type of discrimination against an employee because he has filed charges or given testimony under the National Labor Relations Act.

Joe Thompson filed charges with the National Labor Relations Board claiming that his employer, the Viking Company, was guilty of an unfair labor practice. He was discharged by his employer. Subsequently, the National Labor Relations Board ordered him reinstated with back pay.

The National Labor Relations Board has held countless employers' practices to be discriminatory, and its contentions have been upheld by court decisions. Among those activities that have been found to be antiunion or discriminatory are the following: (1) refusal to hire, (2) failure to recall seasonal employees, (3) discharge of employees, (4) demotion, (5) layoff, (6) transfer to less desirable positions, and (7) reduction to part-time employment.

Strikes

Strikes may be classified for the purpose of this discussion into four groups—economic strikes, unfair labor practice strikes, wildcat strikes, and illegal strikes.

Economic Strikes Employees who strike as a result of a stalemate in negotiations for a contract are on an *economic strike*. They are protected by the National Labor Relations Act against unfair labor practices and retain their status as employees during the strike. An employer may not refuse to reinstate an employee solely on the ground that he participated in the strike, but the employer has a right to replace economic strikers. If they are replaced, the striking employees are not entitled to reinstatement. (Although they may not be entitled to reinstatement, under the Labor Reform Act, economic strikers may now vote in elections conducted by the National Labor Relations Board, at any time within twelve months after the beginning of the strike.)

Employees represented by a union at the ABC Chemical Company plant during contract negotiations demanded a wage increase of 40 cents an hour. The company offered to grant an increase of 10 cents, but the union would not yield and called an economic strike. After it had been going on for 5 months, the union employees decided to call off the strike and go back to work. In the meantime, about 60 percent of the striking employees had been replaced by other workers. The company refused to fire the replacements and take back all the strikers. The strikers took the matter to the National Labor Relations Board, which held that because it was an economic strike the company was justified in refusing to dismiss the replacements and was also justified in refusing to reinstate strikers whose jobs had been filled by others.

Unfair Labor Practice Strike   Employees who strike because of an employer's unfair labor practices remain employees within the meaning of the National Labor Relations Act, and once the employer's acts are determined to be unfair labor practices by the National Labor Relations Board, they may have their jobs back. This is true even though the employer has in the meantime hired replacements.

In the course of the negotiations of the Plymouthe Company with the union representing its employees, the company dismissed several union leaders, who the company said were guilty of insubordination, and refused to continue contract negotiations because of what the company termed the union's hostile negotiations and unfair tactics. The union charged the company with unfair labor practice in discharging the employees and in refusing to bargain; then the employees went on strike to protest the company's unfair action. The National Labor Relations Board held with the union.

Meanwhile, the company had filled the positions left vacant by the strikers. The striking employees asked that their jobs be returned to them. The company refused. The National Labor Relations Board held that if the striking employees unconditionally applied for reinstatement, they had to be reinstated and the replacements had to be dismissed. (The NLRB decision held that the employees were engaged in an unfair labor practice strike and they could not be permanently replaced.)

Wildcat Strikes   A wildcat strike is caused by a group of employees' unauthorized action that does not have the sanction of the law; an illegal strike (discussed in the next section) is absolutely prohibited by the law. Wildcat strikers are those who go out on a strike not authorized by the union which represents a majority of the employees. Such strikers are not entitled to the protection of the National Labor Relations Act and may be discharged.

On October 14 union representatives journeyed to Spartanburg, South Carolina, to attend contract negotiations with the D Corporation. Upon arrival the union leaders were told that the D Company's bargaining representative (and its secretary) was ill in Massachusetts and was unable to attend the conference. The secretary was in fact ill, but some of the employees were angry and resentful because they thought his illness was an excuse for delay. The next morning 41 of the employees (about 25 percent of the total number) gathered in a corner of the factory and failed to go to work. They said they were carrying on a wildcat strike because they believed that the company was stalling; they demanded action. The workers were ordered by the superintendent to go to work or to get out of the plant. They refused to go to work or leave the plant and remained on company property. The next day the 41 workers were paid in full and were discharged for engaging in a sit-down strike.

On October 20, as a result of the efforts of the Federal Mediation and Conciliation Service, the company and the union arrived at a contract settlement. The 41 striking employees presented themselves for work, but the company refused to hire them. The matter was taken to the National Labor Relations Board which ordered the company to rehire the strikers and pay them back wages. An appeal was taken to the United States Court of Appeals (Fourth Circuit), which held that the wildcat strike did not fall within the protection of the strike provisions of the National Labor Relations Act; that the conduct of the workers amounted to insubordination; and that the company was justified in discharging them. It also held that the wildcat strike is a particularly harmful and demoralizing form of industrial strife and is destructive of collective bargaining, which it is the purpose of the law to promote.

Illegal Strikes   The following strikes were made unlawful by the Taft-Hartley Law: (1) strikes to force an employer or self-employed person to join the union, (2) strikes to force an employer to stop doing business with another person, (3) strikes to force an employer to bargain with a minority union after the National Labor Relations Board has certified a majority union, and (4) strikes beginning within sixty days preceding the expiration of a labor contract. Employees who participate in an illegal strike lose their status as employees.

The National Labor Relations Board held an election to determine whether the AFL union or the CIO affiliate would represent the employees of the Bacon Company. The AFL group won the election 210 to 160. The CIO affiliate, contrary to instructions from its national headquarters, had its members go on strike and picket the Bacon plant. The National Labor Relations Board held the strike to be illegal and ordered the union to cease and desist from striking and picketing.

Employer's Rights and Obligations During Union Organizational Drive

The Taft-Hartley Law modified the Wagner Act by giving employers more freedom of speech in the following ways during a union organizational campaign:

The expressing of any views, arguments or opinions, or the dissemination thereof, whether in written, printed, graphic or visual forms shall not constitute or be evidence of unfair labor practice under any of the provisions of this Act, if such expression contains no threat of reprisal or promise of benefit.

This provision of the Taft-Hartley Law gives an employer the right to express his views on unionism generally, his views on a particular union, and his preference for one union over another. However, it is very dangerous for the average employer to criticize a union or its officers without guidance from another skilled in labor relations. For example:

When the Amalgamated Union sent representatives to his plant to convince the employees that they should join the union, Mr. Butterman (president of Butterman Manufacturing Company) said, in a speech to his employees, "The union is made up of a bunch of racketeers, and if the plant is unionized we will be put out of business." The union lost an election and filed unfair labor practice charges against the company. The board held that the remarks of Mr. Butterman constituted an implied threat, which in turn constituted coercion and interference with the right of the employees to self-organization. It directed that the employer recognize and bargain with the union.

During an organizational campaign an employer should not make wage adjustments, threaten economic reprisals or discriminatory treatment, bargain with individual employees, induce employees to sign individual employment contracts, question employees about their union business, or spy on their union activities. After the organizational campaign, an employer can challenge a union's assertion that it represents the majority of employees if he does so in good faith. The election machinery of the National Labor Relations Board comes into play on petition of an employer or on petition of a union to hold an election to determine who is the representative of the employees for collective bargaining purposes. Such an election is conducted under the supervision of a representative of the National Labor Relations Board after the board determines a unit for bargaining purposes. On the basis of the election results the NLRB certifies the appropriate bargaining unit, and this certification is final. For example:

Mr. Cleon, representative of the Amalgamated Union, comes to the office of Mr. Robert, president of Robert's Manufacturing Company, and says, "We represent the employees in your Utica plant and would like to enter into a contract governing wages and working conditions." Mr. Robert says, "That's news to me. How do I know you represent my employees?" Mr. Cleon says, "If you won't take my word for it, we'll go to the National Labor Relations Board." Mr. Robert says, "OK by me." Later a representative of the board calls on Mr. Robert and says, "Will you agree to an election?" Robert says, "Sure." A meeting is held with the board representative, Cleon, and Robert. They enter into an agreement for a consent election. A bargaining unit is decided as "all production employees in the Utica plant excluding office and clerical employees, supervisors, executives, and so on." Ten days later the election is held; the union wins by a vote of 54 to 53 and is certified by the National Labor Relations Board as the bargaining representative of the Utica plant production employees of the Robert's Manufacturing Company.

Collective Bargaining

Collective bargaining is defined by law as the performance of the mutual obligation of the employer and representatives of the employees (1) to meet at reasonable times, (2) to confer in good faith with respect to wages, hours, and other terms and conditions of employment, and (3) to incorporate any agreement reached into a written contract. This obligation does not compel either party to agree to a proposal or require either party to make concessions.

Once the employees' bargaining representative (the union) has been certified by the National Labor Relations Board, the employer is duty bound to agree to discuss wages and employment. Usually in collective bargaining proceedings the union submits a contract and the employer makes counterproposals.

Boycotts and Picketing

Under the Labor Reform Act of 1959 it is an unfair practice for the union to engage in a strike or to refuse to work or to threaten an employer when the purpose of these activities is (1) to force an employer not to handle the goods of another, (2) to stop a person from using, selling, handling, or transporting the products of another employer, (3) to make another employer recognize or bargain with a union unless it has been certified by the National Labor Relations Board, or (4) to force an employer to bargain with a particular union when another union has already been certified by the Board.

This law more strictly than the Taft-Hartley Law bans secondary boycotts. The Taft-Hartley Law prohibited unions from putting pressure on employees of secondary employers, but the Labor Reform Act of 1959 makes it unlawful for a union to put this direct pressure on a secondary employer himself.

Many union contracts formerly contained "hot cargo" clauses, which provided that union employees were not required to handle the goods of a concern whose employees were on strike. Under the current law it is unfair labor practice for a union to engage in concerted activities in order to force an employer to sign an agreement refusing to handle the goods of another.

Before passage of the Labor Reform Act unions sometimes resorted to picketing and other activities to force an employer to sign a union contract when none of his employees belonged or wanted to belong to the union. Under the 1959 law it is unfair for a union to picket or threaten to picket an employer for recognition or to force employees to join the union if (1) a valid National Labor Relations Board election has been held within the preceding twelve months, (2) if such picketing has been conducted before a petition for an election has been filed with the National Labor Relations Board, or (3) if the employer has lawfully recognized another union.

LABOR RELATIONS INVOLVING PUBLIC EMPLOYEES

Until the early 1960s employees of federal, state and local governments lived in a world of undefined rights. They did not have the same privileges to bargain collectively through representatives of their own choosing or other guarantees which nongovernment employees had. Government employees and their unions waged and won a battle. First, the courts recognized the right of government employees to form associations (unions) and to speak freely regarding conditions of their employment. Then President Kennedy and later President Nixon issued Executive Orders granting bargaining and other rights to federal employees.

There are now twenty-two states that give all government employees, state and local, the right to be represented by unions and to bargain collectively. Those states are California, Connecticut, Delaware, Hawaii, Kansas, Maine, Michigan, Minnesota, Missouri, Nebraska, Nevada, New Hampshire, New Jersey, New York, Oregon, Pennsylvania, Rhode Island, South Dakota, Vermont, Washington, Wisconsin, and Wyoming.

Eight states (Alaska, Florida, Georgia, Idaho, Maryland, Montana, North Dakota, and Oklahoma) give limited rights to government employees in special groups such as teachers and fire fighters. Labor relations involving government employees differ from labor problems in the field of private employment principally in that government employees for the most part are denied the right to strike.

12
Corporations

A *corporation* is a legal "person" composed of one or more natural persons and is an entirely separate and distinct entity from the individuals who compose it.

CHARACTERISTICS OF A CORPORATION

The powers of a corporation are fixed by its charter, which is granted to it by the state in which it is incorporated. A corporation may have perpetual existence, notwithstanding the death, withdrawal, or disability of its members. It can sue or be sued; it can purchase and hold lands or other property, enter into contracts, or commit legal wrongs like a private individual. The corporation's ability to do these things depends upon the terms of the charter granted to it by the state; its activities are governed or limited by the state's statutes.

When two or more persons form a partnership, each business partner retains his identity as an individual. A partnership is not a legal entity separate and distinct from the individual members, but a corporation is, and its individual members legally lose their identity in the corporation. The members of the partnership are individually liable for the partnership debts, whereas the stockholders are not usually liable for corporation debts. The death of a partner generally results in the dissolution of the partnership, but the death of a stockholder does not affect a corporation. (See Chapter 13 for more information on partnerships.)

In unincorporated societies and clubs, the individual members may be liable for actions taken by a majority of the members or for actions of its officers. This is not so in the case of a corporation. The corporation is liable for the acts of its officers, but the individual stockholders are immune. Thus, the modern trend is to incorporate most societies and clubs.

Although many states have in recent years revised their corporation laws and have patterned them after the Model Business

Corporation Act of the American Bar Association (called the "Model Act"), the corporation laws still vary greatly among the states. For example, the duration of a corporation according to the laws in one state is twenty-five years; in another state, ninety-nine years; in still another, perpetual. In some states, the name of the corporation must include the word *Corporation* or *Incorporated* or *Limited* or the abbreviations *Inc.* or *Ltd.*, to avoid confusion with individuals doing business under assumed names or partnership forms. Other states permit simply the word *Company* or the abbreviation *Co.*

ADVANTAGES OF INCORPORATION

The advantages to businessmen of incorporation over other forms of business organization are—*limited liability, permanency,* and *flexibility*. Once a stockholder has paid for his stock in the corporation, he is not usually liable to creditors of the corporation. Thus, businessmen can put money into a corporate venture and not run the risk of personal liability if the venture fails. The corporation may continue indefinitely no matter what happens to its original stockholders.

Shares of stock represent fractional ownership interest in a corporation. They may be sold, given away, or pledged as security for loans by the stockholder without affecting the basic corporate organization.

KINDS OF CORPORATIONS

There are many different kinds of corporations, among them public, municipal, and private corporations; stock and membership corporations; and foreign and domestic corporations. Different legal rules determine the powers, liabilities, and privileges of each classification of corporation.

Public, Municipal, and Private Corporations

Public or *municipal corporations* are instrumentalities of government, such as cities, villages, towns, counties, school districts, school boards, and so on. A *private corporation* is owned by individuals.

Stock and Membership Corporations

A *stock corporation* is one the capital stock of which is divided into shares held by the owners of the corporation and which is authorized by law to pay its profits to shareholders in the form of dividends. Private business corporations are generally stock corporations. All corporations listed on stock exchanges are stock corporations. *Membership corporations* are nonprofit, nonstock corporations created for various purposes; examples are organizations or groups to promote or further political, religious, temperance, missionary, educational, scientific, musical, charitable, social, or other nonbusiness activities.

Foreign and Domestic Corporations

A *domestic corporation* is one doing business in the state in which it is incorporated. It becomes a *foreign corporation* when it does business in another state. It is similar to the concept that a citizen of this country becomes a foreigner when he moves to another country.

Other Classifications

Corporations are also classified according to particular statutes as *cooperative, joint stock, religious, cemetery, library, agricultural, transportation, railroad, insurance,* and so on.

ORGANIZING A CORPORATION

The Model Business Corporation Act of the American Bar Association provides that three or more natural persons* (at least two-thirds of whom are citizens of the United States or of its territories) may form a corporation. The Model Act provides, too, that the articles of incorporation shall specify: (1) the purpose of the corporation, (2) its duration, (3) its location and the post office address of its registered office, (4) the total number of shares of par value and the total number of shares of no-par value, (5) the relative rights, voting powers, preferences, and restrictions of each class of shares, (6) the amount of paid-in-capital with which the corporation will begin business, (7) the first directors and their post office addresses, and (8) the name and post office address of each of the incorporators and a statement of the number of shares for which each has subscribed. According to the Model Act procedure, the

---

* The New York State Business Corporation Law provides that one or more persons may act as an incorporator or incorporators of a corporation.

articles of incorporation are first delivered to the state secretary of state. When he has approved them and when all taxes, fees, and charges as required by law have been paid, he issues a certificate of incorporation. At this point corporate existence begins.

Corporate Names

Before the articles of incorporation are approved by the secretary of state, the *corporate name* must be approved by him. It must not be the same as nor deceptively similar to the name of any other domestic corporation or any foreign corporation authorized to do business in the state. The following names have been contested and held to be too similar for duplicate filing of articles of incorporation:

J. S. Dodge Stationery Company
J. S. Dodge Company

Mount Hope Cemetery Association
New Mount Hope Cemetery Association

International Loan and Trust Company
International Trust Company

Glucose Sugar Refining Company
American Glucose Sugar Refining Company

Backus Oil Company
Backus Oil and Car Grease Company

Manchester Brewery Company
The North Theshir and Manchester Brewery Company

The following names have been held to be not so similar as to come within the rule prohibiting the use of both names:

Los Angeles Trust & Savings Bank
Los Angeles Savings Bank

Elgin Creamery Company
Elgin Butter Company

Industrial Mutual Deposit Company
Central Mutual Deposit Company

Corning Glass Works
Corning Cut Glass Company

Buffalo Commercial Bank
Bank of Commerce in Buffalo

Organization Meetings

When the articles of incorporation are filed, the incorporators hold a meeting, adopt bylaws, and approve the initial steps to be taken by the corporation. The directors named in the certificate of incorporation hold their first meeting, elect officers, and decide what assets are to be acquired, what stock should be issued, and so on. The incorporators adopt the bylaws, usually with the approval of the directors. Bylaws are rules and regulations established by a corporation for the government and guidance of its officers and stockholders in the management of corporation affairs. Generally the bylaws contain a restatement of the state's laws governing the conduct of corporations.

Powers of a Corporation

An individual has the legal power to do anything or to engage in any kind of business not prohibited by law. A corporation on the other hand may do only those things and engage only in those businesses permitted by law or set forth in its certificate of incorporation.

The corporation laws of each state specify the purposes for which a corporation may be organized. Under the old rule corporations were organized for a single business, such as to sell real estate, manufacture automobiles, operate a store, or to conduct a specified business enterprise. If the corporation attempted to operate another type of business, its efforts would be considered illegal and it would have to organize a new company to operate the new type of business. Then the rule was changed, and the powers stated in certificates of incorporation were broadened so that a corporation could engage in many different enterprises. Most current certificates of incorporation contain an absurd enumeration of endless powers and purposes; incorporators seem to like to include in the corporate charter almost every conceivable kind of legal business. Modern draftsmen of corporate charters have attempted to end the enumeration of countless types of businesses by general statements of comprehensive scope. The trend to simplify statements of corporate powers is illustrated by the following provision in the Model Business Corporation Act: "It shall not be necessary to set forth in the articles of incorporation any of the corporate powers enumerated in this Act."

The broadening of corporate powers is exemplified by the New York Business Corporation Law, enacted in 1961, which states that every corporation has the power:

1. To have perpetual duration

2. To sue and be sued in all courts and to participate in actions and proceedings, whether judicial, administrative, arbitrative or otherwise, in like cases as natural persons

3. To have a corporate seal and to alter such seal at pleasure and to use it by causing it or a facsimile to be affixed or impressed or reproduced in any other manner

4. To purchase, receive, take by grant, gift, devise, bequest or otherwise, lease, or otherwise acquire, own, hold, improve, employ, use and otherwise deal in and with real or personal property, or any interest therein, wherever situated

5. To sell, convey, lease, exchange, transfer or otherwise dispose of, or mortgage or pledge, all or any of its property, or any interest therein, wherever situated

6. To purchase, take, receive, subscribe for or otherwise acquire, own, hold, vote, employ, sell, lend, lease, exchange, transfer or otherwise dispose of, mortgage, pledge, use and otherwise deal in and with bonds and other obligations, shares, or other securities or interests issued by others, whether engaged in similar or different business, governmental, or other activities

7. To make contracts, give guarantees and incur liabilities, borrow money at such rates of interest as the corporation may determine, issue its notes, bonds and other obligations, and secure any of its obligations by mortgage or pledge of all or any of its property or any interest therein, wherever situated

8. To lend money, invest and reinvest its funds, and take and hold real and personal property as security for the payment of funds so loaned or invested

9. To do business, carry on its operations, and have offices and exercise the powers granted by this chapter in any jurisdiction within or without the United States

10. To elect or appoint officers, employees, and other agents of the corporation, define their duties, and fix their compensation and the compensation of directors

11. To adopt, amend, or repeal bylaws relating to the business of the corporation, the conduct of its affairs, its rights or powers, or the rights or powers of its shareholders, directors, or officers

12. To make donations, irrespective of corporate benefit, for the public welfare or for community fund, hospital, charitable, educational, scientific, civic, or similar purposes and in time of war or other national emergency in aid thereof

13. To pay pensions, establish and carry out pension, profit-sharing, share bonus, share purchase, share option, savings, thrift and other retirement, incentive, and benefit plans, trusts, and provisions for any or all of its directors, officers, and employees

14. To purchase, receive, take, or otherwise acquire, own, hold, sell, lend, exchange, transfer or otherwise dispose of, pledge, use, and otherwise deal in and with its own shares

15. To be a promoter, partner, member, associate, or manager of other business enterprises or ventures or to the extent permitted in any other jurisdiction to be an incorporator of other corporations of any type or kind

16. To have and exercise all powers necessary or convenient to effect any or all of the purposes for which the corporation is formed.

The all-inclusive statements of powers in the New York statute give New York corporations the power to perform almost every conceivable business act which an individual could perform.

BOARD OF DIRECTORS OR TRUSTEES

The fundamental responsibility for the management of a corporation actually lies with the directors, who have full discretionary power. The board of directors or trustees is the corporation's governing body and must, in most corporations, consist of at least three persons. Directors or trustees (terms often synonymous) are elected by the majority vote of the stockholders; the modern trend is to provide either by statute or in the bylaws that a director need not be a stockholder of the corporation. The directors may, if they so desire, consult the stockholders concerning their wishes.

Generally, directors have authority to act only at regularly called meetings and they must act as a board; the individual or separate action of one of the directors does not bind the board or the corporation. Meetings of the board of directors may be held at any time and place, within the state of incorporation or elsewhere, appointed by the majority of the directors.

Directors stand in a fiduciary relation to the corporation and are required to discharge their duties in good faith—with diligence, care, and skill. A director of the corporation should not deal with himself when he is acting in behalf of the corporation, and he may not directly or indirectly derive personal benefit, by reason of his position as a director, that is not enjoyed by all the stockholders.

Mr. Garber was a director of the Union Manufacturing Company. While attending a directors' meeting, he learned that the corporation was contemplating the purchase of land on which to build a new factory. Mr. Garber had his real estate agent go out and buy land in the vicinity and subsequently offered to sell the land to the corporation at a profit. A minority stockholder, learning of Mr. Garber's double dealing, brought a court action against him and succeeded in recovering damages in behalf of the corporation for Mr. Garber's breach of trust.

A vacancy in the board of directors usually can be filled by the remaining board members. A director who obtains his status in this way remains until his successor is elected by the stockholders at their next annual meeting.

Although directors are chargeable with and have the authority to run the corporation and do not need to get stockholder approval of important business decisions, there are certain actions which require stockholder approval. For example, the Model Business Corporation Act provides that a sale, lease, exchange, mortgage, pledge, or other disposition of substantially all the property and assets of a corporation, if not made in the usual and regular course of business, must have the approval of the holders of two-thirds of the outstanding stock. Also a merger, consolidation, or voluntary dissolution of a corporation, according to the Model Act, requires two-thirds stockholder approval.

OFFICERS (AGENTS) OF THE CORPORATION

The Model Act provides that the board of directors of a corporation shall elect a president, a secretary, a treasurer, and one or more vice-presidents and shall appoint such officers and directors as may be necessary for the business of the corporation. None of the officers except the president need be a director. A vice-president who is not a director cannot succeed to or fill the office of the president. Any two of the offices—vice-president, secretary, treasurer—may be combined in one person.

The officers and agents have authority to perform duties in the management and affairs of the corporation subject to such control of the board of directors as may be prescribed in the bylaws or as determined by the board. Officers of the corporation also occupy a fiduciary relationship to the corporation and are accountable for the same high degree of fidelity as are the directors. An officer or agent may be removed by the board whenever in its judgment his removal is in the best interest of the corporation.

RIGHTS OF STOCKHOLDERS

Members are those who have a vested interest in a corporation which has no capital stock. *Stockholders* are the owners of shares in a corporation which has capital stock.

Right to Information

The stockholders are the owners of the corporation and as such have the right to information about the business affairs of the company; they are privileged to visit and inspect the corporation's property and to inspect and examine the books and records of the corporation at a proper time and place and for a proper purpose.

The Model Act provides that every corporation shall keep at its registered office (1) appropriate books of account, (2) a record of the proceedings of the stockholders and of the directors, and (3) a register giving the names and addresses of the stockholders of the corporation, the number of shares owned by each, and the dates acquired. The Model Act also provides that every shareholder shall have the right to examine the corporation's books in person or by proxy (through an agent or an attorney) at all reasonable times and for any reasonable purpose. The act provides further that a corporation shall be liable to the state for a fine of fifty dollars for each day that it neglects to keep these books or records.

Mr. Townsend, holding 15 percent of the stock of the Brewster Corporation, goes to the main office of the corporation and requests that he be permitted to examine its books and records. His request is denied. Mr. Townsend obtains a court order permitting him to examine the records. Later Mr. Townsend learns that the corporation does not keep a record of stockholders as required by law. He reports this to the attorney general of the state, who brings a proceeding to collect fines from the Brewster Corporation.

Stockholders' Meetings

The Model Act provides that stockholders' meetings may be held within or without the state of incorporation and that at least one stockholders' meeting must be held within each calendar year. Stockholders' meetings may be regular or special. Special meetings of stockholders may be called at any time by the officers of the corporation or by the board of directors or by an individual director or under certain conditions even by an individual stockholder. The Model Act provides that stockholders are entitled to written notice at least ten days prior to a stockholders' meeting.

Voting Rights

In a stock corporation, each shareholder is entitled to one vote for each share he owns. The Model Act provides that in the election of directors, each shareholder shall have the right of "cumulative voting"; that is, he has the right to determine the number of votes he has by multiplying the number of his shares by the number of directors to be elected. He may cast all his votes for one candidate, or he may distribute his votes among two or more candidates. For example, if five directors are to be chosen, a holder of five shares may have twenty-five votes.

At stockholders' meetings, a shareholder may cast his vote either in person or by proxy. A *proxy* is a person who has been duly authorized to vote for the stockholder by a written instrument (also called a proxy), filed with the secretary of the corporation. The Model Act provides that the validity of a written proxy shall cease eleven months after the date of its execution unless another definite period shall be specified; even when a definite time is specified in the proxy instrument, the instrument is generally not good beyond three years from the date of issue.

Voting Trusts

A *voting trust* is an agreement whereby several stockholders, in order to control the business and affairs of a corporation, turn over their shares to one or more persons as trustees to vote the stock. The Model Act, in referring to voting trusts, states that two or more shareholders may transfer their shares to any person or corporation to act as trustee for the purpose of vesting in such person or corporation all the voting rights pertaining to such shares for a period not exceeding ten years. It provides that a duplicate copy of the voting trust agreement shall be filed in the registered office of the corporation and shall be open to inspection by any shareholder. Any other shareholder may transfer his shares to the same trustee on the terms and conditions stated in the agreement. The voting trustee must then execute and deliver to the shareholder voting trust certificates which are transferable in the same manner as stock certificates.

The Snell Company encountered financial difficulties. Realizing that the bank was about to foreclose the mortgage on the factory and that the creditors of the corporation were seeking bankruptcy, a group of stockholders went to a man who was reputed to be an "industrial doctor" and persuaded him to act as voting trustee with full power to vote stock of the majority of the stockholders and to throw out the management of the corporation. The voting trust agreement was valid and enforceable and as a result of hard-boiled but prudent business tactics this person saved the company from bankruptcy.

Liability of Stockholders

Since a corporation is a legal entity entirely separate from its stockholders, the latter, except under very rare circumstances, are not liable for the debts of the corporation, nor for the acts or misdeeds of the officers or agents of the corporation. This is a fundamental principle governing corporations—the law of limited liability.

The stockholder who does not pay the corporation for his stock is liable to creditors of the corporation for the amount of the capital he had agreed to pay. As far as the relation of the stockholders to the creditors is concerned, only the capital of the corporation can be used for payment of debts. In the absence of fraud or the creation of a fictitious corporation, the stockholders have no further responsibility once they have paid in the capital. In determining whether stock is fully paid and whether actual or true value has been paid for the stock, the courts say that if the directors have acted in good faith (that is, without actual fraud or intentional overevaluation) stock is deemed to be fully paid up. This is so even though (against creditors) it may afterwards appear that through mistake or error in judgment there was an overevaluation of property received by the corporation in exchange for stock.

It must be borne in mind that the concept of a corporation as a legal entity, or "person" apart from its members, is a mere fiction of the law conceived for convenience in conducting business. In rare cases, the courts have disregarded this corporate fiction and, as the expression goes, have "pierced the corporate veil" in order to place the legal and moral responsibility for fraud on those persons who have attempted to hide behind a corporate entity. This has happened when several corporations have been owned by the same parties. In these cases, the courts have disregarded the legal fiction of distinct corporate entities because the corporations were so organized and controlled that one corporation was merely an instrument or an adjunct of another.

The Sword Steamship Brokerage Company organized the Sword Stevedore Company with identical officers for each company. The brokerage company furnished the facilities and offices of the stevedore company, kept its accounts, handled its funds, paid its losses, and retained its profits as a charge for handling its business. In a negligence action the court held that concerning third persons the two corporations were identical and both were liable for damages caused by the negligence of any employee of either company.

CAPITAL, SHARES, PROFITS, DIVIDENDS

A knowledge of the meanings of the terms *capital, capital stock, capitalization, profits,* and *dividends* is essential to an understanding of corporation law. Here we will differentiate among these several topics.

Distinction between Capital Stock and Shares

The *capital stock* of a corporation is the amount fixed by the articles of incorporation (or in the case of no-par stock, by the directors) as the amount paid in or to be paid in by the stockholders as capital with which the corporation is to do business. In accounting terminology, the single word *capital* is also used to denote the amount of the capital stock.

Shares of stock represent the proportionate interest of the stockholders in the corporate property. The terms *shares of stock* and *stock* and *shares* are used interchangeably, as are the terms *stockholders* and *shareholders*. This distinction is made between *capital stock* and *shares of stock*: The capital belongs to the corporation, and the shares are the property of the individual shareholders.

The legal capital of a corporation and the number of shares into which the capital stock is divided and the amount or par value of each share are fixed by the articles of incorporation. However, in the case of no-par stock, the amount of the capital is fixed by the directors.

Each stockholder is entitled to a *certificate of stock* signed by the president or vice-president and the secretary or treasurer; this is the manner in which stock is issued. The stock certificate states (1) the name of the corporation, (2) the name of the registered holder of the shares of stock, (3) the number and class of shares which the particular certificate represents (that is, preferred or common stock, par stock or no-par stock), (4) the par value of each share or a statement that the shares have no-par value, (5) the total number of par shares and the total number of no-par shares. A certificate of stock is not issued until the shares represented by the certificate have been paid for in full. To determine whether the shares have been fully paid and to fix the obligation of a shareholder to the corporation, the valuation placed by the incorporators or by the directors is final.

Different Kinds of Stock

There are many types of stock shares. The following are the major ones:

Common stock is the ordinary stock of the corporation which entitles the owner to a pro rata share of the profits of the corporation. No profits may be paid to common stockholders until dividends are declared by the directors.

Preferred stock gives the holder preference either in the distribution of earnings of the corporation or in the dissolution of the corporation over the holders of common stock or another class of stock. Holders of *guaranteed stock*, a form of preferred stock, are guaranteed dividends by the corporation.

Nonassessable stock is that which has been legally issued by the corporation and is fully paid and on which no assessment against the stockholder can be made.

Treasury stock is stock which has been sold to stockholders and reacquired and held by the corporation.

Unissued stock is that which is authorized but which has never been issued.

Par stock is given a "price ticket" which indicates the nominal value of each share of stock.

No-par stock is stock without any named par value, but which simply represents a fractional interest in the assets of the corporation.

Profits and Dividends

The dividends and the profits of a corporation are not the same thing. *Profits* become dividends when they are declared or set apart by the directors as such. *Dividends* become the property of the stockholders; they are distributed to the stockholders on the basis of their ownership interest in the corporation.

Dividends can be declared and paid only out of net profits or surplus funds of the corporation, except when a corporation is liquidated. The reason for this is obvious: distribution of capital as dividends depletes the capital of the corporation. In many states it is a criminal offense for directors to declare dividends out of capital, for it perpetrates fraud on the firm's creditors (who have extended credit to the corporation on the faith of its capital).

The Model Business Corporation Act strictly prohibits the payment of dividends except from the surplus profits of the corporation; if the directors knowingly vote in favor of illegal dividends, they are individually liable to the corporation for the amount of the dividend so paid.

MERGER AND CONSOLIDATION

The terms *merger* and *consolidation* are often confused and in-accurately used. A true *consolidation* is brought about when a new corporation comes into existence to take over the assets and liabilities of two or more former corporations, which are then dissolved. A *merger*, on the other hand, is brought about when one existing corporation is continued and one or more others are merged into it without the formation of a new corporation. For example:

The South American Steamship Company and the African Coastal Lines decide to put their assets together and form a new company to be called the Trans-African Transportation Company. A consolidation results.

The directors of the Johnstown National Bank vote to acquire the First National Bank of Meredith. After the acquisition, both banks will be known as The Johnstown National Bank which will have a branch in the Village of Meredith. The First National Bank of Meredith loses its identity. The Johnstown National Bank continues its corporate existence as before. The result is a merger of the Meredith Bank with The Johnstown National Bank.

Neither consolidation nor merger does away with the rights of creditors without their consent, and the surviving corporation (in a merger) or the new corporation (in a consolidation) is liable for the debts of the merged or consolidated companies.

Mechanics of Merger or Consolidation

Merger or consolidation may be limited by statutes or by anti-trust laws. The Model Business Corporation Act (in Sections 65–71) provides that a merger or consolidation can be effected only as the result of a joint agreement entered into and filed as follows:

1. The board of directors of each such corporation enters into a joint agreement, signed by the directors, describing the terms and conditions of merger or consolidation and the methods of effecting it.

2. The agreement is submitted for consideration to the stockholders of each merging or consolidating corporation at a meeting. If at this meeting the holder of two-thirds of the voting power of all the stockholders of each corporation votes for the adoption of the agreement, then that fact is certified by the secretary of each corporation; the agreement so adopted and certified is signed by the president and secretary of each corporation.

3. The agreement is delivered to the state secretary of state, who, if he finds the agreement lawful, files and records it in his office, whereupon the merger or consolidation becomes a fact.

Rights of Dissenting Stockholders

When a corporation plans to merge or to consolidate a stockholder of either corporation who did not vote in favor of the move may (according to the Model Act), within twenty days after authorization to merge or consolidate, reject the proposal in writing and demand payment for his shares. If the corporation and the stockholder cannot agree on the value of his shares, it will be determined by three disinterested persons—one named by the stockholder, one by the corporation, the third by the two other appraisers. The finding of the appraisers is final. If their award is not paid by the corporation within thirty days after it is made, it may be recovered in a suit against the corporation.

DISSOLUTION

A corporation is *dissolved* when its existence is terminated, its affairs wound up, and its assets distributed among creditors and stockholders. Dissolution does not take place with the suspension of business, nor with the abandonment of a corporate franchise nor with the sale of a corporation's entire assets or by the appointment of a receiver. Dissolution may be voluntary or involuntary. The proceedings may be conducted out of court (voluntary dissolution) or subject to the supervision of a court (involuntary dissolution).

Voluntary Dissolution

Voluntary dissolution may be achieved by the corporation stockholders. The Model Business Corporation Act provides that proceedings for voluntary dissolution may be instituted whenever a resolution therefore is adopted by the holders of at least two-thirds of the voting power of all the stockholders at a special meeting called for that purpose. Instead of having a stockholders' meeting to dissolve a corporation there may be a voluntary dissolution on the written consent of all the stockholders. Also there may be a voluntary dissolution by all the incorporators of a corporation within two years after the date of the issuance of its certificate of incorporation, provided (1) that the corporation has not commenced business, (2) that no debts of the corporation remain unpaid, and (3) that the majority of the incorporators desire that the corporation be dissolved.

The resolution for voluntary dissolution may provide that the affairs of the corporation shall be wound up out of court by a trustee or trustees. The appointment of the trustees cannot be made until duplicate copies of the resolution have been signed by a majority of the directors or by the stockholders holding a majority of the voting power and until one of these copies has been filed in the office of the state secretary of state.

Although it has been said that voluntary dissolution results from the expiration of a corporate charter, from merger, from consolidation, and from other proceedings which result in the corporation going out of existence, these are not true voluntary dissolutions. In order for there to be a voluntary dissolution (1) the stockholders must act, (2) a certificate of dissolution must be obtained from the proper state official (obtainable only after all state corporate taxes have been paid), and (3) a notice of dissolution to creditors must be published. Then steps are taken to terminate the affairs of the corporation by selling the assets and distributing the proceeds to creditors and stockholders.

In a few states voluntary dissolution, after approval by the stockholders, is carried out by application of the corporation to the court for supervision of the dissolution. In other states a voluntary dissolution may be effected only by a proper application to the court, and dissolution does not take place until a hearing has been held for the creditors and all interested parties, and the court has entered its decree.

Involuntary Dissolution

Involuntary dissolution may take place as a result of (1) the expiration of the corporate charter; (2) an equity suit by a stockholder or creditor asking the court to appoint a receiver and terminate the affairs of the corporation by reason of fraud on the part of the majority stockholders, mismanagement on the part of the officers or directors, or dissension among stockholders which renders impossible a continuation of the business; or (3) the forfeiture of the charter by the state as a result of fraud practiced on the state by the corporation or failure to pay franchise taxes or failure to exercise corporate powers. The general rules and principles concerning involuntary dissolution have been codified in the Model Business Corporation Act, which sets forth three types of involuntary dissolutions:

1. In an action filed by the Attorney General when it is established that:
a. The corporation has failed to file its annual report within the time

required by this Act or has failed to pay its franchise tax on or before the first day of August of the year in which such franchise tax becomes due and payable; or

b. The corporation procured its articles of incorporation through fraud; or

c. The corporation has continued to exceed or abuse the authority conferred upon it by law; or

d. The corporation has failed for thirty days to appoint and maintain a registered agent in this state; or

e. The corporation has failed for thirty days after change of its registered office or registered agent to file in the office of the secretary of state a statement of such change.

2. In an action by a shareholder when it is established:

a. That the directors are deadlocked in the management of the corporate affairs and the shareholders are unable to break the deadlock, and that irreparable injury to the corporation is being suffered or is threatened by reason thereof; or

b. That the acts of the directors or those in control of the corporation are illegal, oppressive, or fraudulent; or

c. That the shareholders are deadlocked in voting power, and have failed, for a period which includes at least two consecutive annual meeting dates, to elect successors to directors whose terms have expired or would have expired upon the election of their successors; or

d. That the corporate assets are being misapplied or wasted.

3. In an action by a creditor:

a. When the claim of the creditor has been reduced to judgment and an execution thereon returned unsatisfied and it is established that the corporation is insolvent; or

b. When the corporation has admitted in writing that the claim of the creditor is due and owing and it is established that the corporation is insolvent.

Professional Corporations

A professional corporation (commonly referred to as PC) is a corporation organized by members (or even one member) of a profession (such as medicine, architecture, dentistry, law, accountancy, or engineering) to enable them to practice their professions as a corporation. Until recent years professional people were forbidden by state laws from practicing their professions as corporations. The prohibition against their incorporating was thought to work hardships on them. Advocates of professional corporations claimed that the law unfairly discriminated in favor of business executives and employees who received many fringe benefits, such as pension or profit-sharing plans, which professional people were barred from using. The subject was controversial and was debated for many years. Finally the fifty states now have laws which allow members of professions to incorporate. Despite the enactment of these laws many members of professions are reluctant to become corporations.

13
Partnerships*

Chancellor Kent's (New York state) definition of a partnership is one of the earliest and yet one of the most comprehensive: A partnership is "a contract of two or more competent persons to place their money, effects, labor and skill, or some or all of them, in lawful commerce or business, and to divide the profit and bear the loss in certain proportions." A *partnership* is an association of two or more persons formed to carry on a business for mutual profit. The partners (1) are co-owners of the enterprise, (2) intend through the partnership to make a profit, (3) are agents for and have a fiduciary relationship with each other, and (4) consequently, each partner is responsible for the acts of the others.

Although there are many advantages to the corporate form of business, many businessmen prefer the partnership form of organization. This feeling prevails when persons consider important equality of action and freedom from public supervision, corporation taxes, and corporation routine. A partnership, however, is not to be entered into lightly; its freedoms are balanced by equal responsibilities which in certain circumstances may become liabilities. The major disadvantage of the partnership form of doing business is the unlimited personal liability of each partner for all obligations of the business, including liabilities which result from wrongful acts of another partner.

Many years ago an English court stated that it is "an imprudent thing for a man to enter into a partnership with any person unless he has the most implicit confidence in his integrity." This is still true.

* The rules and principles stated in this chapter are based on the Uniform Partnership Act which in 1962 had been adopted by forty-five states; Alabama, Connecticut, Florida, Georgia, Hawaii, Iowa, Kansas, Louisiana, Maine, New Hampshire, and Texas either follow common-law principles of partnership law or have adopted their own statutory provisions to govern the rights and duties of partners.

KINDS OF ORGANIZATION AND PARTNERS

Partnerships may be general or limited (special). Over 90 percent of partnerships in this country are *general partnerships*, those in which all the partners share the liabilities of the partnership debts and in which each partner is an agent for the firm. In a general partnership partners may have the same or different investments of capital and may share the profits and losses in the same or different proportions.

A *limited partnership* is composed of one or more general partners and one or more special partners. A *special partner* may limit his liabilities in the partnership to the amount of his investment by inserting modifying articles in the partnership agreement.

Limited partnerships have existed in Europe since the Middle Ages, but they were never part of the English common law. In 1822 New York became the first common-law state to introduce limited partnership laws. Connecticut followed, and other states later adopted limited partnership laws. Then, in 1916, the Uniform Limited Partnership Act was approved by the National Conference of Commissioners on Uniform Laws, and it has been adopted with slight modifications by all the states except Alabama, Connecticut, Kansas, Kentucky, Louisiana, Maine, Mississippi, Oregon, and Wyoming. This act, which was borrowed from the French Code, provides for the filing of a limited partnership certificate stating information about each partner, the amount of cash or other property contributed by each limited partner, and the share of profits each limited partner is to receive. The limited partnership certificate must not only be filed but must also be published once a week for six successive weeks in two newspapers of the county in which the original certificate is filed. The Uniform Limited Partnership Act delineates the rights and liabilities of general and limited partners between themselves and in respect to other persons. Among other things, the act provides (1) that a limited partner shall not become liable as a general partner unless he takes part in the control of the business, (2) that a limited partner shall have the right to full information about all things affecting the partnership, and (3) that a limited partner shall receive his share of the profits or other compensation by way of income.

A partnership may exist where parties do not intend partnership or where the agreement between them even states otherwise. This happens when persons conduct themselves in such a manner that it may be reasonably inferred that they are partners. This is known as *partnership by estoppel*. For example, if a third party, assuming that two businessmen are partners, extends credit to them, they may be held to be partners by the third party.

Partners have been divided into various classes such as dormant, silent, incoming, retiring, nominal, ostensible, and secret partners. These terms have no well-defined meaning in law. A silent partner is said to be the same as a sleeping partner: one who is neither an active partner nor generally known to the public as a partner; his connection with the firm is concealed in some way. A nominal partner is one who allows his name to appear as a member of the firm in which he has no real interest. This arrangement is similar to that of an ostensible partner, who may appear to be a partner but who has no actual interest in the firm.

FORMATION OF A PARTNERSHIP

No particular form of contract is necessary for the formation of a partnership. The contract may be oral or written or may be implied from the conduct of the parties. An oral contract is as binding on the individual partners as a written agreement between them. The best way to establish a partnership is, however, by a contract in writing.

A partnership agreement is sometimes called "articles of copartnership" and usually contains in detail all things agreed to by the prospective partners. The rules of law applicable to contracts generally, such as those relating to consideration, consent, and capacity of the parties to enter into a contract apply to partnership contracts, but the contract of partnership, as distinguished from other types, must be a contract to conduct a business for the mutual profit of the partners. *The making of money is the essential feature of a partnership.*

People do sometimes enter into business arrangements for purposes other than to share a profit; for example, local merchants may form an association for the purpose of sharing losses in the breakage of plate glass, several persons may agree to share the expense of paying rewards for the capture of thieves, or businessmen may band together for mutual protection or advancement. None of these cooperative ventures is a partnership. A mere community of interest, such as the joint ownership of property, does not make the owners partners. On the other hand, when co-owners of real estate agree to combine their efforts in the business of buying, improving, selling, or leasing it, they may be held to be partners.

Mason, Young, and McGee decide to build houses under an arrangement whereby Mason agrees to furnish the cash and the real estate. Young is to act as architect, and McGee agrees to do all clerical and mortgage work. It is further decided that each one is to receive a fair share of the profit on the sale of the houses. Such an arrangement constitutes a partnership.

Money may be loaned or advanced to the owner of a business with the understanding that the loan is to be repaid from profits of the business and that the profits shall take the place of interest on the loan. This arrangement does not constitute a partnership. Sometimes a store is leased under an agreement that a percentage of the profits of the business of the store is to be paid as rent, but this arrangement does not make the landlord a partner in the business. When people band together for other than business purposes, for instance, for social, religious, moral, patriotic, educational, literary, scientific, political, or charitable reasons, no partnership exists.

PARTNERSHIP NAME

A partnership may choose to do business under a firm name consisting of all the names forming the partnership. However, practically all states have assumed-name laws, which require that any person (or persons) conducting business under any other title than his real name file in a public office a certificate stating his full real name and his residence. Some states prohibit the use of the name of a person and the phrase *and company* when that phrase does not represent an actual partner.

Messrs. Moon and Stellick operated a plumbing business in New York under the name of Empire Plumbing Company. Under the New York assumed-name law, they were required to file a certificate in the county clerk's office showing the name and address of the business and their individual names and residences, but they neglected to do this. One of their competitors brought the matter to the attention of the district attorney who instituted a criminal proceeding against Moon and Stellick for failing to file an assumed-name certificate. Moon and Stellick claimed that they were the victims of needless persecution and pleaded innocent to the charge, saying that no creditor or other interested person was hurt. The court found Messrs. Moon and Stellick guilty of a misdemeanor and they were subjected to unpleasant publicity.

Other states have an additional law requiring that persons may not transact business as partners under a partnership agreement unless they file in the county clerk's office in the county in which the firm operates a certificate showing the name under which the business is transacted and the name and address of each partner. For example, three public accountants operate a partnership firm under their names, Walsh, Wilson & Elgin; even though they are using their true names, they must still file a partnership certificate giving their full names and addresses.

RIGHTS AND DUTIES OF PARTNERS TO EACH OTHER

No formal contract is necessary to form a partnership, but, in view of the complexity of the modern business world, it is advisable that those entering into this type of business organization have a written agreement. The written contract specifies the rights and the duties of the partners. It includes such items as place, name, term of partnership; amount of capital to be invested by each partner; types of partners to be included; distribution of profits; and so on.

Short and Long Agreements

A partnership agreement may be written on only one sheet of paper, or it may be a long, involved document covering the details of important arrangements. Here is an example of points covered by a short partnership agreement:

Weaver and Levene decide to open a stationery store. Their short partnership contract provides:
1. The name of the partnership shall be "Weaver and Levene."
2. The term of the partnership shall be 10 years.
3. The place of the partnership shall be 214 Main Street.
4. The capital of the partnership shall be $10,000, each partner contributing $5,000 cash. Neither party's contribution to the capital shall bear interest.
5. If either party, with the consent of the other, lends money to the partnership, such loans shall bear interest at the rate of 6 percent per annum.
6. Each partner shall devote all his time to the business and shall not engage in any other business.
7. Partnership profits or losses shall be divided equally.

The following is an example of the subject matter of a long partnership agreement:

Messrs. Read, Bailey, Holden, and Ferber, about to engage in the business of wholesale distribution of food products, decide they would be better off if they did not incorporate. They tell their lawyer that they want to cover in detail in the partnership agreement all the points of their arrangement. Read is to contribute $25,000, Bailey $10,000, Holden $7,000, and Ferber $3,000.

The agreement drawn by the lawyer specifies the capital of the partnership; that additional contributions to capital may be made by the parties from time to time; how loans may be made by the partners and how they shall be repaid; how the bank account is to be maintained and what signatures are to be required on checks; the fact that Read will not be required to render active services to the business beyond weekly consultation services, but that Bailey, Holden, and Ferber will devote all their time to it; that Bailey is to be the managing partner, charged with the responsibility of making decisions concerning operational details; that for the first six months of the operation none of the partners is to receive a salary or drawing account but thereafter Bailey is to receive a salary of $300 each week, Holden $150 each week, and Farber $130.00 each week; that the first $10,000 of net profits should be divided equally between the partners but that all profits after the $10,000 should be divided in proportion to the capital contributions; that no partner can withdraw more than 50 percent of his share of the profits in any one year without the consent of the other partners; that full and accurate account of the transactions shall be kept in books of account; that the lives of Bailey and Holden shall be insured for $25,000 each and the lives of Ferber and Read insured for $10,000 each, payable to the partnership.

Also, that each partner should satisfy his own personal debts; that no partner shall assign, mortgage, or sell his interest in the partnership; that no partner shall make any assignment for the benefit of creditors or mortgage his personal real estate without the consent of the other partners, nor borrow, lend money, or indorse commercial paper except for the purpose of the partnership; that each year a complete statement and accounting shall be made of all assets and profits of the partnership; that if any party should elect to retire from the partnership, he should give the other partners notice in writing, and that the amount of his capital contribution shall be paid to him by the other partners; and other detailed machinery about the method of retiring from the partnership; provisions regarding the payment of a small percentage of the partner's share in the profits on the physical or mental disability of any partner; provisions as to how a partner can be expelled for misconduct; that death shall not terminate the partnership, but that the estate of the deceased partner shall be paid the amount of his contributions to the capital in equal annual installments extending over a period of ten years; and a provision for arbitration in the event of a dispute between the partners.

Restrictions on Individual Transactions of Partners

Someone once said that when a person becomes a partner, he enters into a business marriage. Undoubtedly the formation of a partnership is almost as important a step as marriage. In the same way partners owe to each other the utmost good faith in all their mutual dealings, including abiding by the limitations placed on the activities of partners.

All profits made by a general partner in conducting the business of the partnership belong to the partnership. Thus, a partner may not derive a secret personal profit from any transaction of the firm or use partnership property for his individual profit or benefit.

Todd and Murdock were partners who owned several tobacco plantations and sold to many concerns. On one occasion they sold tobacco at a ridiculously low price to the Lost Continent Tobacco Company of which Murdock was the principal stockholder. The transaction, unknown to Todd, resulted in considerable profit to Murdock. Upon discovery, Todd sued. The court set aside the sale and required Murdock to account to the partnership for his personal profit.

When a partner transacts business with another firm in which he has an interest, he must always disclose his personal interest in the matter.

A partner cannot engage in the same kind of business as that of the partnership without the consent of his partners. However, there is nothing to prevent a partner from engaging in a trade or business different from that in which the firm is engaged. If his business is entirely different, he does not have to account to his partners for the profits.

The Kingsley Chalmers Company was engaged in the real estate brokerage business. Chalmers bought a tract of land with his own money, subdivided it, and sold lots. Kingsley Chalmers Company had never been in the business of buying or developing real estate subdivisions, but had limited itself to brokerage business. Therefore, Chalmers was not accountable to the firm for the profit he made in buying and selling lots for his own profit.

When a partner withdraws from the partnership, notice of his withdrawal should be given to all persons with whom the partnership has dealings so the withdrawing individual cannot be held liable for debts contracted after he has severed his connection with the business. Unless the other partners consent, a partner cannot sell his interest in the firm in order to give the transferee the right to become a member of the firm.

LIABILITY OF PARTNERS TO OTHER PERSONS

In the United States each partner may usually be held liable for the total amount of the partnership debt. If the partnership assets are depleted, the creditors may look to the individual partners for payment. This is true not only regarding contractual obligations but also concerning wrongs committed in behalf of the partnership that result in injuries and damages to others. The partnership firm as well as each member thereof is answerable for the acts of its agents and employees provided their acts are performed in the course of their employment.

Kress and Kaplan were partners engaged in the contracting business. They hired Dyer as their general superintendent. In supervising the construction of a building Dyer did not follow the architect's plans and, as a result of weak and defective supports negligently constructed, the building collapsed causing considerable destruction to the property. The partnership assets were subject to the claims of those who had been damaged and Kress and Kaplan were individually responsible for the acts of Dyer, the superintendent.

DISSOLUTION OF PARTNERSHIP

A dissolution of a partnership is the cancellation or breaking up of the relationship of the partners. On dissolution the partnership is not terminated but is continued until the settlement of the partnership affairs. Dissolution does, however, terminate all the remaining partners' authority, except that which is necessary to wind up partnership affairs.

There is no such thing as an indissolvable partnership, because the courts have held that the right of a partner to dissolve a partnership is an inherent right. Any partner to a partnership may at any time take legal steps to dissolve the partnership.

According to the provisions of the Uniform Partnership Act, dissolution is caused:

1. Without violation of the agreement between the partners:
a. By the termination of the definite term or particular undertaking specified in the agreement, or
b. By the express will of any partner when no definite term or particular undertaking is specified, or
c. By the express will of all the partners who have not assigned their interests or suffered them to be charged for their separate debts either before or after the termination of any specified term or particular undertaking;
2. By any event which makes it unlawful for the business of the partnership to be carried on or for the members to carry it on in partnership;
3. By the death of any partner;
4. By the bankruptcy of any partner or partnership; or
5. By decree of a court.

A court of competent jurisdiction may decree a partnership dissolution (1) when a partner has been declared a lunatic or has been shown to be of unsound mind, (2) when a partner in any way becomes incapable of performing his part of the partnership contract, (3) when a partner has been guilty of such conduct as tends to prejudice the partnership business, (4) when a partner has willfully committed a breach of the partnership agreement or so conducts himself in matters relating to the partnership business that it is not practical to carry on the partnership business with him, (5) when the business of the partnership can only be carried on at a loss, or (6) when other circumstances render a dissolution equitable.

In addition to court decree and the other causes listed in the Uniform Partnership Act, dissolution may be brought about by mutual consent of the partners, on the termination of the partnership, by war between belligerent countries of which the partners are respectively citizens, by an abandonment of the business enterprise, or by a partner's sale of his interest.

Effect of Death of a Partner

In the forty-five states where the Uniform Partnership Act has been adopted, the death of a partner operates as a dissolution of the partnership, unless there is a provision in the partnership agreement for the continuance of the partnership notwithstanding the death of a partner. The very nature of a partnership is the reason for its dissolution by the death of a partner; it is largely founded on the personal qualities of its members.

In the absence of a special agreement to the contrary, the surviving partner or partners become the legal owners of the assets of the partnership for the purpose of adjusting and terminating its affairs. The surviving partners hold the partnership property as trustees for the purpose of liquidation. New contracts or obligations should not be entered into by the surviving partners except as an incident to settling the business.

A partnership agreement may provide that the death of a partner shall not dissolve the firm and that the business may be continued by the surviving partner or partners. The agreement may provide that the capital of the deceased partner shall remain in the business and that the surviving partners shall pay interest on and ultimately return the investment of the deceased partner in the business or pay to the representative of the deceased partner a share of the profits of the business. A partner may in his will provide that the partnership shall continue after his death, may direct that his capital remain in the firm, and may give to the surviving partners the right to continue to carry on the business of the partnership and to enter into an agreement with his executor for eventual repayment of his share.

Settlement of Partnership Affairs

On dissolution, the partnership affairs must be settled before the rights of the various partners can be determined and property can be distributed among them. The most desirable way to terminate the affairs is for partners to enter into an agreement about the valuation and distribution of the firm's assets. If a partner insists, partnership assets may be sold and converted into cash. Otherwise, they may be distributed in kind.

Ordinarily a partner is not entitled to compensation for his services in settling the firm's affairs. He is, however, entitled to the expenses which he incurs in accomplishing the dissolution.

The Uniform Partnership Act provides the procedure by which a retiring partner or the estate of a deceased partner may be compensated when there is no definite settlement agreement between a retiring partner or the estate of a deceased partner and the person (or persons) who continues the business. When there is no such settlement, the retiring partner or the estate of the deceased partner may have the value of his interest ascertained at the date of dissolution. He or his estate is entitled to receive—as an ordinary creditor—an amount equal to the value of his interest in the dissolved partnership plus either (1) legal interest or (2) the profits attributable to the firm property used in the partnership after retirement or death.

14
Marriage

In thinking of marriage or getting married, the average person usually thinks of a religious rite or a civil ceremony. But, when a lawyer thinks of marriage he thinks of its legal nature, of the marriage contract. Marriage is a civil contract consented to by both parties. The marriage contract differs from ordinary contracts in that it cannot be dissolved by the parties but only by the sovereign power of the state.

It is the law in all Western countries that the marriage relation can exist only between one man and one woman at one time; hence only a monogamous marriage is legal.

VALID AND INVALID MARRIAGE

The validity of a marriage is determined by the laws of the place where the marriage is contracted and validated.* If the marriage is valid by the law of the place where it occurred, it will be held valid wherever the question arises.

Bertha Jones and Harvey Jones, first cousins, lived in New Hampshire, where the marriage of first cousins is prohibited. But Bertha and Harvey wanted to be married so they went to the neighboring state of Maine, where first cousins may marry. Since they were married in Maine, their marriage is valid everywhere.

In order for there to be a valid marriage, there must be the legal, mental, and physical capacity to enter into the marriage contract and the consent of the parties.

Legal Impediments to Marriage

Legal impediments to the marriage contract may result from (1) one or both of the parties being underage, (2) a marriage between relatives within the prohibited degrees of relationship, and (3) a previous marriage (of one of the persons) undissolved by death or divorce, and (4) miscegenation in those states where prohibited.

* See the end of the chapter for the marriage requirements in each state.

Where legal impediments exist there is a distinction between marriages which are *voidable* (recognized until set aside in court) and those which are *void* (never existed legally). For example, marriages where one or both of the persons may be under the age required by law are voidable and may be set aside only at the election of one of the parties to the marriage.

Mental Incapacity to Marry

Mental incapacity means that a person may be of unsound mind or mentally incompetent; this may include insanity, imbecility, intoxication, or other state of mind that deprives a person of the use of reason. A marriage contracted during the mental incapacity of one of the parties is voidable, but it may later be ratified by this person should he or she subsequently become competent.

Physical Incapacity to Marry

Physical incapacity (or *impotence*) to perform the marriage act may render the marriage voidable. As a general rule, sexual impotence must result from malformation, defect, or disease in order to preclude the possibility of sexual intercourse. (Impotence should not be confused with *sterility,* the inability to procreate.)

Consent of Parties to Marriage

It seems unnecessary to say that *consent of the parties* to the marriage is necessary for a valid marriage; yet there have been many court cases in which the question of consent has been seriously disputed. The law says that there is no valid consent to the marriage, if there has been a mistake on the part of one of the parties concerning whether there was really a marriage.

A New Jersey court has held that a woman of another faith who went through a Jewish marriage ceremony on the supposition that it was merely a betrothal is entitled to have the marriage declared void.

LEGAL RELATIONSHIP OF HUSBAND AND WIFE

Years ago there was a fiction under common law that the husband and wife were one person. Today, all state legislatures have at least modified, if not destroyed, the common-law unity of the husband and wife. Previously, the wife had no property rights, but modern laws give her rights in property, the right to make contracts, and the right to sue.

Husband: Head and Support of the Family

In the eyes of the law the husband is the head of the family. This is true despite the many laws which have attempted to put the wife on the same legal basis as her husband. As head of the family the husband has the legal right to choose the family domicile; when the husband changes his place of residence, the wife is duty bound to follow him to his new address.

The legal idea that the husband is the head of the family carries with it the duty that the husband support and maintain his wife and family. The fact that the wife has property and means of her own does not relieve the husband of his duty to support her. The obligation of a husband to support his wife exists only while they are living together as husband and wife. If they are separated because of her fault, the husband is not bound to support his wife; if, however, the husband is responsible for the separation, he is bound to support her. Furthermore, if the separation resulted from the joint fault of the husband and wife, the husband must continue to support her.

Dr. Plymouth of New York had disagreements with his wife. He went to Nevada to sue for divorce, but she followed him to Nevada, retained a lawyer, and contested the divorce. She lost the case in Nevada, returned to New York, and brought suit against the doctor for support, claiming that he had abandoned her. The New York court held that the issue of whether the doctor was justified in leaving his wife had been properly tried in Nevada, where the court found in his favor; hence the New York court held that she could no longer hold him responsible for her support.

Services and Earnings of the Wife

The common-law fiction still remains that it is the duty of the wife to render service to her husband. These "services" traditionally include the performance of household and other similar chores. Theoretically, the wife is supposed to render these services to her husband free. For this reason, a husband may sue for damages for loss of his wife's services when she is injured by another's negligence.

Mrs. Falkner is disabled as a result of an automobile accident, supposedly caused by the negligence of Mr. Preston. Not only does Mrs. Falkner sue Mr. Preston for damages, but her husband sues Mr. Preston for the value of the loss of his wife's services while she is disabled.

GENERAL PROPERTY RIGHTS

Under the common law, what belonged to a husband was his and what belonged to his wife was also his. But most state legislatures have changed their laws to allow husbands and wives to own property separately and to have rights in each other's property.

Ownership of Household Goods and Wedding Gifts

This question often arises: Who owns the household goods? The answer is: In the absence of a special intent to the contrary, the household goods belong to the husband. It is commonly believed that the wife owns the wedding gifts, but this is not necessarily true. If the husband's relatives give him a present that is particularly suitable to his use, the gift may be presumed to belong to him. If the wife's relatives do likewise, then the item belongs to her. Otherwise, wedding gifts belong to both husband and wife.

Ownership of Property by Husband and Wife

Ordinarily, when husband and wife both acquire a piece of real estate, they are said to own it as "tenants by the entirety." This is a survival of the old common-law theory of unity. *Tenancy by the entirety* does not mean that the husband owns half and the wife owns half, but that they both own the whole property and that neither one can convey away his half. On the death of one of the two tenants by the entirety, the entire property goes to the survivor.

Mary and Frank Baker, husband and wife, buy a home. The deed reads "Mary Baker and Frank Baker, husband and wife." Though they are not specified as "tenants by the entirety," the law says that is the way they have acquired the property.

Property owned by husband and wife as tenants by the entirety is not good security for a creditor who has a claim against the husband alone or against the wife alone, for when the creditor's claim is reduced to judgment, it attaches only against the survivorship interest of the husband or wife, as the case may be. If the creditor's claim is against the husband and the husband and wife own the property as tenants by the entirety, the creditor cannot attach the property during the lifetime of the wife and may levy against the property only if the husband survives the wife. If the wife survives the husband, the creditor has no interest in the property to attach.

Bill and Mary Strater own property as tenants by the entirety. Bill goes into debt and one of his creditors gets a judgment against him. The sheriff sells Bill's interest at public auction. At the sheriff's sale the creditor purchases Bill's interest in the property. Bill dies, Mary survives. The creditor gets nothing.

Obviously, a husband or wife cannot sell his or her interest in property which is owned in tenancy by the entirety without the other spouse's consent.

Husband's Liability for Wife's Debts

A husband is required to supply his wife with all the necessities of life. If he fails to do so, his wife can go out and pledge his credit. To that extent, the wife is the husband's agent.

Mr. Smyley is very stingy. He will not supply his wife with adequate money for groceries. Mrs. Smyley goes to the grocery store and buys on credit. Mr. Smyley is liable to the grocery store for the bill.

There is a limit, however, to the agency of the wife. Her purchases or bills must be in keeping with her husband's income or financial standing and appropriate to his level and manner of living.

Mr. Kedly is a hard-working hardware store clerk who is embarrassed to find that his wife has been making excessive and extravagant charges at the millinery store. Mr. Kedly has adequately clothed his family and provided all the necessities. He is not responsible for the unreasonable, extravagant purchases made by his wife.

Generally, the remedy of a husband whose wife overspends is to notify merchants that he will not be responsible for what she buys. He may do this with a public published notice or by writing to local merchants or both. But, if his published notice disclaiming responsibility for his wife's purchases does not reach the attention of a merchant who furnishes his wife with goods, the merchant will still be able to recover the money for the purchases from the husband. Thus, written notice mailed to the merchants his wife patronizes is an additional advisable remedy. Necessaries, as opposed to necessities, are those things necessary for one to live in the manner appropriate to one's ability and station in life. The following have been considered in law as necessaries: food, shelter, household furniture and supplies, decorations, clothing, medical and dental services, and certain legal services.

Marriage Settlements

In the absence of fraud, mistake, or a failure of consideration, marriage settlements relating to the property of the husband and wife are recognized by the courts as proper. Marriage settlements may be made either before or after marriage and must relate solely to property. The very nature of marriage prevents the settlement from altering the obligations of the marital state. This statement does not summarize the duties of the marital state.

A provision in an antenuptial contract by which a husband attempted to bind himself to pay $500 to his wife annually for her clothing and incidentals was held by the court to be contrary to public policy and void, because the husband had the duty to support his wife according to his ability and station in life—regardless of whether her clothing and incidentals cost $500 or more or less.

Generally, marriage settlements are entered into by persons who have property rights which would be affected by marriage. Such settlements must be fair and reasonable, and both parties must have knowledge of all the facts; any concealment might invalidate the agreement. As long as the prospective wife has full knowledge of her prospective husband's means and wealth, she may make any settlement agreement she wants.

Mr. Ranken, 80, decides to marry his housekeeper, Mrs. Gouch, 55. Mr. Ranken tells Mrs. Gouch, honestly, that he is worth $200,000. Mrs. Gouch enters into a premarital settlement agreeing that on the death of Mr. Ranken she will accept $30,000 as her share of his property. The agreement is valid because she knew all the facts.

Community-Property System

Eight states (Arizona, California, Idaho, Louisiana, Nevada, New Mexico, Texas, and Washington) have adopted the community property system. Other states have had the system and repealed it; in Pennsylvania the courts held that the community property law was unconstitutional.

Under the community property system, all property acquired during the marriage, as a result of the work and efforts of either the husband or wife or both the husband and wife, belongs to both the husband and wife. The only property which a husband or wife can hold separately under the community property system is that owned by the individual before marriage or acquired by gift or inheritance during the marriage.

The community property system can be traced to the laws of France and Spain. Undoubtedly, there are many advantages to this system but under it, it is often difficult to determine the source of community property. The courts of the community property states are constantly required to interpret the rules and rights and liabilities of parties involved in community property disputes.

LAWSUITS ARISING OUT OF BREACH OF PROMISE TO MARRY AND MARITAL FIDELITY

A few decades ago, newspapers and magazines contained lurid stories of suits for breach of promise arising out of promises to marry and of suits for alienation of affection evolving out of betrayal of marital fidelity. Nowadays, such suits are a rarity.

Critics of these "heart-balm" suits felt that the actions for damages offered too many opportunities for abuse. Finally, some of the state legislatures eliminated actions for breach of contract to marry as well as suits for "alienation of affections," "criminal conversation," and seduction. One legislature said:

. . . remedies . . . for the enforcement of actions based upon alleged alienation of affections, criminal conversation, seduction and breach of contract to marry, having been subjected to great abuses, causing extreme annoyance, embarrassment, humiliation and pecuniary damage to many persons wholly innocent and free of any wrongdoing who were merely the victims of circumstances, and such remedies having been exercised by unscrupulous persons for their unjust enrichment and such remedies having furnished vehicles for the commission or the attempted commission of crime and in many cases having resulted in the perpetration of frauds, it is hereby declared as the public policy of the state that the best interests of the people of the state will be served by the abolition of such remedies.*

By the 1960s fourteen states had abolished claims in one or more kinds of these suits. California, Colorado, Florida, Illinois, Indiana, and Wyoming abolished them all. Maine abolished breach-of-promise suits, except when pregnancy exists; Massachusetts and New Hampshire abolished breach-of-promise suits; Michigan, Nevada, New Jersey, New York, and Pennsylvania abolished alienation-of-affection and breach-of-promise suits.

* New York

Breach of Promise

Allowable recovery in breach-of-promise and similar suits came under such unmeasurable headings as mental suffering, injury to affections, wounded pride, loss of social standing, "loss of market," and expenses incurred in the preparation for marriage. Breach-of-promise suits are predicated on the idea that an engagement is a contract or a promise to marry. Before the state legislature disallowed such suits, the New York Court of Appeals said:

We can conceive of no more suitable ground . . . for compensation than that of a violated promise to enter into a contract on the faithful performance of which the interests of all civilized countries so essentially depend. When two parties of suitable age to contract, agree to pledge their faith to each other . . . and one of the parties wantonly and capriciously refuses to execute the contract which is thus commenced, the injury may be serious, and the circumstances may often justify a claim of pecuniary indemnification.

Alienation of Affection

Although not as popular as they once were, there are still many actions brought for alienation of affections. It is often done when a married person can show that someone else has alienated with malice and intent the affections of his or her spouse; in such a case the interferer may be liable for damages. In these suits it is not actually necessary to show that a divorce or a physical separation of the husband and wife resulted, but the wronged person must be able to show that the wrongdoer directly interfered with the married lives of the couple and caused a loss of companionship to the wronged. The entire basis or theory of the rights of actions for alienation is the loss of the companionship and relationship of the husband and wife.

Mere adultery of one spouse does not give the other a right of action for alienation. If it can be shown that adultery was the sole cause of the alienation or separation, there is no basis for the action. Undoubtedly, that is the reason why in so many cases it is difficult to prove alienation of affection.

It is not only an interloper who can be sued for alienation, but also a parent if he or she wrongfully and maliciously alienates his or her married child. Ordinarily, a parent would not be sued for alienating the affection of his child; if he acts in good faith and it results in the breakup of a marriage, the parent is not liable.

Marriage Requirements by State

	MINIMUM AGE WITH PARENTS' CONSENT		MINIMUM AGE WITHOUT PARENTS' CONSENT		BLOOD TEST REQUIRED	WAITING PERIOD	MARRIAGES BETWEEN FIRST COUSINS PROHIBITED	COMMON-LAW MARRIAGES RECOGNIZED
	Men	Women	Men	Women				
Alabama	17	14	21	18	yes	no	no	yes
Alaska	18	16	19	18	yes	3 days	yes	no
Arizona	18	16	18	18	no	no	yes	no
Arkansas	17	16	21	18	yes	3 days	yes	no
California	18	18	18	18	yes	no	no	no
Colorado	16	16	18	18	yes	no	no	yes
Connecticut	16	16	21	21	yes	5 days	no	no
Delaware	18	16	21	18	yes	24-96 hours	yes	no
Florida	18	16	21	21	yes	3 days	no	yes
Georgia	18	16	18	18	no	3 days	no	no
Hawaii	16	16	18	18	yes	3 days	no	no
Idaho	15	15	18	18	yes	no	yes	yes
Illinois	18	16	21	18	yes	no	yes	no
Indiana	18	18	18	18	yes	3 days	yes	no
Iowa	18	18	18	18	yes	no	yes	yes
Kansas	14	12	18	18	yes	3 days	yes	yes
Kentucky	18	16	18	18	yes	3 days	yes	no
Louisiana	18	16	21	21	yes	no	yes	no
Maine	16	16	18	18	no	5 days	yes	no
Maryland	16	16	18	18	no	48 hours	yes	no
Massachusetts	14	12	18	18	yes	5 days	no	no
Michigan	18	16	18	18	yes	3 days	yes	no
Minnesota	16	15	18	16	no	5 days	yes	no

Mississippi	no	no	17	15	yes	3 days	yes	yes	yes
Missouri	15	15	21	18	yes	3 days	yes	yes	no
Montana	18	16	18	18	yes	5 days	yes	yes	yes
Nebraska	18	16	19	19	yes	no	yes	yes	no
Nevada	18	18		18	no	no	no	yes	no
New Hampshire	18	18	18	18	yes	5 days	yes	yes	no
New Jersey	18	18	18	18	yes	72 hours	yes	no	no
New Mexico	18	16	21	18	yes	no	yes	no	no
New York	16	14	21	18	yes	10 days	yes	no	no
North Carolina	16	16	18	18	yes	no	yes	no	no
North Dakota	18	15	18	18	yes	no	yes	yes	no
Ohio	18	16	18	18	yes	5 days	yes	yes	yes
Oklahoma	18	15	21	18	yes	no	yes	yes	yes
Oregon	18	15	18	18	yes	7 days	yes	yes	no
Pennsylvania	14	12	18	18	yes	3 days	yes	yes	yes
Rhode Island	14	12	18	16	yes	5 days	no	no	yes
South Carolina	14	16	18	18	no	24 hours	no	no	yes
South Dakota	18	16	18	18	yes	no	yes	yes	no
Tennessee	16	16	18	18	yes	3 days	yes	no	no
Texas	16	14	19	19	yes	no	yes	no	yes
Utah	16	14	21	18	yes	no	yes	yes	no
Vermont	18	16	18	18	yes	5 days	yes	no	no
Virginia	18	16	21	21	yes	no	yes	no	no
Washington	17	17	18	18	no	3 days	no	yes	no
West Virginia	18	16	18	18	yes	3 days	yes	yes	no
Wisconsin	16	18	18	18	yes	5 days	yes	yes	no
Wyoming	18	16	19	19	yes	no	yes	yes	no
District of Columbia	18	16	21	18	no	3 days	no	no	yes

Criminal Conversation

When somebody invades the marital rights of a couple and has adulterous relations with one of the parties, the interferer may be sued for what is known as "criminal conversation." These suits are so rare as to be almost obsolete. Damages in an action for criminal conversation are for the loss of the love and the society of the plaintiff's spouse, the destruction of home and happiness, the suffering endured, and the distress of mind resulting from the defendant's adulterous acts.

15
Divorce, Separation, and Annulment

Marriage is a social institution protected by the state and, therefore, is often difficult to terminate. The difficulty of termination is further complicated by the great diversity of state laws governing the marriage relationship.

TERMINATING THE MARRIAGE RELATIONSHIP

The marriage relationship may be terminated or set aside by divorce, separation—voluntary or judicial—or by annulment. *Divorce* is a judicial act by which the marriage relationship is dissolved. Unlike ordinary contracts, marriage contracts may be legally dissolved only by divorce or by death. There is a technical distinction between *divorce,* which completely breaks the bonds of marriage and *judicial* or *legal separation* ("divorce from bed-and-board"), which suspends the marriage relation and provides for the separate maintenance of the wife by the husband. A *separation agreement* arises out of a *voluntary separation* (as distinguished from a judicial separation), whereby a husband and wife agree to live apart with an arrangement for the support of the wife and the custody and support of any children of the marriage. *Annulment* is a court decree holding that a marriage is a nullity from the beginning; that is, no valid marriage ever existed. It differs from a divorce in that it must be founded on a cause which existed at the time of the marriage. In a divorce, the court dissolves the marriage; in an annulment, the court holds that the marriage was invalid from the beginning.

DIVORCE

Serious questions often arise about the residence of the parties to divorces, the jurisdiction of the court, and the consequent validity of divorces. Does the husband or wife who moves to another state for the purpose of getting a divorce truly become a resident of that state? Are Nevada divorces valid? When is a decree of divorce rendered by a foreign state (a state other than the state of residence) binding on the courts of other states in accordance with the "full faith and credit" clause of the federal Constitution? When is a divorce decree rendered by one state a bar to a subsequent suit brought by the defendant in another state?

Formerly, the United States Supreme Court resolved the conflict between the courts of the various states by establishing the general rule that only the courts of the state where the parties had their last "matrimonial domicile" (where they last lived together as husband and wife) had jurisdiction to grant divorces.

In the famous *Atherton* case, the matrimonial domicile was in Kentucky. The wife left her husband there and returned to her mother's home in New York. The husband began suit for a divorce in Kentucky because the laws of Kentucky accepted her abandonment as cause for divorce. He gave her notice of his suit through the mails, and she did not respond or contest it. The Kentucky court granted the husband an absolute decree of divorce, and the United States Supreme Court upheld the decree, reasoning that Kentucky had been the last matrimonial domicile of the Athertons and was entitled to "full faith and credit" under the Constitution.

In the equally famous *Haddock* case, the husband and wife were domiciled in New York, from which state the husband abandoned the wife. He acquired a domicile in Connecticut, where he obtained a divorce. The wife did not contest this; but she later sued for divorce in New York (where she had continued to maintain a residence). The New York court refused to accredit the Connecticut decree, reasoning that at no time had there been a Haddock matrimonial domicile in that state. The Supreme Court upheld the New York court and held that full faith and credit need not be given to the Connecticut decree.

Supreme Court Justice Oliver Wendell Holmes dissented in the Haddock case, saying that the rule was "poor fiction and fiction always is a poor ground for judging substantial rights." Thirty-six years later (1942) the United States Supreme Court accepted Mr. Justice Holmes's view and stated that when one state grants a divorce decree, other states must give the decree full faith and credit. In 1944 the Supreme Court explained that even though the divorce decree of a state was presumed to be good, there was nothing to prevent a foreign state from inquiring whether the domicile was acquired in good faith in the state granting the divorce or whether it was merely a sham. The Court said in effect that it was no longer necessary to have a divorce granted in the state of the last matrimonial domicile but that it was necessary for a person to establish a residence in another state "in good faith" to obtain a valid divorce there. The Supreme Court decisions have been known as *Williams I* and *Williams II:*

Williams I, decided in 1942, involved two married couples who lived in North Carolina. The husband in couple number one and the wife in couple number two went to Nevada and obtained divorces against the wife of couple number one and the husband of couple number two. The husband and wife who had obtained divorces in Nevada were thereafter married in Nevada; they returned to North Carolina where they lived as husband and wife. They were subsequently tried and convicted of bigamy in the courts of North Carolina. The case was appealed to the Supreme Court which held that the courts of North Carolina had to give full faith and credit to the Nevada divorce decree because Nevada's finding of a bona fide residence had not been questioned.

In *Williams II*, the appeal from the second trial, the big issue was whether the husband of couple number one and the wife of couple number two had established bona fide domiciles in Nevada and, hence, whether or not the Nevada courts had jurisdiction. The jury was told that if the two people went to Nevada "simply and solely for the purpose of obtaining divorces" and intended to return to North Carolina on obtaining them, they never lost their North Carolina domiciles and did not acquire new domiciles in Nevada. The jury convicted the defendants of bigamy, and the Supreme Court upheld the conviction.

Despite the efforts of the Supreme Court to clarify the rules of law governing foreign divorces, much confusion ensued. In *Cook* v. *Cook,* decided in 1951, the United States Supreme Court reversed the decision of the Supreme Court of Vermont for a marriage annulment. The ground for annulment was that the woman at the time of the marriage was the lawful wife of a third person, although she had prior to the marriage obtained a Florida divorce decree against the third person. The Vermont court held the Florida decree invalid. The Supreme Court in reversing the Vermont Supreme Court held that the Vermont court had no right to invalidate the Florida decree.

In the case of *Vanderbilt* v. *Vanderbilt,* decided in 1957, the Supreme Court held that a husband could not be relieved from his financial obligations by a state that had no jurisdiction over his wife.

The Vanderbilts, who lived in California, separated in 1952. In 1953, the wife established residence in New York. In March 1953 the husband filed suit for divorce in Nevada. The wife was not served with process in Nevada and did not appear before the court. Later in 1953 the Nevada court granted a final divorce decree. Subsequently, the wife instituted an action in the Supreme Court of New York for separation and alimony. While the New York court found the Nevada decree valid and held that

it had effectively dissolved the marriage, it nevertheless entered an ord
directing the husband to make designated support payments to the v
The United States Supreme Court upheld the New York court; a majoi.,
of the Supreme Court justices held that the Nevada court had no personal
jurisdiction over the wife and no power to extinguish her personal rights
under New York law to financial support from her husband.

Grounds for Divorce

There are at least fifteen major grounds (or causes) for divorce,
but these grounds are not uniformly recognized among the fifty
states. The problem is left to the individual state legislatures, each
of which has a different basic policy. The principal grounds for
divorce follow:

Adultery Adultery is a universal cause for divorce in this country. But the commission of a single act of adultery is not sufficient
grounds for divorce in some states.

Conviction of a Crime or Felony The laws of about forty states
provide that conviction of a felony or an infamous crime or imprisonment for a certain number of years in a state prison or penitentiary is ground for divorce.

Extreme Cruelty Cruelty in one form or another is a ground for
divorce in most states. The language of the various statutes differ.
Some refer to it as "cruel and inhuman treatment," others as "cruel
and barbarous treatment," and so on. The courts of some states have
become quite liberal in interpreting the word "cruelty." It may
include acts of violence; conduct which causes fear of personal harm
or mental suffering, such as offensive language; false charges of
adultery; conduct imposing hardship, such as failure to provide
necessities; conduct directly injuring health; communication of
disease; habitual intemperance; refusal to cohabit; and so on.

Desertion Over forty states list desertion as a ground for
divorce. The courts have defined *desertion* as a voluntary separation
of one spouse from the other without consent, without justification,
and with the intention of not returning. Whether a continued refusal of one spouse without cause or justification to have marital
relations with the other constitutes desertion, although the parties
still live under the same roof, is a question on which the courts of
the various states differ. Some hold that refusal to have relations
amounts to desertion and constitutes grounds for divorce; other
states disagree.

Fraud Seven states list *fraud* as a ground for divorce, if it involves the concealment of something that was, in those states, essential to the validity of the marriage itself. The following examples of fraud and concealment could be grounds for divorce: (1) nondisclosure by the husband that he was an escaped convict, (2) nondisclosure by the wife that she was pregnant by another man at the time of the marriage, (3) nondisclosure that one party to the marriage is intermittently insane, although sane at the time of the marriage, or (4) concealment of unchastity or a false representation concerning fortune, social standing, or previous marriage.

Habitual Drunkenness or Habitual Use of Drugs   In over thirty states, habitual drunkenness is a ground for divorce; in fourteen states the habitual use of drugs is a ground.

Duress   Duress is the legal word for force. Four states provide that divorces may be granted when the marriage was contracted by force or by threat of bodily harm.

Insanity.   Over twenty states list insanity or idiocy as grounds for divorce, and a few states include mental incapacity at the time of the marriage.

Impotence.   Twenty-six states consider impotence a ground for divorce, but if the condition is present at the beginning of the marriage, it may be a cause of action for annulment. Generally impotence refers to physical incapacity which prevents either copulation or (in some places) procreation.

Personal Indignities   "Indignities" are a form of mental cruelty and must consist of rudeness, vulgarity, abusive language, malicious ridicule, or other forms of hateful action. Divorces are granted on the ground of indignities in nine states. Examples of personal indignities are (1) false charges of infidelity or crime, (2) habitual intemperance, (3) excessive use of opiates, (4) lewd conduct, (5) sexual excesses, (6) refusal of marital relations, (7) nonsupport, and (8) abuse and personal insults, name calling, public defamation.

Nonsupport of Wife   Nonsupport is allowed by twenty-two states as a ground for divorce. It consists of a husband's willful refusal and neglect to provide suitable maintenance for his wife, generally for at least one year. What constitutes maintenance and support required of the husband depends upon the condition and standing of the parties in the community and is generally determined by the circumstances peculiar to each case. The courts have held that the failure of a husband to give his wife money is not of itself failure to support, nor is stinginess necessarily nonsupport.

Fuller at the time of his marriage had accumulated considerable property by a lifetime of thrift. He was regarded as wealthy; yet he failed to give his wife the niceties that she felt her station in life justified. A Michigan court held that Fuller's stinginess did not constitute failure to provide, even though his means would have justified much larger expenditures.

Pregnancy at Time of Marriage Eleven states list pregnancy existing at the time of marriage as a ground for divorce, provided the pregnancy is proved to have been caused by a man other than the husband.

Disappearance (Enoch Arden Laws) In four states, disappearance for specified periods, varying from two to seven years, constitutes grounds for a divorce when the absence of a spouse might indicate that he or she is dead.

Other Grounds for Divorce A few states have unique grounds for divorce. Incompatibility is not as common as one might believe; it is allowed by only a few states. Among the other isolated grounds for divorce are: (1) joining a religious sect believing cohabitation unlawful, (2) loathsome diseases, (3) malformation preventing sexual intercourse, (4) unnatural behavior, (5) vagrancy, and (6) venereal disease.

Residence Requirements

In forty-one states there is a minimum period (varying from six months to two years) during which a person must have been a continuous resident before he or she may begin a divorce proceeding. Most states try to discourage the residents of other states from shopping around for easy divorces, but Arkansas, Colorado, Nevada, Utah, and Wyoming allow "quickie divorces"—those which may be obtained after residence periods of from forty-two to ninety days.

Defenses to Divorce Actions

There are two sides to every court dispute; this is particularly true in the field of matrimonial disputes. Although there are fifteen major causes of divorce in the United States, a divorce is not always granted when an appropriate cause for a divorce appears to be probable. Often there are extenuating or aggravating circumstances that cause a court to deny a divorce. These circumstances are known as "defenses" and include cases in which the person seeking the relief has either deliberately brought on the grounds for divorce, has forgiven the offending party, or where there has been some justification or excuse for the offense. Condonation, provocation and justification, and collusion are typical defenses.

Condonation Condonation is the legal word for forgiving a matrimonial offense which would otherwise constitute a ground for divorce. The idea behind condonation as a defense is that the offender is forgiven with the understanding that the offense will not be repeated. Although condonation applies to all charges of matrimonial misconduct, it most frequently arises in the case of adultery. When one spouse learns that the other has been guilty of adultery and thereafter cohabits with him or her, the law says that the adultery has been forgiven and is no longer a ground for divorce.

Provocation and justification When a divorce is sought on the ground of cruelty, desertion, nonsupport, or similar grounds, the defendant may very often reveal misconduct on the part of the one seeking the divorce and thus defeat the action for divorce. The misconduct may amount to *provocation and justification*.

Collusion Sometimes a husband and a wife agree that one of them will commit a matrimonial offense for the purpose of permitting the other to obtain a divorce. Such *collusion* is a fraud on the court and is one of the chief vices in our divorce system. When one of the parties changes his mind and discloses to the court that the ground for divorce was set up by collusion, the court may deny the divorce.

NO-FAULT DIVORCE

In 1970 there were 2,179,000 marriages in the United States and 715,000 divorces—1 divorce for every 3 marriages. For several centuries the only way to obtain a divorce was to prove that the other party to the marriage was guilty of something "wrong." The guilty party had to be at fault. Just as no-fault auto accident insurance has caught the imagination of the public, so no-fault divorces are winning increased acceptance.

Divorce in California, Florida, and Iowa is called "dissolution of marriage." In California there are two grounds for marriage dissolution: (1) irreconcilable differences that have caused irremediable breakdown of the marriage and (2) incurable insanity. A number of state laws, including those of Colorado, Florida, Iowa, and Michigan, follow that trend. They list irretrievable breakdown of marriage relationship (Colorado), marriage irretrievably broken (Florida), and breakdown of marriage relationship (Iowa and Michigan) as grounds for divorce.

Statistics show that the laws facilitating divorces have brought a dramatic increase in the number of divorces and a considerable decrease in the number of annulment cases. This may be happening because under the old divorce laws in some states it was difficult to get evidence for divorce, so annulment was an easier way to dissolve the marriage. Now when it is easier to get a divorce, resort to an annulment is no longer necessary.

SEPARATION

The law cannot compel husband and wife to live together. Therefore, they may separate with or without judicial decree. Some contend that *separation* is only a makeshift, not a permanent, solution. They argue that after separation the parties are "neither fish nor fowl." They are married, yet they do not live together; neither party is free to remarry. But separation is sometimes the only solution possible for people who are prohibited divorce by the rules of their religion.

Marital separations, whether by agreement or by court order, are not necessarily permanent; there is always a chance of reconciliation. The breakup of a marriage may work hardship on the parties and their children, and sometimes, especially in a separation arrangement, husband and wife try to repair a broken marriage.

Voluntary Separation

Where marriage has become intolerable for either or both parties, they often *separate voluntarily*. Although many men and women walk out on a marriage, they may be prejudicing their future legal rights by so doing. If the husband on the one hand gets fed up with the wife's faults and leaves her, he immediately leaves himself open to court action by the wife wherein she will claim alimony, counsel fees, and so on. The wife who can no longer tolerate a husband's faults should, instead of leaving his bed and board, consult her lawyer. If, after living separately for a period of time, the husband and wife are unable to settle their differences, they usually begin to think in terms of a separation agreement.

Separation Agreement

Separation agreements, which are the result of voluntary separations, state that the parties are living separate and apart and shall continue to live separate and apart, provide settlement of property rights, and state that the parties shall not molest nor interfere with each other. The law gives considerable flexibility and latitude to a separation agreement; if a husband and wife must separate, a separation agreement is considered much more advantageous and civilized than going to court and wrangling over differences.

Specifically, a separation agreement may settle the household goods and the property to be retained by each. It may likewise provide that one party have possession of the family home or apartment, and, unless there is a lump-sum property settlement, provide for the payment of a weekly or monthly amount of money to the wife by the husband. An important feature of a separation agreement is a provision for the custody, control, and upbringing of the children, if any. Sometimes separation agreements provide that the husband shall keep in force insurance on his life for the benefit of wife and children. Depending on the property settlement, the wife may be entitled to certain benefits in the event of the husband's death or she may waive her right to receive any benefits under her husband's will.

Judicial Separation

In order to maintain an action for *judicial* or *legal separation* there must be the ground prescribed by the laws of the particular state. Grounds for judicial separation in most states include desertion and cruel and inhuman treatment. Other grounds for separation may be adultery, habitual drunkenness, idiocy or insanity, impotence, violent temper, conviction of felony, incompatibility, willful neglect to provide, indignities rendering life intolerable, conduct calculated to make living together unsafe or improper, habitual use of drugs, attempt on life of other party, refusal to cohabit, absence without tidings for three to seven years, or leprosy or other loathsome disease. In certain states a judicial separation may be decreed for any cause for which a divorce may be granted.

The facts of each separation case differ so widely and the concepts of adequacy vary so much throughout the country that it is almost impossible to set up a general guide to determine the amount or the extent of the property settlement which should be made.

ANNULMENT

Annulment is a judgment of a court (of competent jurisdiction) declaring a marriage void.

Voidable and Void Marriages

The legal distinction between a voidable marriage and a void marriage is tenuous and fine-spun. A *voidable marriage* is one that a competent court rules to have been invalid from the beginning, such as a marriage that one party claims to have been induced by misrepresentation or fraud. But the courts will not grant an annulment when an originally voidable marriage has been sanctioned by the couple's living together with full knowledge of the facts. A *void marriage* is one which the courts arbitrarily say never existed legally because it was invalid from the beginning (such as bigamous or incestuous marriages). When such a marriage has been contracted in good faith, the parties to the marriage should not rely on their own interpretation of the law and decide for themselves that their marriage is void; they should apply for a court decree stating so. One court has said, "It is often of the very highest importance to the individuals and to the community that there should be a judicial adjudication in reference to void marriage."

Grounds for Annulment

An action for annulment may be brought for any of the reasons which would render the marriage invalid. In some states, however, cohabitation after knowledge of the facts on which annulment could have been granted removes the right to annulment. In New York, if either of the parties is sentenced to prison for life (and hence is civilly dead), the marriage is automatically dissolved without a court decree, just as in the case of physical death, and it is not resumed or revived by a pardon or commutation of sentence.

Twelve states in the United States do not list specific grounds for an annulment but leave it up to a court of equity to decide whether the marriage is valid under law. A few states, such as Maine, Massachusetts, New Hampshire, South Carolina, Utah, Washington, and Wyoming, have laws providing that either party may petition the court in equity to "avoid" a marriage, when "doubt is felt about the validity of the marriage." In a few states, it is left to the discretion of the courts to grant an annulment when "any impediment" renders the marriage contract void. *Grounds for annulment* may include nonage, want of understanding (insanity), miscegenation (despite the holding of the United States Supreme Court that anti-miscegenation statutes are invalid), physical incapacity (impotence existing from the beginning of the marriage), prohibited degree of blood relationship, fraud, duress (force), previous undissolved marriage, or communicable, loathsome disease.

CUSTODY OF CHILDREN

Since the courts have general jurisdiction over infants (in thirty-nine states, persons under eighteen years of age), they have the power to award the custody and control of infant children during the pendency and at the conclusion of actions for divorce, separation, and annulment. The primary test for awarding custody is the welfare of the child. The wishes and desires of the parents and even of the child, must yield to the judgment of the court concerning the best interests of the child.

Under the common law, the father was generally entitled to the custody and control of the children. But the modern tendency is that, unless it is proved to the court that she is unfit or incapable of looking after children of tender age, the mother is entitled to custody

Many courts make it a rule to award custody of the children to the innocent party in a divorce proceeding. When the question is close, the court in using its discretion sometimes takes into consideration the wishes of children, particularly if they are approaching maturity and have good reasons for their preferences.

ALIMONY

The idea of alimony comes from the common-law obligation of the husband to support his wife. At the beginning of matrimonial court proceedings, the court will award temporary support to the wife during the pendency of the case. The courts realize that the wife, if she has no independent income, has to have some means of support, so they generally give her the benefit of the doubt about the probable outcome of the case and make an allowance for her *temporary alimony* at the beginning of the lawsuit. *Permanent alimony* is the allowance which the court compels the husband to pay his wife for support and maintenance after judicial separation or divorce.

Some states limit alimony to a certain percentage of a husband's income. Other states may award a wife a definite amount to be paid either at once or in installments. In community property states, the courts have the power to make a division of community property and to fix a lien on separate property of the husband in order to insure the support and maintenance of the wife and children.

In those states where alimony is not controlled by statute, the amount is left entirely to the discretion of the court. Some courts have said that alimony should never exceed one-half of the husband's estate, others that one-third of a husband's income is a proper portion. Basically the courts take into consideration all the circumstances, including the size of the husband's estate, his earnings and capacity to earn, other obligations (such as supporting aged relatives), his age and health, and his conduct in the particular circumstances. The courts also take into consideration the actual needs and obligations of the wife, her age and health, her personal wealth, her earnings or capacity to earn, and her conduct in connection with the subject matter of the litigation. From time to time, after the permanent alimony is fixed, the court may modify the amount of alimony because of the changed circumstances of the parties.

In Delaware and Texas permanent alimony is not granted to the wife. In a few states, such as Illinois, West Virginia, and California, husbands sometimes are granted alimony.

In most states, the usual method of enforcing an order for alimony is to hold the husband in contempt of court if he fails to pay the alimony. If the husband has the ability to pay the alimony awarded by the court and refuses to do so, he may be imprisoned.

When a husband breaches a separation agreement by failing to supply to the wife the amount of money to be paid to her periodically under the agreement, the same legal steps may be taken to enforce his compliance as in any breached contract.

Generally a court order for alimony provides that it should cease upon remarriage of the wife. In some states it is specifically provided by law that alimony terminates upon the divorced wife's remarriage.

COUNSEL FEES

Except when a wife is a plaintiff in an annulment action, the husband is often required to make payment for expenses incurred by her, including the fees of her lawyer. The court orders the payment to be made at the beginning of the lawsuit; this is because it may be a considerable length of time before the case is brought to trial and the wife's lawyer should be paid for preparing the case. Generally, the opening round in a divorce or separation action is the determination of the amount of counsel fees to be paid, along with temporary alimony. Before making the award of counsel fees, the court looks into the merits of the case superficially to determine whether the wife has some chance of success. If it appears to the court that there is merit in the wife's case, it will award her an amount for lawyer's fees on the theory that it is one of the necessaries for which the husband is responsible. The court determines from its experience in similar cases the amount of the lawyer's fees.

16
Real Property Law

Real property has been defined by the courts as "land, and whatever is erected or growing thereon, and all things connected with it which are permanently fixed and immovable."

PURCHASE OF REAL ESTATE

Some people buy and sell real estate without seriously considering the legal problems connected with their transactions. They claim to have bought and sold parcels of land for years without title searches or representation by lawyers. Real estate title complications, however, lie dormant often for years and when uncovered may cost the persons involved in the transactions thousands of dollars and unnecessary litigation. For this reason, sound legal advice should be obtained at the outset of the negotiations.

Purchase Contract

Although real estate brokers sometimes advise an individual to sign a contract as a "memorandum agreement" or a "binder," neither these nor any other contract for the purchase or sale of real estate should be entered into by anyone without benefit of legal counsel. A buyer or seller should also beware of printed forms, for each purchase or sale has its own problems that cannot be fitted to the provisions of a stereotyped printed contract.

The purchase contract is the blueprint for the entire purchase and sale transaction. It must be in writing, and it should be prepared by an attorney.

Identity of Seller

Particularly in large cities where persons who are strangers to each other buy and sell real estate, the identity of the alleged owner of real estate is important. The problem of identification in small communities is not so great because lawyers and real estate brokers frequently know the persons involved in real estate transactions.

A man representing himself as James Brown, the owner of a house and lot which he wishes to sell for $20,000, accepts a deposit of $2,000 from a purchaser. The man who represents himself to be James Brown takes the $2,000 and disappears.

An even more serious (but fortunately rare) loss takes place when the purchaser has the title searched and finds that James Brown owns the house and pays over the balance of the purchase price of $20,000 to a man who is not James Brown. When the real James Brown (who may be out of the area when the transaction was closed) shows up, the purchaser finds that he has purchased a forged deed.

In the case immediately above, if the purchaser had bought title insurance at the time of the transaction, the title insurance company would reimburse him, because he did not get good title. But insurance companies are very careful about establishing the correct identity of sellers of properties.

Marketable Title

No deed or mortgage should ever be accepted unless the title to the property has been properly examined and the purchaser has been advised by his attorney that (when he gets the deed) he will have good and marketable title to the property. The title should also be examined for restrictions which might limit the uses to which the property might be put.

In some communities lawyers or abstract companies make title searches which indicate the validity or invalidity of titles to real property. In other communities the purchaser of real estate buys a title insurance policy to protect himself against loss in the case of faulty title.

Title Search   In many small communities throughout the United States real estate buyers do not purchase title insurance. They rely on an abstract of title made by an abstract company, a lawyer, or by the clerk of the court. Whether the search is made by a lawyer or by an abstract company or the clerk of the court depends on the area where the property is located and the local custom.

An *abstract of title* is a summary of deeds and other instruments, which have been recorded in the county clerk's office or other public office, arranged in chronological order, and containing a statement of all liens and encumbrances against the real estate covered by the abstract. The *existence* of an abstract, which is a summary and digest of the public records relating to the land, does not prove anything about the title. What the abstract *shows* is important.

The examiner of the abstract must consider the history of the ownership of the property and all facts relating to the title to the property as shown by the abstract of title, and then he must determine whether or not the owner of the property has marketable title. The title examiner must check the abstract description throughout the years and see that every link in the chain is present. If a link is missing, title may be defective.

Where title insurance policies are not frequently used, the seller usually agrees to furnish to the buyer an abstract of title showing good and marketable title, free of all liens and encumbrances, to the property. In such a case, the attorney for the buyer examines the abstract to determine whether the abstract of title shows that the seller has good title to the property.

Title Insurance   Title insurance is used in practically all large cities in the United States. Its premiums and rates vary from place to place. A title insurance policy specifies an amount of money, which is usually the amount which the purchaser has paid for the property, and guarantees the owner (of the policy) against all the loss and the damage that he shall sustain by reason of defects in the title to the real estate described in the policy or by reason of liens or encumbrances affecting the title at the date of the policy, except liens and encumbrances and other matters specified in the policy. Thus, if the purchaser pays $20,000 for his property, his title insurance policy must be taken in that amount. And, if the purchaser's property is subject to an existing $5,000 mortgage, this amount would be specifically excepted from the responsibility of the title guaranty company.

In those cases where title insurance has been obtained, the seller does not pass along to the buyer his title insurance policy; the buyer buys his own policy. Before the transaction is closed, the buyer makes an application to the title guaranty company for a title policy. Sometime before the closing of title, the title guaranty company furnishes the buyer a preliminary report and if that report indicates that the title company will not guarantee the title, the buyer knows that the seller cannot give him good title. Questions or objections frequently considered in connection with the marketability of title are the following:

1. *Afterborn or posthumous children*: (These phrases refer to children born after the making of a will and after the death of their father.) When title is derived through a will, the question may arise concerning whether

there is a posthumous child or afterborn child. If there is, he inherits the property in the same manner as though there had been no will. In such a case, the will might be a bad link in the chain of title.

2. *Adverse possession*: Titles acquired through adverse possession are difficult to prove, and ordinarily lawyers and title companies do not honor them.

3. *Covenants and restrictions in a deed*: Often prior deeds in a chain of title contain restrictions concerning the use of property. Violation of covenants or of restrictions generally renders the title unmarketable.

4. *Debts of a decedent*: Debts may be a charge on real estate and may make title unmarketable.

5. *Insufficient or defective descriptions in prior deeds*: Unless correction deeds can be obtained, the defective descriptions may render title unmarketable.

6. *Release of dower rights*: Some states give the wife a right of dower in real estate. A wife must execute a release of dower before marketable title can be given. A dower question may arise when a previous owner of property conveyed the property and failed to set forth in the deed his marital status. There is always the risk that the owner may have been married at the time of the conveyance and that his wife may have a dower interest in the property.

7. *Encroachments*: Often a slight encroachment by the wall of a structure on adjoining property may render the title unmarketable. The only way the question can be settled is by a survey. A caveat to be watched for in connection with contracts for the purchase of real estate is a clause "subject to any state of facts which an accurate survey may show." A survey might show that a building is not entirely within lot lines or that the building of a neighbor may encroach on the property being sold.

8. *Easements*: Easements held by others may render title unmarketable. One of the most common easements is a right-of-way which someone else may have on the property in question. A survey should show the exact location of the easement.

9. *Federal or state estate or inheritance taxes*: Federal estate taxes are a lien on real estate generally for a ten-year period from the date of an owner's death. Unless the tax is paid the title is unmarketable. The laws of most states provide that the state inheritance tax is a lien on real estate for a specified period of time and may prevent the property from being marketable.

10. *State corporation taxes:* Taxes unpaid by the corporations which are or have been owners of the property may be liens on the property.

11. *Judgments*: A judgment obtained against the owner or a former owner of the property may be a lien against the property.

12. *Mechanic's liens*: A lien filed by a laborer or one who has furnished material in connection with the improvement of real estate is a lien against the property.

13. *Petitions in bankruptcy*: Bankruptcy or assignment for the benefit of creditors would render the title unmarketable if the bankrupt person were the owner of the property or had been the owner at the time of the filing

of the petition. Often the problem of identification arises when a petition in bankruptcy is filed by a person with a name identical or very similar to the property owner.

14. *Land taxes and assessments*: Real estate taxes and assessments be paid before the seller can give good title.

15. *Tax sales*: Sometimes, although a person is currently paying his taxes on schedule, a search of the records may show that a prior owner had not paid taxes and that the property had been sold for taxes by the city, village, or town. This may mean that a stranger is holding a tax deed which renders the title defective.

16. *Mortgage foreclosure*: If a mortgage against the property exists and someone has started a foreclosure action, the owner cannot give good title. Likewise, if the property had previously been sold on a mortgage fore-closure, the question arises whether proper steps were taken in that fore-closure action so that the purchaser on the foreclosure action acquired good title.

17. *Leases or other tenancies*: A lease may be recorded in the proper public office or unrecorded. In either event, a purchaser is required to in-vestigate carefully and verify the nature of the lease or tenancy of any person in possession of all or part of the property.

18. *Legacies under a will*: Unpaid legacies under a will may constitute a prior charge on real estate. Proof of payment of the legacies must be made before good title can be given.

19. *Mortgages—ancient or modern*: A recent mortgage must be satisfied or released before good title can be given. An ancient mortgage may be disregarded after the lapse of many years, but generally it is considered advisable to institute a court proceeding to cause the ancient mortgage to be discharged from the record.

20. *Proceedings in decedent's estate*: Careful examination must be made of the records in a probate court to determine whether the court has jurisdiction of the estate and whether proper steps have been taken and all interested parties have received notice.

Title Restrictions Before accepting a deed to property, a pur-chaser should also determine whether there are in the title restric-tions that would prohibit the use of the property intended by him. The courts have held that a contract to sell property free and clear from encumbrances is broken if there are restrictive covenants on the property to be conveyed.

The courts permit property owners to put in deeds almost any reasonable restriction on the use of the property. If an owner sells a piece of property and puts a restriction in the deed that the property may not be used for the sale of alcoholic beverages, the courts will uphold the restriction. If a provision in the deed specifies that the property may be used only for residential, not business, purposes, again the courts will enforce the restriction. There are many kinds of restrictive covenants contained in deeds including those which prevent the use of the property by any business that is "dangerous, obnoxious, or offensive." There are also title restrictions against boardinghouses, hotels, barns, garages, gasoline stations, apartment houses, funeral establishments, public markets, chicken houses, theaters, restaurants, breweries, and the like.

A common form of restrictive covenant is the "set-back restriction," that is, a restriction which provides that buildings must be set back a certain distance from the street. In connection with this restriction, questions arise whether the construction of bay windows, fire escapes, permanent awnings, verandas, porches, steps, sun parlors, and so on, which are built within the set-back line constitute violations. In most cases such structures are held to be violations of the set-back restriction.

How are the restrictive covenants enforced? A neighbor or other interested person asks the court to issue an injunction against violation of the restrictive covenants and, in some cases, to remove the building or objectionable structure. The courts, however, are practical in their enforcement of restrictive covenants. When an ancient restrictive covenant exists in a neighborhood, the character of which has in the meanwhile changed, the court will take into consideration the changed conditions and will frequently refuse to enforce the restrictive covenant.

The courts have held zoning restrictions not to be an encumbrance which would justify the purchaser in rejecting title to a piece of real estate. It is important that zoning ordinances be thoroughly investigated before one contracts to purchase real estate. Many a purchaser has contracted validly to buy property that he later discovers is not "zoned" to his purposes.

Delivery of Deed and Closing of Title

There are various kinds of deeds. Their use varies even within states. The popular type of deed in New York City and vicinity is the bargain-and-sale deed that contains no guarantee of title but simply the owner's covenant that since he has owned it he has done nothing to encumber the property. In other parts of New York state this type of deed is not accepted, but warranty deeds, whereby the seller warrants and guarantees the title, are. A quit-claim deed is a third kind of deed through which the owner releases all title to the property.

A well-drawn contract simplifies the closing of a real estate transaction. But many unforeseen issues may arise, and, therefore, all important matters should be methodically reviewed; a sufficient time (sometimes several months) should be allowed for considering and carrying out all the important items in the contract.

If no difficult problems arise and the procedure is relatively simple, the following matters are taken care of by the closing of title:

1. Disposition of objections to title found in examining the abstract of title or in examining the title guaranty company's preliminary report. Sometimes unpaid taxes or an old unsatisfied mortgage of record is a lien on the property, and sometimes all the heirs of an estate have not signed off their interests. Often the title objections are mere irregularities that can be straightened out at the closing.

2. Adjustment of financial matters, such as proration of taxes, rents, and insurance premiums.

3. Final checking and execution of deeds, mortgages, and other legal documents.

4. Payment of the purchase price.

5. Delivery and recording in the public office of the deeds, mortgages, and other closing instruments.

Title companies and lawyers who frequently handle real estate transactions usually make their own checklists of matters to be handled at the closing. The following is an example of a typical checklist:

1. Complete execution of deed from seller to purchaser.

2. Obtain old deeds and other title papers in the possession of the seller.

3. Examine instruments, including leases, which are not recorded in public offices and which affect title.

4. Affidavits regarding death of prior owners, occupancy of premises, and so forth.

5. If seller is a corporation, obtain proof of the officer's authority to execute deed.

6. Get bill of sale of personal property on the land.

7. Obtain copies of leases.

8. Obtain list of tenants, rents, and estoppel certificate from holder of mortgage showing amount due and date to which interest has been paid.

9. Examine tax and water bills and proration computation.

10. Prepare closing statement showing all debits and credits and net amount of purchase price.

11. Deliver instruments and pay purchase price.

12. Affix cancellation and revenue stamps to deed.

13. Notify insurance companies of ownership change and see that necessary mortgagee clauses are effective.

14. Notify utilities and other interested parties of change of ownership.

MORTGAGES

A *mortgage* is a conveyance of land as security for a debt and in most states is accompanied by a note or bond as the evidence of the indebtedness. The *mortgagor* is the owner of the land and giver of the mortgage. The *mortgagee* is the person who loans the money and who takes the mortgage as security.

Mortgages are one of the oldest forms of investment. Under English common law, a mortgage was an absolute conveyance and not merely security for a debt. Through this interpretation land was commonly forfeited at much less than its true value; the mortgagee was legally entitled to possession at any time.

Despite later rulings protecting debtors, the courts in England and in some of our states still view a mortgage as an absolute conveyance of land to which the mortgagee has legal title until the debtor has paid the entire debt. Connecticut, Maine, New Hampshire, North Carolina, Rhode Island, and Vermont still hold to this archaic theory. The majority of the states, however, accept the "lien theory": The mortgage is merely a lien for the security of the debt. Many authorities believe the old common-law interpretation will eventually disappear from our jurisprudence.

Mortgage Loans

A mortgage is given to secure a loan or a debt evidenced by a promissory note and mortgage; hence, the phrases "bond and mortgage" and "note and mortgage." The mortgage is not the written evidence of the debt; the debt is evidenced by the bond or the note. The mortgage is security for the payment of the debt.

A mortgage may be a first mortgage, second mortgage, third mortgage, and so on. Obviously, the first mortgage is the one which has a preferred lien against the property. Subsequent mortgages are subordinate and secondary in lien to a first mortgage.

Before the prudent lender will lend money on the strength of mortgage security, he will have the property appraised by an expert and make a careful study of the physical condition and the marketability of the property. Then he will have the title carefully searched. Ordinarily the lender will investigate the financial status of the borrowers, too. He wants to know that the mortgaged property is good security for the debt, and that the mortgagor (the one who borrows the money) has the financial ability to pay the debt.

Establishing Identity in Mortgage Transactions

Establishing the identity of the property owner is even more important in a mortgage transaction than an ordinary real estate transaction, because more losses have occurred through false claims of ownership in mortgage transactions than in the sale of property. The following is an example of a loss which resulted from failure to establish the identity of the property owner:

A man who said his name was Joe Hoffman went to the office of a real estate broker specializing in mortgage loans and asked for an $8,000 mortgage loan on choice building lots in the metropolitan area. The mortgage broker at the end of a few weeks' time notified Mr. Hoffman that he had found a man who was willing to lend $8,000 on the lots. He told Mr. Hoffman to obtain a search and other title data. The title search disclosed that the title was vested in Joe Hoffman free and clear of all encumbrances. The attorney for the lender was satisfied that Joe Hoffman owned the property and he prepared the necessary bond and mortgage which was properly executed and delivered by Joe Hoffman. The lender gave a certified check to Joe Hoffman for $8,000, and Hoffman paid the real estate broker.

Seven months later, the lender, who had not received interest on the bond and mortgage, contacted his lawyer; an investigation disclosed that Joe Hoffman, the owner of the property, lived in Denver, Colorado. Upon communicating with Joe Hoffman, it was discovered that the bond and mortgage were forgeries. The phony Joe Hoffman had taken the $8,000 less a 5 percent brokerage fee and vanished. Failure to identify correctly the fake Joe Hoffman who got the money resulted in a loss to the lender.

Kinds of Mortgages

Mortgages may be divided into three general classes: mortgages for monies loaned, purchase-money mortgages, and building-loan mortgages.

Mortgages for Moneys Loaned   Mortgages for moneys loaned are sometimes referred to as straight bond and mortgage loans. (The person who borrows the money gives a mortgage on his property as security for the repayment of the loan.)

Purchase-Money Mortgages   Purchase-money mortgages are those given by purchasers to sellers in part payment of the purchase price. In some cases a purchase-money mortgage has superiority over other liens on the property.

Building-Loan Mortgages   Building-loan mortgages are those by which the total amounts of the mortgage loans are advanced in installments as the work progresses on improvements to real estate. A building-loan mortgage may be used for a new house or for the renovation of an old house. A building-loan agreement is executed and filed with a mortgage; it provides that advances are to be made according to a schedule and that on the completion of the building the lender will lend to the borrower the full amount of the mortgage loan which will be repaid at the end of a specified period in the same way as any other mortgage. A building-loan agreement may provide, for example, that in the case of a $10,000 mortgage loan, $2,000 is to be advanced when the roof is on, an additional $1,000 when the exterior trim is completed, another $2,000 when the rough plumbing and heating is in and the rough plaster completed, another $1,000 is to be advanced when the white plaster is finished, and the balance of the mortgage loan is to be advanced when the premises have been completely graded, landscaped, and all interior trim and fixtures have been installed and the building finished according to plans and specifications.

Trust Deeds

In Alaska, Arizona, California, Colorado, Georgia, Idaho, Illinois, Mississippi, Missouri, Montana, North Carolina, Texas, Virginia, and West Virginia it is popular to use trust deeds or loan deeds instead of mortgages. When used, a trust deed or loan deed secures a debt to a trustee subject to the condition that the deed shall be void upon payment of the debt. Trust deeds usually give the trustee power to sell the property in case of default.

Foreclosure

In ancient times, English courts of chancery or equity relieved the hardship resulting from mortgages (absolute conveyances of land) with the doctrine known as the debtor's "equity of redemption," that is, the debtor could recover the ownership of the land by paying the debt even long after it became due. This doctrine in turn led to evils, for unless it was restricted, the creditor might never know whether or not the land was rightfully his. The courts, therefore, set up a procedure known as "foreclosure" whereby the equity of redemption was cut off (foreclosed). Foreclosure actions in the United States today are the usual remedies for nonpayment of mortgages, although there are other remedies which a creditor may exercise instead of going through a court action for foreclosure of the mortgage.

In states where trust deeds are used, the trustee is frequently given a power of sale so that if the debt is not paid, the trustee can sell the property for the benefit of the creditor. In order for the creditor to sell the mortgaged property in some states, there must be a foreclosure action. In other states, foreclosure of a mortgage may be obtained by means of an "advertisement procedure," that is, by publishing notice of the sale of the property to satisfy the debt.

A number of states give the debtor the *right of redemption*; the right to reclaim the property even after foreclosure. The right of redemption in at least ten states is preserved for periods varying from six months to three years.

Legal Documents in Mortgage Transactions

The most common of the many types of legal documents used in connection with mortgages are discussed below:

An *assignment of mortgage* is an instrument through which the owner of the mortgage transfers ownership of the mortgage to another person.

In an *estoppel certificate* the mortgagor (the one owing money on a bond and mortgage) specifies the amount of principal and interest due on the mortgage and also that there are no offsets or defenses to the mortgage. An estoppel certificate protects the purchaser of a mortgage and prevents the debtor from claiming that he has already paid all or a large part of the mortgage.

A *release of part of the mortgaged premises* is an instrument often used when the owner of property wishes to sell part of the mortgaged premises. Before he can give good title to the section of the mortgaged premises the owner must obtain a release from the holder of the mortgage; this instrument should quit-claim and transfer all interest in the part of the mortgaged premises to be released.

An *extension agreement* extends the time of payment of the mortgage.

A *consolidation agreement* has the effect of combining several mortgages into one.

A *spreader agreement* extends an existing mortgage to cover property other than the original mortgaged property for the better security of the debt.

A *subordination agreement* is an instrument whereby the holders of several mortgages or other liens agree among themselves which liens are to be superior and which are to be subordinate.

A *satisfaction of mortgage* (sometimes called a discharge of mortgage) is an instrument executed by the owner of the mortgage acknowledging that the mortgage has been paid in full and may be discharged of record.

OTHER LIENS ON REAL PROPERTY

Several other types of liens besides mortgages may be made against real property. Among them are mechanic's, judgment, attachment, and tax liens.

Mechanic's Liens

A *mechanic's lien* is a legal (statutory) claim against land (or the buildings and the improvements thereon) for priority of payment to one who performs labor or furnishes material for improvement on the land. Sometimes the state statutes name the classes of persons entitled to mechanic's liens—laborers, mechanics, material men, and so on. In some states, such as New York, a material man, laborer, or sub contractor, may not claim a lien for a sum greater than that which is due the contractor at the time the notice of lien is filed. In other states such persons have a direct lien on the property regardless of the amount owing to the general contractor; in such cases the owner acts at his peril if he makes payments to the contractor without first being sure that claims of subcontractors, material men, and laborers have been paid.

The statutes generally provide that one who has a mechanic's lien must file a notice of the lien in a public office where deeds or mortgages are filed and also serve a notice of the lien on the owner of the land. The lienor is required to file a sworn statement about the contract he made with the owner or contractor, the work he has done, the materials he has furnished, the property on which the lien is claimed, and certain other details. Once the lien is filed, the lienor may eventually sell the property to satisfy the lien.

Judgment Liens

By statute in the various states, a *judgment creditor* has a lien for his judgment against his debtor's land within the jurisdiction of the court rendering the judgment. Generally, this is restricted to the limits of a particular county, but the statutes provide that a transcript of the judgment may be filed in other counties; thus, the lien of the judgment may be extended to real estate in other counties.

A creditor gets a judgment against his debtor for $525. The judgment is entered in Ontario County. The debtor owns no real property in Ontario County; hence the lien of the judgment extends to no real property. But, the debtor owns real property in Erie County, and the creditor files a transcript of the judgment in that county. Thereupon the real estate in Erie County becomes subject to the lien of the judgment obtained in Ontario County.

Attachment Liens

For good reasons—such as when fraud has been committed or when a debtor plans to leave the state in order to defraud his creditors—many states will grant a *writ of attachment* before judgment is entered. As soon as the attachment is filed, a lien becomes effective against the property attached.

Tax Liens

Many state statutes provide that taxes on land—corporation taxes, inheritance taxes, and others—become a lien on real property of the person or corporation against whom the tax is assessed. Also, United States Internal Revenue taxes may be made a lien on the real estate of one liable for the taxes, by the filing of a written notice called a *tax lien*. This remedy is regarded as drastic and is resorted to by the federal government only in rare cases.

LEASES

A *lease* is a contract transferring the right to possession and enjoyment of real estate for a definite period of time. A lease is a binding contract whether it is for a short term or a long term. Many leases, especially for business property, should not be entered into by owner or tenant without legal advice. The *lessor* is the owner, the one who leases the property. The *lessee* is the tenant.

Verbal Leases

Tenancies from month-to-month and week-to-week are verbal in most cases, and some year-to-year tenancies are verbal. Such leases are called *periodic tenancies*. They are terminable at the end of one of the periods by means of a previous notice from the landlord to the tenant or from the tenant to the landlord. At common law, a six months' notice was necessary to terminate a year-to-year tenancy. Today, most states require one month's notice to terminate a month-to-month tenancy.

L rents an apartment to T on a month-to-month basis. T moves in and starts paying rent on the fifteenth of the month. One spring T decides that he would like to move out on May 15. On April 20 he gives notice to *L* of his intention to move on May 15. The notice is insufficient; it should have been given by April 14 at the latest. Because of the insufficient notice *T* is liable for rent for the period from May 15 through June 14.

Written Leases

In forty states a lease for more than one year must be in writing. In Indiana, Maryland, New Jersey, New Mexico, North Carolina, Ohio, and Pennsylvania a lease for more than three years should be in writing. In Maine a lease for more than two years must be in writing. In Maryland, Massachusetts, and New Hampshire a lease for more than seven years may be invalid unless recorded in the Registry of Deeds. In Louisiana leases may be either oral or written.

Leases may be very simple documents, printed or typed on one page, or they may be complicated business arrangements consisting of several hundred pages. Sometimes important business leases run for ninety-nine years. Generally a printed lease is a landlord's lease, for it contains clauses which favor the landlord. For this and other reasons it is advisable to have legal advice before signing a lease.

Sublease and Assignment

In the absence of a provision in the lease to the contrary, a tenant may assign or sublet the lease. An assignment is different from a sublease: In an *assignment* the tenant transfers his entire interest in the lease; in a *sublease* the tenant retains some interest or control in the lease.

Holding Over

A tenant who continues in possession of leased premises after the expiration of the term of his lease is said to "hold over." Holding over is usually regarded as wrong, and the landlord may take steps to oust the tenant. In general practice, a tenant for a year or more who wrongfully holds over may be compelled by the landlord to leave or be treated as a holdover tenant for another period of one year.

The A & B Holding Corporation owns store property and leases it to the Haberdashery Corporation for a period of three years, expiring March 31. The Haberdashery Corporation, instead of moving out on April 1, continues to occupy the property until June 1 and then tells the holding company that it is moving out of the property. The officials of the holding company say to the Haberdashery Corporation people, "Nothing doing, we elect to treat you as a holdover tenant for an additional period of one year and we will treat you as a tenant for one year commencing April 1."

Dispossess Proceedings

At common law when the tenant did not pay his rent or when he held over after the expiration of the term of the lease, the landlord had to bring an action for ejectment (a slow and cumbersome proceeding) in order to get the tenant out. To speed up the procedure, most states today provide that the landlord may bring dispossess proceedings (commonly known as "summary proceedings") to force the tenant out on short notice.

Landlord's Lien for Rent

In the absence of a state statute covering the subject, the landlord has no lien on the personal property of his tenant for unpaid rent. That means the landlord has no right to hold the tenant's property for payment of the rent. On the other hand, sometimes leases contain special provisions whereby the tenant agrees that the landlord can hold his property for payment of the rent.

In some states the legislature has given the landlord a lien against the tenant's personal property on the leased premises, except property exempt by law from execution. The following states have adopted laws giving landlords liens against property such as crops of the tenant: Alabama, Arizona, Arkansas, Florida, Georgia, Illinois, Iowa, Kansas, Kentucky, Louisiana, Missouri, New Jersey, New Mexico, North Carolina, Oklahoma, Oregon, South Carolina, Tennessee, Texas, Utah, Virginia, and Washington.

Types of Leases and Lease Arrangements

There are no clear definitions of short-term and long-term leases. Arbitrarily speaking, a lease for a period of ten years or less is a *short-term lease*. Obviously a *long-term lease* (for example, one for ninety-nine years) must be drawn with the greatest care because it may be reviewed later by persons who were not alive at the time the original agreement was drawn; therefore, nothing should be left to the imagination. All provisions of the lease should be spelled out. Even in short-term leases printed forms should be avoided, unless inspected and found acceptable to the situation by an attorney. A layman should never attempt to draft a lease agreement himself.

A *percentage lease* is one in which the tenant pays as rent a stipulated percentage of either (1) the gross volume of sales of merchandise or services or (2) a percentage of the net profit of the tenant's business. Generally under a percentage lease the landlord is paid a minimum rental; thus, if the tenant's sales are low or he makes no profit the landlord still receives an income from his property. In a *sale-and-leaseback* transaction, which is a relatively new development, property is sold and immediately leased by the buyer to the seller for a long term at a stipulated annual rental.

NEW TRENDS FAVORING TENANTS

Until recent years the law governing landlords and tenants was that, unless otherwise expressly provided in the lease, a tenant took the leased premises "as is," and assumed all risk as to their condition. Today legal scholars and some courts are coming around to the view that a lease is a contract which contains an implied warranty of fitness for use by the tenant.

In Hawaii Mr. Lem rented an apartment for his family. They took possession and found the building infested with rats. After three harrowing nights and after attempts to exterminate the rats failed, Mr. Lem and his family moved out. Mr. Lem sued for the return of the advance rent he had paid. The courts ruled in Mr. Lem's favor.

In New Jersey Mr. H rented an apartment under a lease which contained no specific agreement on the part of the landlord to make repairs. After repeated attempts by Mr. H to get his landlord to repair a cracked toilet, he hired a plumber and deducted the plumber's bill from the rent. The New Jersey court held that the lease contained an implied warranty to keep the premises in repair, and that the tenant was right in deducting the plumber's bill from the rent.

17
Debtors and Creditors

Broadly defined, a *judgment* is a decision given by a court as a result of legal proceedings instituted therein; it may direct that certain acts be performed, that property be transferred, or that one person recover a certain sum of money from another person. Although there are many different kinds of judgments, this chapter is concerned only with money judgments.

MONEY JUDGMENTS

A *money judgment* adjudges that one person is entitled to a certain sum of money from another person. The form of a money judgment is as follows:

Adjudged that John Jones, the plaintiff, recover of Tom Brown, the defendant, the sum of three hundred dollars ($300) damages, with seventeen dollars ($17) costs and disbursements, amounting in all to three hundred seventeen dollars ($317), and that the plaintiff have execution therefor.

William Smith
Judge of the District Court

Money judgments bear interest at the legal rate from the date that the judgment is entered in the court.

Before judgment is entered the person seeking the judgment is known as the *plaintiff,* and the person against whom the judgment is sought is called the *defendant.* After the judgment is entered, however, the person who has obtained the judgment is known as the *judgment creditor,* and the person against whom the judgment is rendered is called the *judgment debtor.*

ENFORCEMENT OF MONEY JUDGMENTS

Money judgments are not self-enforcing. When a money judgment is rendered, it is simply a final and binding statement by the court that one person owes money to another. After the judgment is entered, the judgment creditor has to take steps to enforce or collect it. Although most of the states have gradually abolished them, the states of Georgia, Delaware, Kentucky, Maryland, New Hampshire (writ of *scire facias*), Virginia, and West Virginia (writ of *fieri facias*) still use the common-law writs in enforcing judgments. The other states use a straight form of execution. The result is the same by either method: the sheriff is directed to levy upon the personal property (or goods and chattels) of the debtor and sell the same and pay the judgment from the proceeds.

There are various auxiliary proceedings to assist creditors in enforcing judgments; among these are receiverships, garnishee proceedings (to levy on wages or earnings of a judgment debtor), and proceedings supplementary to execution, but there is great lack of uniformity and countless discrepancies and contradictory provisions in the proceedings to collect money judgments in the United States. Moreover, although creditors have a vast number of remedies, the procedures are often cumbersome, clumsy, inequitable, and technical. A legislative advisory committee on practice and procedure in New York state commented that a large number of money judgments are paid only after years of postjudgment litigation, frustration, harassment, and deception involving substantial expenditures of time and money. This indicates the pressing need for modern laws governing the collection of money judgments in this country.

Executions against Property

After the judgment is entered in most states an execution is issued. An execution or writ of execution is a mandate or official order by the court to the sheriff, marshal, or constable, or other officer of the court directing him to take into possession property of the judgment debtor, to sell it, and to satisfy the judgment out of the proceeds of the sale.

Certain property is exempt from execution. Generally, only personal property is subject to an execution. Real estate can be sold to satisfy a judgment, but the procedure is more complicated; an ordinary execution does not usually extend to real estate. When the execution is delivered to the sheriff, he makes a *levy*, the act by which he takes the property into his possession. Property under levy may be redeemed by payment of the judgment before the sale.

Sale of Property When the sheriff intends to conduct a public sale, he must give notice of the time and place of the sale according to the law of the state where the sale takes place. If sufficient money is realized from the proceeds of the sale, the judgment is satisfied and discharged of record. If more than enough money is realized, the excess is paid to the judgment debtor. If the funds from the sale are not sufficient, the debt is satisfied to the extent of the net proceeds.

Warrant of Attachment   An execution should not be confused with an attachment. A *writ of attachment* is a special proceeding authorizing the sheriff or other court officer to seize the property at the beginning of an action and hold it pending the outcome of the action. An attachment is granted in certain types of cases when it can be proved that the debtor intends to defraud his creditors by leaving (or having left) the state or removing property from the state or that he has been guilty of other gross wrongdoing (such as fraud or obtaining property under false pretenses). Before a writ of attachment is granted the plaintiff, he must post with the court a bond which will cover losses to the defendant as the result of an unjustified attachment.

After the plaintiff obtains judgment he may proceed in the usual manner to obtain satisfaction of judgment. Having obtained the attachment, he is then in the advantageous position of selling the very property that has been held for him by the sheriff while he was obtaining a judgment.

Proceedings Supplementary to Execution ("Sup-Pro")

It is one thing to issue an execution against property and another to find property which can be sold to satisfy the execution. In nine executions out of ten, the sheriff cannot find any property on which to make a levy. Thus, the judgment creditor usually has to institute supplementary proceedings, commonly known as "sup-pro."

The purpose of supplementary proceedings (authorized in most states) is to give the judgment creditor an opportunity to establish under oath the status of the property of a dishonest debtor or of an honest debtor whose property cannot be reached by execution. The testimony given by the judgment debtor or others in sup-pro determines the steps the judgment creditor then takes to collect the judgment. Most times, the judgment creditor just tells the sheriff what property he can seize and sell. Sometimes the judgment creditor has to have a receiver appointed to handle the judgment debtor's property. At other times the judgment creditor may get an order directing the payment or delivery of the property to the sheriff or an order for the payment of money, in one sum or in periodic installments, to satisfy the debt.

Executions against Persons (Body Executions)

Even in this age debtors may be sent to jail for nonpayment of obligations that originated in moral wrongs. Most state constitutions prohibit imprisonment for debt, but many courts hold that this prohibition applies only to ordinary debts and that there are certain obligations which are not ordinary debts. The theory is that if the debtor has been guilty of wrongdoing that is the equivalent of a crime and if he has no property to satisfy the debt, he himself should pay a penalty by being put in jail. In the case of an *execution against the person* or *body execution,* the sheriff arrests the judgment debtor and imprisons him until he satisfies the judgment or is otherwise discharged by law.

Among the debts for which it may be permissible to imprison a debtor are those cases where judgments have been entered in actions for fraud or deceit; in actions for official or professional misconduct; in actions for libel or slander, seduction, malicious prosecution, conversion of personal property, misappropriation of public funds, and similar actions. Many students of the law believe that body executions should be abolished entirely: The punishment for these crimes should rest with the criminal courts.

Executions against Wages or Other Income

Many state laws provide that a judgment may be collected by regular deductions from wages or other income of the judgment debtor. Executions against income due the judgment debtor have been variously designated as "garnishee execution," "suggestee execution," "installment execution," and so on. In some states the execution against wages or income of a judgment debtor may not be issued until the judgment creditor has first tried unsuccessfully to recover under a general execution. By law a special execution requires the sheriff to collect a fixed percentage of wages, debts, earnings, profits, or income due from trust funds owing to the judgment debtor provided that such income exceeds a certain designated sum per week. The sum designated varies from state to state.

The federal Wage Garnishment Law (passed in 1970) restricts the amount payable under a state garnishee execution to the lesser of 25 percent of the weekly earnings of an employee (after deductions) or 30 times the federal minimum hourly rate. This law forbids the practice of employers firing employees when their wages are garnisheed.

Property Exempt from Execution

All fifty state legislatures have enacted laws exempting certain kinds of property from execution. When property is exempt from execution, neither sheriff nor marshal nor constable can seize the property and sell it to satisfy a judgment. Furthermore, federal bankruptcy laws recognize the exemptions created by the state in which the bankrupt person lives. Thus, when a debtor goes into bankruptcy, he may retain the exempt property as his own.

Most states allow a homestead exemption of real estate. In some states there is a flat homestead exemption of a specified amount which varies from $1,000 to $20,000. In other states there is a specified amount of land which may be claimed as a homestead for a farm and a lesser amount for a home in the city. The legislatures of most states seem loath to modernize property exemptions, though in many cases the lists are a carry over from colonial or pioneer days and have little application to modern living. Many states also establish unrealistic monetary limits for exemptions. Some states put an overall limit of $500 for the furniture, wearing apparel, and so on for a whole family and $200 for an unmarried person's.

The following property is typical of that exempted by the various states from the claims of creditors:

Ohio exempts these six items of personal property: (1) wearing apparel and certain household and kitchen furniture, (2) livestock or household furnishings not exceeding $600 in value, (3) books used in the family and all family pictures, (4) $150 worth of provisions, (5) tools and implements of the debtor for earning or carrying on business or trade not exceeding $600 in value, (6) all articles, specimens, and cabinets of natural history or science, except such as are kept for exhibition for gain.

A percentage of the debtor's current wages (varying from 90 percent in Indiana to 75 percent in Oklahoma); or all or a portion of wages for a certain period prior to the time when exemption is claimed (South Carolina allows an exemption of 60 days' wages, Wyoming allows one-half of wages earned 60 days previous to the time of execution.

The proceeds of life insurance or fraternal, cooperative, health, or accident insurance, or annuities. (There is no uniform rule concerning insurance. In most states life insurance is not totally exempt; in other states it is exempt up to $10,000; in still other states, it is exempt if the annual premiums do not exceed $500); pensions, veterans' and old-age benefits, workmen's compensation payments and so forth, family Bibles, and burial lots (in almost all states).

Variety in the exemption laws among the states is endless. Some states provide that exemptions may not be waived. Other states provide that when the debtor does not own property in the enumerated list, substitutions may be made; still other states do not.

TRUTH IN LENDING

Truth in lending is a key portion of the Consumer Credit Protection Act which was passed by Congress in May 1968. Congress assigned to the Federal Reserve System the job of writing regulations that would serve as guidelines for the interpretation and enforcement of the truth in lending law. The board of governors of the Federal Reserve System released what has become known as Regulation Z covering truth in lending, effective July 1, 1969. Regulation Z applies to banks, savings and loan associations, department stores, credit card issuers, credit unions, automobile dealers, consumer finance companies, and other organizations that extend or arrange for credit for which a finance charge is payable.

When personal property is sold on credit, the seller is required to set forth (1) the cash price, (2) the downpayment itemized as to cash and trade-in, (3) the unpaid balance of the purchase price, (4) other charges, (5) any prepaid finance charges or required deposit balances, (6) the amount financed, (7) the total finance charge, (8) the time sales price, and (9) the annual percentage rate of finance charges, and so on.

The purpose of Regulation Z of the Federal Reserve System is to let the consumer know the costs of his credit so that he can compare the credit plan offered him with those of other credit sources and avoid the uninformed use of credit. Regulation Z does not fix maximum, minimum, or other charges for credit. The finance charge and the annual percentage rate are the two most important disclosures that it requires. Many states have credit laws which require that the interest and credit service charge be disclosed. Few define the disclosures required in the same detail in which the federal Truth in Lending Act does. As a result, an effort is being made to get the states to adopt a uniform consumer credit code which will be consistent with the federal law.

Creditors Entitled to Favored Treatment

In order to collect his money, the ordinary creditor has to look to a debtor's general financial responsibility, earning capacity, and general assets. But, the class of creditors called "lienors" are given favored treatment against those who owe them money. A *lienor* is one who holds a lien, a preferred claim against particular property. For example, when a garageman repairs an automobile, or a livery stable boards a horse, or a jeweler repairs a watch, the garageman, the proprietor of the livery stable, or the jeweler may hold on to the automobile or the horse or the watch until the bill is paid.

Certain liens have always been recognized by traditional law. But, today most liens are created by statute. In analyzing the special statutory liens created in the states it becomes obvious that each state made those workmen and suppliers on which the state's economy depends special classes of creditors: Maritime states have special laws giving liens on boats or vessels to those who repair boats or furnish fuel or provisions for them. States with large mineral deposits recognize miners as a special class of creditors. Inland states give special protection to threshermen, corn shellers, wood choppers, and the like. The following are the general classifications of persons for whom liens are given by statute in most states: repairmen; keepers of inns, hotels, and lodging houses; artisans; owners of stallions or bulls (on their progeny); garagemen; those furnishing seeds for crops; blacksmiths; lumbermen; boatmen; owners of laundries and dry cleaning establishments; and warehousemen. The following lienors are recognized only in a limited number of states: employees on railroads, newspapers and oil wells; spinners, throwsters, and dyers; fishermen; detective associations for the recovery of stolen money; abstractors preparing real estate abstracts; house movers; farm equipment dealers having established places of business; printers, photographers, type setters; laborers in orchards; factory employees; and so on.

Many states give hospitals or other institutions of similar function liens on the proceeds of the injured person's damages awarded in actions for the injuries. It would seem that the interests of the hospitals are better represented in the legislatures than medical personnel, for only a very few states protect physicians, nurses, and dentists in the same way. In New York state, for example, when an injured person has a claim for $1,000 arising out of an automobile accident, the hospital where the injured person was treated may file a lien against the proceeds of the settlement, and the insurance company, before paying the claimant, must make sure that the hospital gets the money. Doctors and nurses, on the other hand, may receive nothing from the proceeds of the insurance settlement.

ASSIGNMENT FOR THE BENEFIT OF CREDITORS

An *assignment for the benefit of creditors* is a voluntary transfer of property by a debtor to someone in trust. Generally, the assignment is made pursuant to state statutory law where the debtor resides and for the purpose of discharging the debtor's obligations to those creditors who file claims and consent to the (assignment) proceedings. The statutes in forty-two states permit debtors to make assignments for the benefit of creditors. (Alaska, Illinois, Maine, Maryland, Nebraska, Oregon, Washington, and Wyoming lack special statutes for this purpose.) According to these statutes a debtor may transfer (assign) all his property to another, an *assignee*. The assignee must file a bond, and debtor and assignee each must file an inventory of the debtor's property. The assignee then gives notice of the assignment (usually by publication) to the creditors; after this, the creditors present their claims, and the assignee liquidates the debtor's property to pay the creditors.

Some regard assignment for the benefit of creditors as bankruptcy under state law, but these proceedings are not as effective as bankruptcy under the federal law. Under the assignment plan, the debtor's debts are discharged only to the extent of the money received by the creditors. For this reason the law of assignment for the benefit of creditors is seldom used; indeed, the federal law suspends these proceedings and makes them an act of bankruptcy.

An assignment for the benefit of creditors should be distinguished from a *composition with creditors,* which is a contract between a debtor and his creditors discharging debts on the payment of less than the full amount owing them. An assignment does not contain any agreement on the part of creditors to discharge their claims on the payment of less than the full amount of indebtedness. Sometimes a composition plan can be worked out with creditors as part of an assignment for the benefit of creditors. The federal Bankruptcy Act even encourages a composition with creditors in order to accomplish a settlement whereby the debtor secures his discharge in bankruptcy in return for the payment of a specified sum to be distributed among the creditors.

BANKRUPTCY

Some authorities say that the definitions of the terms "bankrupt" and "insolvent" are practically the same and that the words should be used interchangeably; however, under the Bankruptcy Act, the terms have technical meanings. A *bankrupt* is a person who has been adjudged a bankrupt under the act or one who has filed a petition in bankruptcy or one against whom a petition has been filed. An *insolvent* is one whose property (appraised at a fair valuation) is insufficient to pay his debts. This definition of insolvency is slightly different from that used in nonbankruptcy (financial, rather than legal) matters, namely, the inability to pay debts as they become due.

Bankruptcy laws, which probably originated in Roman law, have been in force in England since the eighteenth century, when they assured a bankrupt person a place in a debtor's prison. About the same time the legal principle that the bankrupt's surrender of *all* his worldly goods ought to erase *all* his debts began to develop. Several of the American colonies were, under statute, already compelling the bankrupt to surrender his goods to pay his creditors. Later, the adoption of the Constitution placed bankruptcy legislation in the Congress under the power "to establish uniform laws on the subject of bankruptcies throughout the United States." In this jurisdiction Congress has enacted many laws. (In the 1940s the then new codification of bankruptcy laws was referred to by its popular name, "Chandler Act." Today that name is not generally used.)

Technically, the United States district courts have jurisdiction over cases in bankruptcy, but because it is physically impossible for the United States district judges to administer the Bankruptcy Act, most of the powers under the act have been delegated to referees in bankruptcy. For practical purposes, the referees are the judges in the bankruptcy courts, and only a few bankruptcy matters are reserved to the United States district judges.

Voluntary and Involuntary Bankruptcy

In both voluntary and involuntary bankruptcy, bankruptcy proceedings begin with the filing of a petition under oath in the office of the clerk of the United States district court. In *voluntary bankruptcy* the petition in bankruptcy is filed by the debtor; in *involuntary bankruptcy* the petition is filed by creditors. A voluntary petition may be filed by any person, partnership, or corporation—except a municipal, railroad, insurance, or banking corporation—to obtain a discharge of debts. Any sane person who owes debts may become a voluntary bankrupt.

An involuntary petition in bankruptcy may be filed against any natural person, except a wage earner or farmer, and against any corporation except a municipal, railroad, insurance or banking corporation, or a building and loan association. When the debtor's creditors number less than 12, 1 of them may file an involuntary petition of bankruptcy; if his creditors number more than 12, 3 of them must sign the petition. It is important to note, however, that an involuntary petition may be filed only if (1) the debtor owes $1,000 or more, (2) the petitioning creditors have provable claims totaling at least $500, and (3) the debtor has committed an "act of bankruptcy" within 4 months of the filing.

A bankrupt, whether voluntary or involuntary, is required by law to file *schedules* (list of his creditors, all details of his property and assets) and a *statement of affairs* (questionnaire stating information about the bankrupt's income, bank accounts, safe deposit boxes, books, records, property held in trust, pending suits, transfers of property, financial statements, inventories, accounts receivable, and other data). The purpose of the statement of affairs is to furnish the trustee in bankruptcy with sufficient information regarding the bankrupt's financial condition to avoid the expense of long-drawn-out examinations of the bankrupt that are otherwise necessary to furnish such information. It is a criminal offense to knowingly conceal assets, except property exempted by the state.

Proofs of Claim

If a creditor wants to receive from the bankrupt estate a payment or a partial payment of the debt owing to him, he must file a written *proof of claim*. A proof of claim must set forth (1) the nature of the claim, (2) the consideration therefor (for example, it might state that the claim was for "services rendered" or for "goods, wares, and merchandise" or "for printing done"), (3) the security, if any, held therefor (for example, if a bank filed a claim for $2,000 against the bankrupt estate and held securities in the value of $1,000, then the value of the securities would be credited against the claim), (4) payments, if any, made thereon (for example, if $60 had been paid on the sale of merchandise worth $200, the balance of $140 would be covered by the proof of claim), and (5) that the claim is justly owing from the bankrupt to the creditor. Proofs of claim must be filed in a bankruptcy court within 6 months from the first date set for the first meeting of creditors.

The trustee in bankruptcy or any creditor may object to a claim. Objections to claims are passed on by the referee in bankruptcy.

A creditor who has no security for his claim is called a *general creditor*. One who has security pledged for the debt is called a *secured creditor*.

Preferred Creditors

A preferred creditor is one whom the debtor favors either by paying his claim in cash or through the transfer of property within four months of the filing of the petition in bankruptcy. Such transfer of property in payment of a debt is called a *preferential transfer*. The elements of a preferential transfer are (1) the transfer of cash or property by the debtor to the creditor, (2) while the debtor was insolvent, (3) within four months of bankruptcy, (4) the effect of the transfer being to enable the creditor to obtain a greater percentage of his debt over other creditors of the same class, and (5) proof that the creditor receiving the preference had reasonable cause to believe that the debtor was insolvent. When all the elements of a preferential transfer can be proved, the trustee in bankruptcy may take legal action to recover the property or cash transferred so that it will become a general asset of the bankrupt's estate for the benefit of the general creditors.

Prior Claims

Certain classes of creditors' claims are required by law to be paid first, before the bankrupt's assets are distributed among the general creditors. These are known as *prior claims*. They include wages earned by workmen, servants, clerks, or salesmen (not in excess of $600) within 3 months of the commencement of the bankruptcy proceeding, debts due the United States, and taxes owing to the United States or any state or municipality.

Acts of Bankruptcy

There are six acts of bankruptcy set forth in the Bankruptcy Act. It is important to know whether a debtor has committed an act of bankruptcy because a petition in involuntary bankruptcy must allege that the debtor has committed within four months prior to its filing at least one of the six acts of bankruptcy. Brief descriptions of the six acts of bankruptcy follows:

Fraudulent Transfer of Property   The statute defines a fraudulent transfer as one in which the debtor has "concealed, removed, or permitted to be concealed or removed any part of his property with intent to delay or defraud his creditors." For example, a debtor would be guilty of fraudulent transfer if he transferred his house to his son when he realized that his creditors were closing in on him. He would also be guilty of fraudulent transfer if in the same situation he left for parts unknown with a substantial sum of money. Fraudulent intent is part of the offense of making a fraudulent transfer, but fraud is generally inferred from the circumstances.

Preferential Transfer of Property   A preferential transfer of property is one made by a debtor to or for the benefit of creditors while he is insolvent, within four months of the filing of the petition of bankruptcy, and when the effect of such transfer is to enable the creditor to whom the property is transferred to obtain a greater percentage of his debt than other creditors in the same class. For instance, an insolvent furniture retailer is guilty of preferential transfer when he pays his debts to one of a group of furniture manufacturers who have supplied him with merchandise on credit and does not pay the other manufacturers' bills.

Permitting a Lien on Property   The third act of bankruptcy concerns the debtor who permits a creditor to acquire a lien on his property and who then fails to vacate or discharge the lien within a specified time. The most common example of this act occurs when a debtor suffers a judgment to be docketed against him and that judgment creates a lien on his property.

General Assignment for the Benefit of Creditors   When a debtor makes a general assignment for the benefit of his creditors, the assignment must be for the benefit of all his creditors. It is generally made under state law.

Appointment of Receiver or Trustee   When a receiver or trustee has been appointed to take charge of a debtor's property while he is insolvent or unable to pay his debts, the receivership or trusteeship must be one for the benefit of all creditors in order to constitute an act of bankruptcy. Thus, a limited receivership, such as one established to manage real property during the pendency of a mortgage foreclosure action, would not constitute an act of bankruptcy under the fifth classification.

Written Admission of Inability to Pay Debts   The courts require that before one is considered bankrupt under the sixth act, the debtor must (1) admit that he is unable to pay his debts, (2) be willing to be adjudged a bankrupt, and (3) admit both these facts in writing. For example, the fact that a businessman tells his brother-in-law that he is unable to pay his bills does not make him bankrupt under the sixth act, because he has not also said that he wishes to go into bankruptcy and he has not admitted both these matters in writing.

Meeting of Creditors and Election of a Trustee

Within a month of filing the petition of bankruptcy, the referee sends notice of the first meeting to all creditors listed in the bankrupt's schedules. The referee presides over this meeting, at which creditors with verified claims elect a trustee in bankruptcy. (Those creditors who do not then file proofs of their claims may do so within six months.) If the election of a trustee is contested, the candidate who receives the votes of a majority in number and amount of creditor's claims is declared elected. When there are assets to be administered and creditors do not elect a trustee, the referee in bankruptcy appoints a trustee.

The election or appointment of a competent trustee is important to the successful administration of the bankrupt's estate, because the trustee takes over the assets of the bankrupt; in addition, he has the responsibility of examining the bankrupt and those witnesses who happen to have knowledge of the bankrupt's affairs. Furthermore, it is the trustee's responsibility to uncover irregular bankruptcy dealings: to discover bankruptcy frauds, to trace concealments, to recover preferential or fraudulent transfers, and to protect the rights of all creditors.

Debts Not Discharged by Bankruptcy

The Bankruptcy Act provides that a discharge in bankruptcy shall release the bankrupt from all his provable debts except the following, which the bankrupt will still have to pay:

Taxes levied by the United States or any state, county, or municipality. Liabilities for (1) obtaining money or property by false pretenses or false representations, (2) willful and malicious injuries to person or property of another, (3) alimony due or to become due, (4) damages for seduction of an unmarried female, (5) maintenance or support of wife or child, (6) damages for breach of promise (of marriage) accompanied by seduction, or (7) damages for criminal conversation.

Debts which were not listed in the bankrupt schedules unless the creditor had notice or actual knowledge of the proceedings in bankruptcy.

Liabilities arising out of fraud, embezzlement, or misappropriation or defalcation of the bankrupt while acting as an officer or in a fiduciary capacity.

Wages due workmen, servants, clerks, or traveling salesmen and earned within three months before the date of commencement of the bankruptcy proceeding.

Monies due an employee but retained by an employer to secure the faithful performance by such employee of the terms of a contract of employment.

Objections to a Discharge in Bankruptcy

An honest debtor will be granted a discharge in bankruptcy unless he has been guilty of wrongdoing prior to the filing of the petition in bankruptcy or during the pendency of the proceedings.

The referee in bankruptcy gives the creditors thirty days' notice within which they must, if they wish to do so at all, file objections to an individual's discharge in bankruptcy. Objections are filed either by the creditor or by the trustee in bankruptcy and are considered by the referee in determining whether or not the debts of the bankrupt should be discharged. If occurring prior to the filing of the bankruptcy petition, the following acts may result in the denial of the discharge in bankruptcy:

Destruction, falsification, or concealment of account books or financial records, unless a bankruptcy court finds that such acts are justified.

Making of a materially false financial statement by means of which money or property was obtained on credit.

The transfer or concealment of any property by the bankrupt within one year of the filing of the petition with intent to hinder, delay, or defraud his creditors.

The obtaining of a previous discharge of bankruptcy or certain other specified reliefs under the national Bankruptcy Act within six years prior to the commencement of the bankruptcy proceeding.

If occurring subsequent to the filing of the petition, the following acts may result in a denial of the discharge in bankruptcy:

The fraudulent concealment by the bankrupt of property from an officer of the bankruptcy court.

The concealment, mutilation, or falsification of any document relating to the affairs of the bankrupt in any proceeding in the bankruptcy court.

The refusal of the bankrupt to obey any lawful order of the bankruptcy court.

The failure of the bankrupt to explain satisfactorily loss of assets needed to meet his liabilities.

Corporate Reorganizations

To avoid the complete liquidation of bankruptcy, a corporation unable to meet its debts may ask the protection of the court during its reorganization. During reorganization proceedings, the business of the corporate debtor may be continued without interruption. Lawsuits against the debtor may be stayed by the court, and the rights of secured and general creditors, stockholders, and bond-holders may be altered and revised, pursuant to the plan of reorganization.

Before the plan of reorganization can be approved by the court, it must be accepted by creditors holding two-thirds of the amount of claims filed and approved by a majority of the corporation's stockholders. If the court is satisfied that the plan of reorganization is fair and feasible, it will confirm it, making it effective. An example of a corporate reorganization follows:

Mr. B, president of the B & X Corporation, stole money from his corporation, his family, and his friends and ended up in jail, leaving the B & X Corporation $200,000 in debt. Twenty creditors holding claims amounting to $50,000 brought suit and threatened liquidation or bankruptcy of the corporation. Mr. X, vice-president and treasurer of the corporation, convinced people in the community who had invested over $100,000 in the stock of the corporation, that if the company were honestly managed, the corporation could weather the financial storm and operate profitably. The problem was what to do with the suing creditors who held claims for 25 percent of the total amount owed by the corporation. Mr. X caused a petition for a corporate reorganization to be filed with the court. The court issued an injunction restraining the creditors from prosecuting suit or entering judgment. The corporation filed a plan of reorganization which provided that these creditors would receive within 3 years 50 percent of the amount of their claims against the corporation.

Creditors holding more than two-thirds of the total amount in claims approved the plan and practically all the stockholders filed their consent. The court, satisfied that the reorganization plan was filed in good faith and that the corporation had a reasonable chance of working out the plan, confirmed it.

Arrangements

Arrangements are really a compromise of debts. An *arrangement* is a plan for the settlement of debts or extension of the time of payment. The arrangement plan may provide for payments on account, installment payments, or a general moratorium on the debtor's debts. Sometimes a provision is made for the supervision of the debtor's business by a committee of creditors or a court receiver, during the time when payment is being made on the debts. An arrangement under the Bankruptcy Act must be accepted by a majority in number and amount of all creditors. The court will approve an arrangement if it is satisfied that it is in the best interests of the creditors, is fair and feasible, and that the debtor has not been guilty of any violation of the Bankruptcy Act.

18
Agency

Every day of our lives we deal with agents, employ others to act as agents for us, or act as agents ourselves. Much more than 50 percent of all business is transacted through agents, such as real estate brokers, salesmen, store clerks, commission merchants, bank tellers, gas station attendants, and so on. Our dependence on the functions that agents perform makes the law of agency important.

Agency is the relationship between two or more persons by which one (the *principal*) consents that the other (the *agent*) or others shall act on his behalf. The law distinguishes between kinds of agents and kinds of principals. A *general agent* is a person authorized to conduct a series of transactions with continuity of service; a *special agent* is one authorized to conduct a single transaction; an *apparent agent* is a person who, although not really authorized to act as an agent for another, seems to third persons to have that authority; a *subagent* is a person employed by an agent to assist him in conducting the affairs of his principal.

A principal may be disclosed, partially disclosed, or undisclosed. A *disclosed principal* exists in a transaction when the third party is notified of the identity of the principal for whom the agent is acting; a *partially disclosed principal* exists when the third party is notified that an agent may be acting for a principal but without identifying the principal; an *undisclosed principal* exists when the third party is not informed that the agent is acting for a principal.

The law also distinguishes between agents and servants and agents and independent contractors, as well as trustees. A *servant* is a person employed to perform services for another, a *master*, who himself controls the conduct of these services. An *independent contractor* is a person who contracts with another to perform work but who is not controlled by the principal in the methods of performing it.

CREATION OF AN AGENCY

There is no particular way in which an agency must be created. On the one hand, an agency may be created by an express formal contract, such as in conferring a power of attorney. On the other hand, it may be spelled out from the dealings of the principal and agent over a period of time. Or, an agency may be formed when the principal appoints the agent and the agent accepts the appointment. Although no writing is necessary to establish an agency and although verbal authorizations to an agent are generally good, the Statute of Frauds requires written authorizations to sell real estate or to enter into certain other types of contracts.

Actual and Apparent Authority of Agents

The principal is responsible for the acts of his agent when he has given actual authority to the agent to act. Sometimes it is difficult to determine whether or not the principal has actually given an agent this authority. Many circumstances are taken into consideration in this determination. Generally speaking, authority to conduct a transaction includes authority to perform acts which are incidental to it or which usually accompany it.

Cable employs Enright to obtain photographs illustrating life in central Africa. Enright finds it necessary to employ an interpreter to make small goodwill gifts to the natives. Enright's authority includes the authority to spend money for an interpreter and gifts.

Stillwell directs Baker to sell goods at auction in a community where an ordinance forbids anybody but a licensed auctioneer to conduct sales by auction. Baker's authority includes authority to employ a licensed auctioneer.

The extent to which an agent can bind his principal often depends on whether a third person would normally believe that the agent is empowered to go as far as he does in handling a transaction. If the principal entrusts an agent with all evidence of authority, the principal may be responsible (and liable) if the agent misleads third persons.

Bowler turns over his automobile to Garber to sell, telling him he is authorized to take any reasonable price but that he is not to guarantee the performance of the motor or the speed of the car. Garber sells the car with the warranty that it can be driven at eighty m.p.h. Garber had apparent authority to give the warranty, and if the automobile can only do sixty m.p.h., Bowler may be liable for breach of warranty.

Types of Apparent Authority

Authority to make a contract may be inferred from authority to conduct a transaction. This should not be confused with authority to solicit business.

Pembrow employs Austin Estate Brokers to find a purchaser for his farm at a stated price. This employment does not give Austin authority to contract for the sale of the property.

When an agent has been given broad powers to handle certain property or to carry out a transaction, is he authorized to sell a portion of the property involved in the transaction? An agent who is empowered to handle a particular transaction has apparent authority to handle all customary things incidental to the transaction.

Birdman sends Apell down the Mississippi River in charge of a flatboat loaded with produce that Apell is to sell in the market at New Orleans. Nothing is said about what Apell shall do with the boat after the produce is sold. It would cost more than the boat is worth to send it back, and it is the usual practice, in such cases, to sell such flatboats in New Orleans. Apell is authorized to sell the boat.

Ordinarily, an authority to manage a business does not include authorization to sell items of property necessary in its operation.

Putnam, a farmer, goes on an extended trip and gives his neighbor a general power of attorney to manage all his business affairs "as fully as if Putnam were personally present." In Putnam's absence, the neighbor gets an opportunity to sell a portion of Putnam's farm at a handsome price. The sale is not valid. The neighbor is not authorized to sell any part of the farm.

An agent has implied or apparent authority to act in an emergency.

Eggleston, a fruit grower, ships fruit to Megler, his agent in the city. Twenty-four hours before the fruit is due to arrive, Megler learns that in this city, owing to excessive shipments, fruits will not bring enough to satisfy freight charges, but if it is sent to another city, it will. Megler cannot communicate with Eggleston in time to make the change. Megler is authorized to reroute the fruit, and the fact that it is unexpectedly destroyed in a train wreck in another city does not subject Megler to liability to Eggleston.

Apparent Authority

When a principal has taken such actions as would indicate to third parties that someone is his agent, he is held to have given apparent authority to the "agent" and will be liable for his acts.

Many times the principal raises the question of whether the agent has gone beyond his bare authority to buy and sell. Here are some examples of implied authority of the agent stemming from his authority to buy and sell:

Howard telegraphs Paul, "Sell my cotton F.O.B. Memphis at 106." Paul, although not specifically authorized to do so, sells the cotton at a cash 1 percent discount in accordance with local custom. Paul had the authority to give the discount.

Buckels gives to Barnes a power of attorney to sell and convey land but does not actually authorize him to receive the purchase price. Barnes negotiates the sale, gives a deed, and receives the purchase price in cash. Barnes had implied authority to receive this.

Lorillard employs Palmer to sell farmland 1,000 miles away from Lorillard's home. To prospective buyers, Palmer represents the farmland as fertile and the countryside prosperous. Neither statement is true. Lorillard is bound by Palmer's misrepresentations.

Thurston authorizes Fritz to sell gas furnaces. Fritz tells a purchaser that a certain size gas furnace is large enough to heat his house adequately. The gas furnace is much too small to heat the house. The purchaser may sue Thurston.

Generally, authority to sell includes only the authority to sell for cash.

Torbitt authorizes Jordan to sell his house and lot for $30,000. Jordan finds a buyer and conveys the house for $15,000 and takes back a mortgage for $15,000. Torbitt can disaffirm the deal because Jordan was not authorized to accept the mortgage.

The H & H Railroad employs Steadfast as its station agent at Podunk. Occasionally when Steadfast leaves the station he permits Herbert, the town ne'er-do-well, to take charge of the station and wear a railroad cap, a custom known to the railroad superintendent. During one of Steadfast's absences, a customer, thinking Herbert is the station agent, checks his trunk with Herbert, who rifles the trunk of valuables. The customer has a valid claim against the H & H Railroad.

Ratification of Authority by Principal

Despite the fact that he did not give his agent authority or the fact that the agent exceeded his authority, the principal may later be bound by his agent's actions if he has ratified or approved them. There are many ways in which a principal may ratify or confirm an agent's acts; two examples follow:

McNeil, pretending to represent Gregory, contracts with Harris to take care of his horse for a year. McNeil places the horse in Gregory's stable.

Gregory learns of the facts and does nothing about it for a week. Normally, his behavior would be considered an affirmation or ratification of the contract.

Durst authorizes Ross to sell a refrigerator at a specified price and without a warranty. Ross, pretending to have the authority to do so, sells the refrigerator with a two-year guarantee. Durst knowing all the facts receives the purchase price. He is bound by his silence to the two-year guarantee, although originally Ross had had no authority to make the warranty.

Once a principal acquiesces in the acts and conduct of an agent, such acquiescence indicates authorization to perform similar acts in the future.

Lyman appoints Bernette as purchasing agent for his plant. During the first six months Bernette purchases grades of material not previously used in the plant. Lyman pays the bills, knowing that the grade of merchandise has been changed, but later claims that he gave no express authority to Bernette to make the purchases. However, Lyman is responsible for Bernette's acts; Bernette had apparent authority since his previous purchases had been approved.

Delegation of Authority by Agent

Ordinarily, an agent is not clothed with authority to delegate his responsibility to someone else.

Snyder employs Calkins, an auctioneer, to sell his cattle. Calkins sends the cattle to another auctioneer requesting him to put the cattle up at public sale. Calkins had no authority to do this, and Snyder can repudiate the sale.

An agent has apparent authority to appoint subagents if it is in accordance with the established custom or when the very nature of the business indicates that subagents are required.

Butler is appointed general manager of a store. He is authorized from the very nature of the business to employ clerks who thereby become sub-agents.

An insurance company employs King as state manager. A reasonable interpretation of this appointment is that King has authority to appoint selling agents throughout the state.

It is a general rule that a person who holds a fiduciary position cannot delegate his responsibility to someone else. Therefore, a trustee, executor, administrator, or guardian cannot delegate those of his responsibilities which involve elements of discretion.

DUTIES AND LIABILITIES OF AN AGENT

The law seems to impose many more duties on an agent to his principal than on a principal to his agent. In most circumstances the duties and liabilities of an agent are governed by the terms of the agreement between the principal and the agent, but there are certain rules which apply to most agencies.

Agent's Obligations to Principal

In general, an agent has the following duties: (1) to use care and skill, (2) to act with such propriety as not to bring disrepute on his principal, (3) to give his principal all pertinent information, (4) to keep and render accounts if the nature of the work requires them, (5) to stay within the limits of his authority, (6) to obey his principal and carry out all reasonable instructions, (7) to act with utmost good faith and loyalty in advancing the interests of his principal, and (8) above all to act solely for the principal's benefit in all matters connected with his agency.

The last duty is commonly misunderstood; it is simply a duty of loyalty—first, last, and always—during the period of agency. The relationship between agent and principal should be one of trust and confidence. Sometimes, in this helter-skelter life, the agent succumbs to the morals of the marketplace and overlooks the high duty he owes his principal, but when he does the courts penalize him.

VanNess gives to Martin, his selling agent, a broad power of attorney to sell his real estate. Acting under this power, Martin sells the property to himself. This is self-dealing by an agent, and if he desires VanNess can have the conveyance set aside.

If an agent makes a profit in transactions he handles on behalf of his principal, he is obliged by his duty of loyalty to offer the profit to the principal.

Pike, acting for Hun, sells a parcel of land to Bridgeman for $50,000. As an inducement to sell the property to him rather than to other persons, who are interested, Bridgeman pays Pike a bonus of $1,000. This money really belongs to Hun, and Pike must pay it to him on demand.

An agent is further obligated not to act on behalf of an adverse party in a transaction connected with his agency and moreover not to receive any compensation directly or indirectly from the adverse party.

Springman employs Connelly to sell his house at the best price and agrees to pay Connelly a commission of 5 percent. Unknown to Springman, Connelly has been employed by Franklin to obtain a house for him at a low price. Connelly introduces Springman to Franklin and, without disclosing his relationship with Franklin, urges Springman to sell the house at the price offered by Franklin. This is a breach of duty on Connelly's part and could be Springman's defense if Connelly sues him for his 5 percent commission.

An agent is duty bound not to act adversely to his principal concerning the subject matter of the agency. He must not act during the period of the agency for persons whose interests would conflict with the interests of his principal.

Delafield is employed by Potts as manager of Potts's business. He decides to go into business himself, and he secretly contracts with Potts's employees to work for him. Delafield has committed a breach of loyalty to Potts.

Burrmann, a real estate agent, has been asked by the Bankers Bank whether they should renew their lease on a building or buy it. Burrmann secretly visits the owner of the building and obtains a lease on his own account. Owing to his breach of duty, Burrmann may be required to hold this lease for the bank's benefit (as "constructive trustee" or "trustee ex maeficio").

The principal who is the victim of a disloyal agent has various legal remedies at his disposal. He may bring actions for (1) damages for breach of contract, (2) damages for wrongful breach of duty (tort action), (3) impressing a trust on the property acquired by an agent, (4) an accounting, and (5) an injunction. The injured principal may also discharge the agent and refuse to pay him compensation or rescind the contract of employment.

Agent's Liabilities to Third Parties

The liability of the agent himself to third parties involves the important question of whether the principal is disclosed, partially disclosed, or undisclosed. An agent who makes a contract for a disclosed (identified) principal is not personally bound by the contract.

Finley, known by Stone to be the agent for Hawkins, writes to Stone, "I will sell you 100,000 broiler chicks at 10 cents each." Stone accepts. Hawkins defaults on the contract. Finley, having disclosed the fact that he was acting as agent for Hawkins, is not personally liable.

An agent acting for a partially disclosed principal (he discloses his agency, but not the principal's name) becomes a party to the contract.

Clifton writes Felix offering to sell goods and states that he represents a manufacturer who would prefer at this time that his name not be disclosed. Felix accepts. Clifton becomes a party to the contract.

An agent who does not disclose to a third person the fact that he is acting for another is a party to the contract. If the third party later finds out the identity of the principal, he has the option of holding either the agent or the principal responsible.

Forster agrees to sell Hadley's lumber to York without revealing Hadley's identity. When York discovers Hadley's identity, he tells Forster that he will sue Hadley. Later, York changes his mind and sues both principal and agent. Hadley and Forster are liable for their obligations under the contract.

DUTIES AND LIABILITIES OF THE PRINCIPAL

A principal's duties are not so numerous nor on such a high plane as those of an agent to his principal. The principal's duties are mainly contractual.

Principal's Obligations to Agent

The principal owes his agent just compensation. The basic right of an agent to recover compensation rests on contract, express or implied, and on custom or usage in the particular field. But, when an agent has been guilty of such gross negligence as to render his services of no value, the agent can recover no compensation.

A principal is liable to his agent for damages if he breaches his contract by prematurely terminating the agency. In such a case of wrongful discharge, the agent, in addition to damages, may recover from the principal all monies advanced and expenditures made in behalf of the principal. When the agent has in his possession money or property of the principal, he is entitled to retain them to satisfy his lien (for compensation or monies advanced or expended for the principal).

Principal's Obligations to Third Parties for Agent's Acts

A principal is liable to third parties for contracts made by the agent within his authority, whether actual or apparent. When the agent violates his secret instructions, the principal may be liable on the contract.

Bowers instructs Green to purchase a house for him and gives Green a letter indicating that he represents Bowers. Bowers advises Green that he should pay $20,000 for the house, $10,000 in cash and a $10,000 mortgage. Green buys the property for Bowers, but in violation of his instructions he agrees to pay $20,000 in cash. The transaction binds Bowers, and he must complete the purchase of the house in cash or respond to a suit for damages.

In order for a principal to be considered liable for a wrongful act of his agent, the law must presume that the principal intended the wrongdoing. Intent on the principal's part may spring from specific instructions to complete the act complained of, or it may result from wrongful instructions on the principal's part.

Sims, fearing intruders, directs Coe to shoot any person entering Sims's premises. Coe shoots a business visitor rightfully entering the premises. Sims is liable for Coe's wrongful act.

Prentice directs Stamply to wash his windows three stories above the street and not to use safety catches. Stamply carries out instructions, slips, and falls to the ground injuring a passerby. Prentice is subject to liability to the injured persons.

Generally the principal is not liable for physical harm resulting from the conduct of an agent who is not an employee and who is not under his control for the completion of his activities. Examples of such agents would be attorneys, brokers, real estate agents, or the like.

Ebers employs Brush as his real estate agent to convey land for him. While Brush (who has made a sale) is signing a deed, he negligently knocks over an ink stand and ruins a valuable rug. Under such circumstances, Ebers would not be liable for the damage to the rug.

However, when an agent who is not an employee performs wrongful acts which do not involve physical damage, the principal may be subject to liability. The principal may be liable to another for loss occasioned by deceitful representation by his agent if the agent was actually authorized to make such a statement or if it was within his general power to make such representations.

Schopp, as the agent of Carpenter, sells a farm to Winthrop, misrepresenting that the well and the spring on the farm have never run dry. Winthrop purchases land relying on the statement. Carpenter is liable to Winthrop in a lawsuit for deceit just as though he himself had made the statement.

The principal, however, would not be liable for his agent's deceit if the person dealing with the agent had reason to believe that the misrepresentations were not authorized by the principal.

Vergason, employed by Marshall to sell lots in a residential development, misrepresents to Ryan that oil has been discovered on an adjoining tract of land. Ryan buys a lot. Ryan, knowing Vergason's reputation for falsehood, does not believe that Vergason's statements were authorized by Marshall, so Marshall is not liable for deceit.

LIABILITY OF MASTER FOR SERVANT'S ACTS

Related to the status of principal and agent is the relationship of master and servant. A master is usually liable for injuries caused by the wrongful conduct of servants acting within the scope of their employment.

When is a person a servant (or an employee), and when is he an independent contractor? A person working for another is a servant or employee when the master or employer has control of the method and means by which the work is done. If the person doing the work, however, retains control over the manner or method of doing the work, he would be held to be an independent contractor and under most circumstances the person for whom the work is being done would not be responsible for negligence or other wrongful acts.

Bear in mind that the master (employer) is liable only for injuries caused by the wrongful acts of his servant (employee) when committed "within the scope of his employment," that is, when they are of the same general nature as that authorized by the employer or are incidental to such employment.

Sam, a millhand, develops considerable skill in one particular operation and is assigned to that operation. Another employee in the mill has some difficulty operating the machine and calls on Sam for assistance. Sam has not been directed to assist the other employee; yet his doing so is within the scope of his employment.

Nye, proprietor of a pharmaceutical concern, requires all his employees to wash their hands in his washroom before beginning work. Although hand washing is not part of the specific work covered by the employment, it is incidental to it and within its scope. One of the employees turns on the water to wash his hands and fails to turn it off and flooding results. Although employees may perform irresponsible acts, they may sometimes be held to be within the "scope of employment" and the responsibility of the employer. Such was the conclusion here.

A professional ball club requires its ballplayers to eat what the manager directs under his supervision at a training table. Any act of a ballplayer during mealtime while the players are under the manager's control is "within the scope of employment."

A proprietor of a sporting goods store directs his salesman never to insert a shell while exhibiting a gun to a customer. Dexter, a salesman, does so, and a customer is injured. The act is within the scope of Dexter's employment, and the proprietor may be held liable, despite his instructions to his salesmen.

Even deliberate criminal acts may sometimes be within the scope of employment.

A chauffeur, on an errand for his boss, driving on the left-hand side of a double line and greatly exceeding the speed limit is still acting within the scope of employment and his employer may be responsible for the consequences of a serious accident.*

Acts of an employee are held to be within the scope of employment only within the particular locality of employment or in a locality not unreasonably distant. If an employee leaves the area of employment or deviates from his regular route for his own personal benefit, he may be acting beyond the scope of his employment.

McChesney directs Preble, his chauffeur, to drive to the railroad station to meet an incoming guest. Preble, hearing that the train will be late, leaves early and drives to a village 10 miles distant to call on his girlfriend and en route has an accident. In those states which limit liability in accident cases to agents or employees acting within the scope of employment, McChesney would not be liable. However, if Preble had seen his girlfriend and had had the accident on his way back on his regular route, McChesney would be liable.

The common law held that the employer (master) was not liable to an employee (servant), acting in the scope of his employment, who was injured solely by the negligence of a fellow servant. This harsh *fellow servant rule* has been partially displaced by the states' adoption of workmen's compensation laws, but it still applies to employees, such as farm laborers or domestic servants, who generally are not covered by these laws. Employees engaged in the same enterprise and by the same employer are not fellow servants unless their work is so related that they are likely to come in close contact with one another or unless there is a special risk of harm to one by the negligence of the other.

Duff is employed by Bergdorf in a meat-processing plant. While he is carrying meat from one floor to another in Bergdorf's plant, Duff is in-

---

* This rule is important in a majority of states that do not follow the rule that every owner of an automobile is liable for the negligence of the person driving the car with the consent or permission of the owner.

jured by the negligent operation of the plant elevator. The elevator operator is regarded as a fellow employee in daily working contact with Duff; hence, Bergdorf is not liable to Duff.

Archibald employs McGillis as a maintenance man whose duties take him to all departments in his machine shop. McGillis is injured by the negligence of the packing-room foreman who throws a crate in the passageway just as McGillis approaches. Archibald is not liable to McGillis because of the fellow servant rule.

Fortunately, the almost universality of workmen's compensation limits the application of the fellow servant rule.

TERMINATION OF AGENCY

An agency is usually terminated by mutual consent. It may also be terminated if the principal revokes the agent's authority or if the agent renounces his agency. Such revocation or renunciation may constitute a breach of contract between the principal and agent and may be the basis for a lawsuit for damages. Nevertheless, as far as third persons are concerned, the agency itself is terminated.

Jackson writes Mobey, "I authorize you to sell my house on Front Street any time within six months." Mobey writes back and says, "I agree to try and sell your house." Two months later Jackson writes to Mobey, "I've changed my mind; I do not want to sell now." Mobey's authority as an agent is terminated.

An agency may be terminated even though the parties themselves agreed that it was to be irrevocable for an indefinite period. This is the very nature of an agency: *It can be terminated at any time.*

Jenners gives Winans a power of attorney to sell Jenners's property at a stated price and agrees to pay a commission of 20 percent. The power of attorney ends with the statement, "I agree that this power shall be irrevocable for a period of 1 year." At the end of 4 months Jenners says to Winans, "I revoke the power of attorney." Under those circumstances, the agency is terminated. Winans may have a claim for damages against Jenners for breaking his agreement, but the authority for his agency is terminated.

Agency may also be terminated by the death of either the principal or the agent or when it becomes impossible to carry out the agent's authority, as in the destruction of the subject matter or in the bankruptcy of the principal.

19

Criminal Law

Most of the law cases made famous in the newspapers are criminal rather than civil. People usually are interested in the trials of criminal cases, probably because they are more dramatic than civil cases. This chapter presents principles of criminal law with which every person in the community should be informed, for ignorance of the law is no defense in a criminal prosecution. Such information is necessary also to better understand the rights of others justly or unjustly accused of crime.

A *crime* is a wrong which affects the public welfare, a wrong for which the state has prescribed a punishment or penalty (see glossary for explanations of particular crimes). It is an act or omission prohibited by law because it is injurious to the public (as distinct from a private wrong).

POWER TO DEFINE AND PUNISH CRIME

The individual states have broad powers to prohibit and punish crimes. The state legislature has inherent power to define crimes and to enact laws punishing them. It does so, first, by a definite description of the act or acts constituting a crime and, second, by prescribing a penalty for the particular crime.

Unlike the state legislatures, the United States Congress has no inherent power to punish crimes. All its power derives from the Constitution; thus, Congress may define and punish crimes in the District of Columbia and the territories and may punish crimes relating to postal matters, interstate commerce, securities and United States coinage, federal elections, and other matters expressly referred to in the Constitution.

Classification of Crimes

Crimes may be classified as treason, felonies, and misdemeanors. *Treason* is the offense of a citizen in attempting to overthrow the government or in betraying a state into the hands of a foreign power. *Felonies* are those crimes punishable by death or by imprisonment in a state prison, although a lesser punishment may be imposed by the court. Crimes not so serious in nature as felonies are *misdemeanors*.

Sometimes crimes are labeled as *mala in se* (crimes inherently or morally wrong) or *mala prohibita* (crimes not inherently wrong, but crimes because they are prohibited by statute). Examples of crimes which are *mala in se* are murder, rape, arson, burglary, larceny, forgery, and the like. Examples of crimes which are *mala prohibita* are crimes which violate government requirements for licensing, failure of corporate directors or officers to follow requirements of the corporation law, failure to comply with government regulations or government requirements for the labeling of products, printing or publishing copyrighted musical compositions without the consent of the owner, bookmaking and the use of gambling apparatus, violations of the labor law, and so on.

Punishment and Prevention of Crime

It is generally agreed that the purpose of punishment for a crime is to deter the criminal and others from committing similar crimes. When a court imposes punishment for a breach of the law, the object is not vengeance but rather is to discourage the person who has broken the law from repeating his act.

A legislature may impose more than one penalty for the same offense; thus, a statute may provide for imprisonment in the state prison for a term of years and also for a fine which may be double the amount of money stolen or embezzled or double the value of the goods involved in the crime. The federal Constitution and most state constitutions prohibit cruel and unusual punishments.

Although the legislature may fix the limits of punishment, the trial court has the power to fix the actual punishment within statutory limits. In those states where the jury makes a recommendation for mercy in connection with its verdict, the recommendation is no part of the verdict; in fixing the punishment in the exercise of its discretion, the court may disregard the recommendation of the jury.

It is normally the function of police officers to prevent the commission of crime. But a private individual who sees another person actually perpetrating or about to perpetrate a felony may interfere and employ such force as is necessary to prevent the commission of the crime.

DEATH PENALTY

While the high courts of the various states were upholding the constitutionality of death penalties, the number of executions in the United States dropped as follows:

1962: 47
1963: 21
1964: 15
1965: 7
1966: 1
1967: 2
1968: 0

Finally in 1972 the long-awaited death penalty decision was made by the United States Supreme Court in the case of *Furman* v. *Georgia*. By a vote of five to four, the highest court in the land held that discretionary death penalties are unconstitutional because laws that give unlimited discretion to judges and juries to impose the penalty are "pregnant with discrimination." Only two of the nine Justices, however, voted to hold mandatory death penalties invalid, and some states have moved to reinstate the death penalty as mandatory for specific crimes.

Classification of Parties to Crimes

Persons involved in felonies may be classified as principals in the first or second degrees and as accessories before or after the facts. Parties to treason or misdemeanors, if guilty in any degree, are all classified as principals.

The *principal in the first degree* is the person who actually perpetrates the crime. He need not actually be present when the harm is done (for example, if he mixes a poison potion for another who takes it in his absence). A person who causes a crime to be committed through the instrumentality of an agent is the principal in the crime and is punished as such. The *principal in the second degree* is one who aids and abets in the commission of the crime, one who advises, encourages, or helps in the actual perpetration of the crime. A common example of a principal in the second degree is one who stays a distance from the scene of a felony but who keeps watch in order to warn of the approach of danger.

The *accessory before the fact* is one who is not present at the time the crime is committed but who counsels, urges, or commands the crime to be committed or in some way aids the principal in the commission of the crime. The *accessory after the fact* is one who knows that a felony has been committed and who receives, comforts, and assists the principal criminal or criminals. In this situation, the accessory after the fact is not connected with the commission of the crime; his offense occurs afterwards and is, therefore, distinct from the principal crime.

CRIMINAL CAPACITY, INTENT, ATTEMPT

If a person lacks the mental or other *capacity* to commit a crime, his acts, no matter how forbidden by law or how damaging to the public, are not criminal. Want of capacity is a complete defense and not merely an extenuating circumstance.

In law, *intent* is considered the purpose to use a particular means to cause a particular result. In nine out of ten cases, a crime must be accompanied by such intent, or *criminal intent*. The crime must be accompanied by (1) intent to commit the crime or (2) such negligence or indifference to duty or consequences that the law regards it as equivalent to intent.

An *attempt* to commit a crime has been defined by the courts as an act performed in partial execution of a criminal design, amounting to more than mere preparation but falling short of actual completion of the crime. Ordinarily, an *attempt* to commit a crime is a misdemeanor, although at times legislatures have classified attempts to commit particular crimes as felonies.

In order to be convicted of an attempted crime, the accused must take at least one step beyond preparation. The step must be in the direction of the completion of the crime but obviously not the last act of completion.

Webb and Johnson decide to break into a house. They meet at a saloon and talk over their plans. Webb has a revolver, and Johnson goes into a drugstore to buy some chloroform. Johnson is arrested when he comes out of the drugstore. Neither Webb nor Johnson has committed an attempted crime; they are simply in the preparation stage.

The courts have pointed out that there is a wide difference between preparation for the commission of the crime and the actual attempt. The step which may constitute an attempted crime need not be an act which is ordinarily a criminal act but one which may lead up to it.

Quince decides to set fire to a building in order to collect the insurance. He buys kerosene, spreads it around the property, and makes a deal with another person to set fire to the property. His accomplice decides he wants no part of the crime of arson. Quince, however, has made an attempt to commit the crime of arson and can be convicted.

DEFENSES FOR COMMISSION OF CRIMES

When a person is charged with committing a crime, he may plead guilty or not guilty. If he pleads not guilty, he must be prepared to establish his innocence in order to overcome whatever proof the prosecutor offers to establish that he committed the crime; these facts constitute a *defense*. A general defense may be that the accused person did not commit the crime. There are other defenses that may admit for the moment that the accused did certain acts but claim that there are special circumstances or reasons why the accused person should not be found guilty.

Under our system of law, every accused person is entitled to avail himself of all legal defenses no matter how technical they may be.

Ignorance of the Law

The courts in the United States have supported the principle that every person is presumed to know the law of his country and that ignorance of the law is no defense to criminal prosecution. For example:

The agents of the California, Oregon & Santa Fe Railroad Company did not know the law prohibited the solicitation of alien contract laborers for work in this country and prohibited the prepayment of transportation of alien laborers. When confronted with a criminal prosecution the railroad agents, who had sought Italian immigrant laborers in Canada to work in Oregon for the railroad and had paid the immigrants cash and had issued railroad passes to them, pleaded that they did not know of the existence of the law. The court held that their ignorance was no defense.

Although ignorance of the law is no defense in a criminal prosecution, it may sometimes be a matter considered by the judge in determining punishment for a crime.

This rule rests on public necessity, for the welfare of society and the safety of individuals depend on the enforcement of criminal laws. If persons accused of crime could shield themselves behind a defense of ignorance of the law, criminal laws would be practically impossible to enforce.

Ignorance of the Facts

On the other hand, if a person technically commits a crime but is ignorant of a *fact* essential to the crime or makes a mistake regarding the facts, he may have a good defense. In the following instances the accused person may actually have a good defense: (1) if one takes another's property in the honest belief that it is his own, (2) if stolen goods are received by one who does not know that they have been stolen, (3) if one has possession of forged instruments or counterfeit coins in ignorance of their character, or (4) if one marries believing that a former spouse is dead.

Sometimes, however, the legislature specifically provides punishment for a crime regardless of whether the party committing the crime had the necessary actual knowledge. For example, the legislatures of many states prescribe penalties for those who sell intoxicating liquors to minors and specify that it makes no difference whether the persons who sell the liquor are unaware that the purchasers are under age.

Custom or Usage

The practice of law enforcement officers in some situations to overlook certain crimes does not establish a legal precedent or a legal defense. Even though the failure to enforce a law or erroneous interpretation of a law may have permitted violators to escape punishment, no right to violate the law is created; furthermore, it does not provide a defense against criminal prosecution for a person committing a crime heretofore considered lightly in the community. For instance, ship officers have been convicted of the crime of appropriating small portions of the ship's cargo, even though it had been a custom to overlook such offenses, and others have been subject to criminal action for indecent exposure for indulging in the seemingly accepted practice of exposing themselves while bathing in public places.

Direction or Duress

A person is considered guilty of his illegal acts even when he commits them under the *direction* of his superior. For instance, an employee who on orders of his employer pays money to a public official to induce him to neglect his official duty is guilty of bribery.

Occasionally, though rarely, a crime may be excused on the ground that it was committed under *duress* or *compulsion*. The compulsion which will excuse a criminal act must be grounded on fear of death or serious bodily harm. A threat of future injury is not sufficient defense. For example:

Adams and Decker are buddies. Adams plans to rob a store on February 1 and threatens to kill Decker if he does not help him complete the crime. On February 4, both Adams and Decker rob the store and are caught. The mere fact that three days before the crime Adams has threatened Decker with death is no defense for Decker. They are both convicted.

ENTRAPMENT

The courts of the United States are not in complete accord as to when a defendant in a criminal case can successfully assert the defense of entrapment. The general rule is that entrapment is a valid defense only when the crime is the product of "creative activity" on the part of the government (police).

Pedro was suspected of importing heroin into the United States from Mexico. He was promised $500.00 by a man working for the United States government if he would bring heroin to Mexicali, a town across the border from California. The narcotics agent sent word to Pedro at Mexicali that he would have to bring the heroin to Calexico, California, to get his money. Pedro did so, got his money, and was arrested for bringing heroin into the United States. The federal court dismissed the case against Pedro holding that the government induced Pedro to bring the heroin into the United States and therefore Pedro was entrapped.

Mr. K. was charged with using the mails for delivery of obscene, lewd, and lascivious films. The Post Office Department had placed an advertisement in a magazine known for its obscenity. Mr. K. responded to the ad, corresponded with the Post Office Department, which used an alias, and delivered the film to a government agent. The court held that the government induced the offense and failed to show that Mr. K. was predisposed to commit the offense without government encouragement. The court said that the Post Office Department's action was typical of "creative activity" on the part of the government necessary to constitute the defense of entrapment.

Mr. M., a reputed Mafia boss, was charged with assaulting an officer of the FBI. Mr. M., when arriving at an airport, angrily confronted a group of news photographers, asking if they had taken enough pictures. Collins, an FBI agent who was in the crowd answered, "No." Mr. M. asked, "Are you looking for trouble?" Collins answered, "I can handle trouble." Mr. M. assaulted Collins and was later arrested. The court held that Collins's refusal to back down in the face of Mr. M.'s threats did not constitute entrapment.

Instigation amounts to encouraging or soliciting a person into the commission of crime, as distinguished from entrapment, the final act of springing the trap to catch the criminal.

Whether the defense is called entrapment or instigation, it must be shown that the officers of the law or their agents instigated and incited the accused into committing an offense that he otherwise had no intention of committing; such entrapment is a valid defense.

Consent, Forgiveness, or Settlement

Crimes are public wrongs which a private individual has the power neither to condone nor to absolve. The crime is determined by the act of the person in committing the crime. Therefore, the fact that the victim of the crime subsequently forgives his wrongdoer is usually no defense in a criminal prosecution.

Nick Bonn, desperate for money, breaks into Cromwell's home and steals some heirlooms. Nick is apprehended by the police, but Cromwell is so glad to get his heirlooms back and so sympathetic with Nick's plight that he forgives Nick and so informs the police. The district attorney, however, says Nick must be prosecuted. The court agrees, for a crime of burglary was committed, and the homeowner has no power to nullify the law.

There is no requirement that a complainant in a criminal case follow through with the prosecution but, in the case of a felony, there may be the temptation to accept money offered in return for an agreement not to prosecute the felony. Such an act may constitute the new crime of *compounding a felony*.

Alibi

An *alibi* has been called a perfect defense. It is proof that at the time the crime was committed the defendant was not at the scene of the crime and could not have participated in it. In order to constitute a complete alibi, it must be proved that it was impossible for the defendant to have been at the place where the crime was committed.

Religious Doctrine or Belief

As a general rule, religious beliefs cannot be recognized as justifications for committing crimes. Usually neither the law nor the government interferes with religious beliefs, but they may interfere if religious practices constitute crimes. For example, the courts of Utah have in the past century forced Mormon residents of the state to stop practicing their belief in plural marriages. Religious practices are subject to the rules of government.

Turning State's Evidence

When an accomplice in the commission of a crime becomes a witness for the prosecution and discloses his guilt and that of his associates, the law says there is an implied promise that he will not be prosecuted and that a pardon will be granted to him. This right to freedom from prosecution or to a pardon is based on fair dealing and is considered a pledge of faith by the public. It is within the discretion of the public prosecutor to determine whether to use an accomplice as *state's evidence*. Once an accomplice has testified for the prosecution, the court is honor-bound to pardon him or to reduce the charges against him.

This rule has many refinements in the various states. The federal courts have held flatly that, although the United States district attorney has no power to guarantee an accomplice that he will not be prosecuted, an accomplice who gives testimony essential to the conviction should not be prosecuted.

Insanity

One who is so mentally deranged that he is incapable of having a criminal intent cannot be guilty of a crime or be held criminally responsible for his acts. In order for *insanity* to be a good defense, it must appear that the accused was insane at the time of the commission of the crime and not merely before or after the crime.

Mere mental weakness is not an excuse for criminal acts. When the defendant has a low order of intelligence but sufficient mental capacity to know that his act was wrong, he has no defense on this ground. The test used in most jurisdictions is whether the defendant was so unsound mentally at the time he committed the offense that he did not know the difference between right and wrong.

In some jurisdictions the courts have held that a person is not responsible for criminal acts if the jury finds that by reason of mental disease or defect he had lost the power to know right from wrong or had insane delusions or irresistible impulses to do wrongful acts. On the other hand, the courts of some states refuse to accept the "irresistible impulse" theory. In one leading case, the New York Court of Appeals said:

Whatever medical or scientific authority there may be for this view, it has not been accepted by courts of law. The vagueness and uncertainty of the inquiry which would be opened and the manifest danger of introducing the limitation claimed into the rule of responsibility, in cases of crime, may well cause courts to pause before assenting to it. Indulgence in evil passions weakens the restraining power of the will and conscience; and the rule suggested would be the cover for the commission of crime and its justification.

Alcohol and Drug Intoxication

Voluntary drunkenness is no defense for commission of a crime. If a person voluntarily becomes intoxicated and while in that condition commits a crime, he is responsible for his acts. However, in certain crimes a specific intent is an essential part of the crime and if the defendant was stupefied by the consumption of alcoholic beverages, he may not have had the specific intent necessary for commission of the crime. A state of drunkenness is not an excuse for a crime, but the defendant in that state may not have the mental capacity to form a deliberate intent. This situation should not be confused with one in which a person voluntarily becomes intoxicated for the purpose of committing the crime.

A person broods upon his unhappiness and gets drunk; in this condition he kills his wife. He probably would be acquitted by a jury if it feels he did not have the ability to plan a premeditated murder.

Another man first makes up his mind to kill his wife and then becomes drunk and commits the crime. He is likely to be found guilty of murder.

The use of drugs has resulted in court rulings similar to those involving alcoholic intoxication. Temporary insanity resulting from the voluntary use of drugs constitutes no defense to a criminal charge. On the other hand, mental incapacity caused by medicinal use of drugs may excuse the commission of what otherwise would constitute a criminal act.

CRIMINAL JURISDICTION, EXTRADITION, AND PLACE OF TRIAL

There are two kinds of *criminal jurisdiction*: first, the jurisdiction of the subject matter of the crime, that is, the power of the court to hear and determine the particular case; second, the jurisdiction over the person accused of the crime. Jurisdiction is necessary to a valid prosecution and conviction; if the court has no jurisdiction the conviction is a nullity. Thus, the question of prime importance to a criminal lawyer is whether or not a particular court has jurisdiction in his case.

Jurisdiction of Subject Matter

No state or sovereignty can enforce the penal laws of another county or punish offenses committed in another country. (For that reason, the legal profession has been shocked at the attempt of certain courts to punish international criminals for acts committed outside the jurisdiction of those courts.) The jurisdiction of particular courts to hear and determine crimes is determined by the constitution of each state. The statutes of the various states say that certain crimes shall be heard and determined in each level of courts. The particular offense, therefore, must be heard and determined by the court designated by the legislature.

State courts have exclusive jurisdiction in state offenses, and federal courts have exclusive jurisdiction in federal offenses. Sometimes the same act constitutes a violation of both state and federal laws, and state and federal courts have *concurring jurisdiction*.

Jurisdiction of Accused

Before a court can have personal jurisdiction of the accused, he must be in the custody of the court. The presence of the accused is essential to jurisdiction. The court has no jurisdiction to hear and determine the charge of crime unless the accused (1) is in its custody, (2) has been admitted to bail, or (3) has consented to the jurisdiction. In other words, the jurisdiction of a court to try and punish one accused of a crime cannot be acquired by mere assertion or the filing of a complaint or indictment. There is no excuse for failure to bring the prisoner before the court so that the court may have custody of him. It has been held that when the accused is a prisoner in a state penitentiary, the mere filing of an indictment against him does not give the court jurisdiction of the new offense.

Extradition

Extradition is the surrender by one state or nation to another of an individual accused of a criminal offense. The average case of extradition in the United States arises between various states. The right of a foreign power to demand extradition exists only when that right is given by treaty. In the absence of a treaty the United States will not surrender a fugitive criminal to a foreign government.

The right of extradition between states is controlled by article IV, section 2, of the federal Constitution, which provides "that a person charged in any state with treason, felony, or other crime, who shall flee from justice, and be found in another state, shall on demand of the executive authority of the state from which he fled be delivered up, to be removed to the state having jurisdiction of the crime." The responsibility for demanding extradition of a person charged with a crime and the duty to deliver up such a person on proper command are vested in the governors of the states involved.

Generally, a person may be extradited only when he is a "fugitive from justice," who has been charged with a crime in one state and has left that state and is found in another state. Many court decisions have involved the question of whether a person was knowingly running away from a crime. The courts have held that when a person leaves the state where he is charged with a crime, it is immaterial what his purpose or motive is for leaving the state; he will usually be considered a fugitive and will be returned to the state where he is charged with the crime.

In seeking the return of a fugitive from justice, the governor of the prosecuting state sends a requisition to the governor of the asylum state requesting that the fugitive be delivered up. The requisition must be accompanied by a copy of papers charging the person with a crime. For example, when the alleged fugitive has been indicted, there must be a copy of the grand jury's indictment or a copy of the magistrate's warrant seeking the arrest of the alleged criminal. Proceedings are held before the governor of the state to which the alleged criminal has fled. Before sending the accused person back to the state seeking his extradition, the governor must first determine that the person demanded has been legally charged with a crime and is a fugitive from justice.

Place of Trial (Venue)

Venue, an old common-law term still in use in modern court practice, has been defined as the locality where the offense is triable; in criminal matters it means the locality (ordinarily the county) where the criminal act is alleged to have occurred. When the offense consists of the omission of an act, venue is usually the locality where the act should have been performed. There is a certain amount of flexibility in the rules of venue for the prosecution of crimes; some of this is indicated in the following examples of particular crimes:

The venue of a prosecution for abandonment or nonsupport of a wife or child is the place where the abandonment occurred or where the duty to support should have been performed.

The crime of kidnapping is properly laid in the county where the victim is seized even though he is carried into another county.

The crime of bigamy is triable in the county where the bigamous marriage took place, although some statutes provide that the bigamist may be tried in the county where he or she resides or where the parties afterward reside.

Bribery may be triable in the county where the offer is made or accepted.

Burglary must be prosecuted in the county where the breaking and entering took place, not in the county where the property was carried.

The crime of robbery is triable in the county where the property was originally taken.

When one steals property, he may be prosecuted for larceny in the county where he stole the property or where he brought it.

The crime of receiving stolen goods may be prosecuted in the county where the property was received.

Venues for the crimes of conspiracy and monopolies may be tried either in the county where the conspiracy was entered into or where the further acts of the conspirators took place.

Embezzlement may be tried in the county where the property was taken or in the county where the accused was supposed to have accounted for the embezzled property.

The crime of escape from imprisonment must generally be prosecuted in the county where the escape occurred although in some states the convict may be tried in any county of the state.

The venue of a prosecution for extortion is the county where the offense was committed.

The trial of the crime of obtaining money or property under false pretenses should be tried in the county where the money or property was obtained.

Forgery must be prosecuted in the county where the forgery was committed.

The general rule is that the crime of homicide is prosecuted in the county where the crime was committed, but in some states it is prosecuted at the place where death occurred.

The venue in a criminal prosecution may be changed only on the application of the accused. Changing the place of trial is within the sound discretion of the court. Most state laws permit a court to grant the accused a change of venue when it seems necessary in order to secure an impartial and fair trial for him. Disqualification or prejudice on the part of the judge is ground for a change. Other grounds include local prejudice and inability to obtain a fair jury. In order to justify a change of venue, the prejudice must be against the accused and exist throughout the entire locality; for instance, newspaper articles and other means of public communication may have so aroused public hostility as to preclude a fair trial for the accused.

PLEA BARGAINING

Most criminal cases are never tried. They are disposed of before trial because either the defendant pleads guilty or the case is dismissed. Plea bargaining plays a large role in the disposition of criminal cases. In the year 1970 it occurred in 90 percent of all criminal cases disposed of in New York City. In plea bargaining the accused defendant, on the advice of his lawyer and the consent of the prosecuting attorney, pleads guilty to a lesser crime than that with which he was originally charged.

A person is charged with a crime of burglary for which he might expect a sentence of five to ten years in jail. After discussion with his attorney, the defendant pleads guilty to the lesser crime of larceny, for which the likely sentence would be two years.

Many people object to plea bargaining. The subject is debated regularly by lawyers, professors, criminologists, and others, but there is little dispute as to the importance of plea bargaining in our criminal justice system. Our courts are understaffed and simply cannot resort to trials to dispose of all the indictments that are handed out by grand juries. For example, in 1967 there were 20,231 felony indictments in New York City alone. At best only 4,000 of these felony charges could be tried. The rest had to be handled by dismissal or guilty pleas. Former Chief Justice of the United States Supreme Court Earl Warren said, "Plea discussions leading to disposition of cases are indispensable to any rational administration of criminal cases."

CONSTITUTIONAL AND COMMON-LAW PROTECTION OF ALLEGED CRIMINALS

Unthinking persons today claim that there are too many safeguards for the protection of criminals. They overlook the fact that such safeguards also protect the innocent. The safeguards have come down to us through the English common law (they were wrested

from King John at Runnymede and were included in the Magna
Carta for the protection of Englishmen), and several of them are
explicitly stated in the Constitution of the United States.

Presumption of Innocence

It is a fundamental principle of American criminal law that a
person charged with the commission of crime is presumed to be innocent until proven guilty. The *presumption of innocence* extends to
every person accused of a crime.

The presumption of innocence cannot be changed into a presumption of guilt even if the accused fails to testify or call witnesses
to the stand. An accused person does not have to take the stand in
his own behalf and the prosecuting officer may not comment to the
jury on his failure to do so.

Necessity for Arraignment and Plea

A person accused of a crime is *arraigned* by being called to the
bar of the court to answer the accusations contained in an indictment or other form of criminal charge. The accused must be called
by name and definitely identified. The indictment or charge must be
read to him, he must be advised of his rights, and he must make a
plea of guilty or not guilty.

In some jurisdictions, the person accused of a crime may make a
plea of nolo contendere, which means that he will not dispute the
prosecuting authority. *Nolo contendere* is considered an implied
confession of guilt for the purpose of the case only and is accepted as
equivalent to a plea of guilty.

Personal Presence of the Accused

It is essential to a valid trial and the conviction of a defendant
for a felony that he be personally present, not only when he is arraigned but also at every subsequent stage of the trial. The same is
true in misdemeanor cases when the punishment may be imprisonment. In some states, when the punishment is by fine only, the trial
may be held in the defendant's absence.

Speedy Trial

A *speedy trial* is another fundamental constitutional right guaranteed to all persons accused of crime. The right to a speedy trial is

intended to avoid oppression and to prevent delays, to relieve the accused of the hardship of being held in jail indefinitely, the anxiety of a pending prosecution, and the resulting public suspicion. A speedy trial is one which can be had as soon as the prosecution with reasonable diligence can prepare for trial.

The courts have never been able to devise a single test to determine what amounts to undue delay. In certain cases a trial held within six months has been held to be a speedy one, while in other cases the same period of time has been held to be excessive and in violation of the accused's rights and sufficient justification to grant a discharge of the accused on denial of his right for a speedy trial. It all depends on how complicated the case is.

Time Limits for Commencing Criminal Proceedings

There is no time limit within which prosecution for murder must be commenced. It may be begun at any time after the murder. The same situation exists in various states for kidnapping and other crimes.

Time limits for beginning other criminal actions vary in the fifty states. In some states prosecution for any misdemeanor must be commenced within two years after its commission and within five years for more serious crimes. In some places, when the accused has been absent from the state of jurisdiction, the time limit for prosecution becomes operable only after his return to the state. If the defendant departs from the state or remains within the state under a false name after the crime is committed, the time of his absence or of such residence within a state under a false name is not part of the time limit for the commencement of the prosecution. To determine whether it has been commenced within the proper time limit, the prosecution is said to have begun when an information, charging the commission of the crime, is laid before a magistrate and a warrant is issued by him or when an indictment is duly presented by a grand jury in open court.

Double Jeopardy

The word *jeopardy* means the danger of conviction and punishment which an accused in a criminal action incurs when he is charged with a crime. The prohibition against *double jeopardy* is a sacred principle of criminal law. It was incorporated into the Fifth Amendment to the Constitution of the United States, which states that no person "shall be subject for the same offense to be twice put in jeopardy of life or limb." The constitutions of nearly all the states contain similar provisions.

Simply applied, the rule is that once a person is acquitted or has paid the penalty for his crime, he may not thereafter be arrested for the same crime. The rule has no application to civil proceedings, such as deportation, contempt of court, prosecutions for abandonment or failure to support children, proceedings under motor vehicle laws to revoke or suspend licenses, and other proceedings for forfeiture, penalties, and damages. When a number of offenses grow out of the same criminal act or the act seems to be comprised of a sequence of criminal acts, it is a highly technical matter to determine whether the accused is being tried for several crimes or being tried for one several times—being put in double jeopardy in violation of his constitutional rights.

Miranda Rules

The United States Supreme Court has laid down rules for in custody interrogation by the police of those suspected of crime. The suspect must be advised before interrogation (1) that he has a right to remain silent, (2) that anything he says may be used against him, (3) that he has a right to have present an attorney during the questioning, and (4) that if he has no money to pay for a lawyer, he has a right to a lawyer without charge. These warnings to be given by the police to a person suspected of a crime have become known as "Miranda warnings" because they were promulgated by the United States Supreme Court in the case of *Miranda* v. *Arizona*. If the fourfold warnings are not given, then no evidence may be given in court of any admissions or confession made by the prisoner as a result of police interrogation.

Students of the Supreme Court say that there are signs that the Court is swinging away from the doctrine of *Miranda* v. *Arizona*. But one cannot predict a position that might be taken by the Supreme Court on the subject of constitutional safeguards for the protection of those accused of crime.

CRIMINAL LAWS VOID FOR VAGUENESS

Some courts hold that state laws which are vague and indefinite invite arbitrary police action and are unconstitutional.

Laws in the states of New York, Pennsylvania, and Colorado making vagrancy a crime were struck down by the courts of those states because the legislatures did not sufficiently define what constituted vagrancy.

In Philadelphia, after a series of mass arrests in Rittenhouse Park, a gathering place for hippies and other undesirables, a United States district court ruled that the obvious motive for the arrests had been to clear hippies from the area and that mass arrests, directed at the status of the arrestees rather than at criminal actions, were illegal.

When rioters were arrested in Washington, D. C., one of the defendants appealed, claiming that such statutory terms as "public disturbance," "tumultuous and violent conduct," and "grave danger of damage or injury" did not provide an "ascertainable standard" by which to judge conduct and that the statute should be held void for vagueness. By a two to one decision the court held that the statute was not ambiguous and that few people would not recognize a riot if they saw one. One of the federal judges dissented, holding that a person might be reluctant to exercise his constitutional right of peaceful assembly for fear of being charged with aiding a riot if the demonstration became violent.

An Oregon court held that a law making it a crime to encourage, cause, or contribute to the delinquency of a minor was unconstitutionally vague since the causes of delinquency are broad and uncertain.

By a five to four decision the United States Supreme Court in *Coats* v. *Cincinnati* held a loitering ordinance unconstitutional for vagueness. The ordinance made it criminal for "three or more persons" to assemble on any sidewalk and "conduct themselves in a manner annoying to persons passing by."

POLICE INVESTIGATION AND ACTIVITIES

The courts continue to restrict police activities that are claimed to infringe on the constitutional rights of those charged with crime.

Electronic Surveillance (Bugging)

A man was convicted of narcotics violations largely on the basis of conversations transmitted to law enforcement agents by a device concealed on the person of an informer. A United States court of appeals (7th circuit) reversed the conviction on the ground that the defendant's "reasonable expectations of privacy" were violated.

Search and Seizure

Mr. Chimel was arrested at his home, under an arrest warrant. Despite Chimel's objections, police conducted a one-hour search of his home and found various items which were used against him as evidence on his trial. The United States Supreme Court reversed his conviction, holding that the mere arrest of an individual at his home does not give police the right to search the entire house. A valid search warrant is necessary.

TRIAL PROCEDURES

Six-Member Jury

For years civil cases have been tried before six members, but criminal cases have not. In 1970, however, the United States Supreme Court overruled an 1898 decision and held that twelve jury members were not required under the Constitution. All that is required is that the number of jurors "be large enough to promote group deliberation and a fair possibility for obtaining a representative cross-section of the community."

Unanimous Jury Verdict

In landmark cases in 1972 the Supreme Court held in two five to four decisions that unanimous verdicts are not required for conviction in state criminal courts.

Disruptive Tactics in Court

Under the United States Constitution, one accused of a crime has the right to confront and cross-examine his accusers and the witnesses against him. This is often referred to as the "right of confrontation." For a time there was much confusion and doubt as to what trial judges should do with defendants who threatened and abused judges and tried to break up court proceedings. Some feared that if they were bound and gagged or put behind jail bars they might be deprived of their right to be present at the trial at all times (the right of confrontation).

The United States Supreme Court in deciding an Illinois case in 1970 gave courts the tools to maintain order and decorum in the courtroom. The Court outlined three methods of handling obstreperous defendants:

1. They could be bound and gagged and remain present at the trial. (This remedy to be used only as a last resort because it would be an affront to the dignity of the court.)
2. The trial court could cite an unruly defendant for criminal contempt and imprison him, discontinuing the trial until such time as the

defendant promised to behave. (This method has its disadvantages because it may cause the very delay which an unruly defendant is seeking.)

3. The disruptive defendant may be excluded from the courtroom while the trial continues. (Before his removal he must be warned that his continued misconduct will result in his waiving his right to be present in the courtroom.)

20
Sales

A *sale* is a contract by which one party (the *seller*) transfers property for a valuable consideration to another (the *buyer*). Since a sale is a contract the general rules of the law of contracts apply to sale transactions except where modified by the Uniform Commercial Code, which has been adopted in every state except Louisiana.

In an *executed sale* (a complete sale, one in which nothing remains to be done by either party to complete the transfer of title to the property) or an *executory sale* (an incomplete sale, one in which something remains to be done by either party to complete the transfer of title), there must be (1) parties capable of entering into the contract of sale, (2) consideration, (3) valid subject matter (existing goods or goods likely to exist), and (4) mutual assent (with intent to pass title).

Contracts of sale and contracts to sell goods valued at more than a specified amount must be in writing. This is a part of the Statute of Frauds. The written contract may be a formal agreement or just a written memorandum embodying the terms and signed by the party to be charged. When a written contract does not exist, the contract to sell may still be enforceable if the buyer (1) accepts part of the goods or (2) pays a deposit on the purchase price.

In addition to the law of contracts, the Uniform Commercial Code plays an important part in everyday commercial transactions. Questions of interpretation of sales transactions are among those covered by these laws: Who owns goods while they are in shipment? If the goods are destroyed in shipment, who stands the loss? If a person in New York makes a contract to buy goods in California, when does the title pass? When does the buyer become the owner? What responsibility does the seller take when he sells goods? What does he warrant, if he says nothing about the warranty? What are the remedies of an unpaid seller? May he stop goods in transit? May he take back the goods? When may he rescind the contract? What are the remedies of the buyer, if the goods are not as represented or are not delivered?

The Uniform Commercial Code covers not only the law of sales but also negotiable instruments and nearly all other phases of commercial transactions. Louisiana, because of its French heritage, follows the civil law in sales contracts. Because the Uniform Commercial Code is in effect in all other states and the District of Columbia, the information in this chapter (unless otherwise noted) is based on that law and is applicable only to the sale of personal property.

TRANSFER OF TITLE TO GOODS

A *bill of sale* is a written instrument evidencing the transfer of title to property. A *document of title to goods* (chattels and property other than intangibles or money) is any bill of lading, dock warrant, warehouse receipt, or order for the *delivery* (voluntary transfer of possession from one person to another) of goods. There are two kinds of goods: *Specific goods* are those identified and agreed on at the time of sale or when the contract to sell is made. Any specimen or part of *fungible goods* may be used as the equivalent of another specimen or part in the satisfaction of an obligation; for example, a storage bin of oats may be referred to as fungible goods, because every bushel of oats is the same as every other bushel of oats in the same bin.

When Title Passes

Under the Uniform Sales Act, which was the predecessor to that portion of the Uniform Commercial Code dealing with sales, title to specific goods passed to the buyer at such time as the parties intended. Under the Uniform Commercial Code, passage of title does not depend entirely upon the intention of the parties; in the Code, title to goods cannot pass before the goods are identified as being part of the contract.

Goods may be identified to a contract at any time and in any manner explicitly agreed to by the parties. In the absence of an explicit agreement, identification occurs: (a) when the contract is made if it is for the sale of goods already existing and described, or (b) if the contract is for the sale of future goods, then when the goods are shipped, marked, or otherwise designated by the seller as goods to which the contract refers.

Fox visits the Proctor Lumber Company, selects the quality of lumber he wishes to buy, and places an order for it. As the goods are already existing and described at the time the contract is made, title passes to Fox at that time.

The Simplified Vacuum Company agrees to sell 100 vacuum cleaners to the Bradley Distributing Co. and agrees to hold the cleaners in its warehouse for 60 days. As soon as Simplified ships the cleaners or otherwise designates the specific cleaners as the ones covered by the contract, title to the cleaners passes to Bradley.

The parties are free to agree when title transfers to existing goods. In the absence of an explicit agreement, title passes at the time and place at which the seller completes physical delivery of the goods. Of course, the acts of the seller which complete physical delivery will vary according to the contract involved in the transaction. Where the contract requires the seller to ship goods but does not require him to deliver them at a destination, title passes to the buyer at the time and place of shipment. On the other hand, if the contract requires delivery at a destination, title passes on tender of the goods there.

The Smith Importing Company purchases 100 tons of hemp from the Peru Exporting Company with the understanding that the exporting company would ship the hemp by boat. Since the contract did not require the exporting company to deliver the goods at a particular destination, title passes to the Smith Importing Company on shipment.

The Bargain Department Store ordered 10 gross of toy trucks to be shipped for the Christmas trade, instructing the manufacturer to have the trucks delivered to its store in Albany, New York. Title to the trucks passes to the department store when the manufacturer tenders delivery of them in Albany.

Risk of Loss

Under the Uniform Sales Act the problem of determining whether the buyer or seller was required to bear the loss of goods that were lost or destroyed in transit was usually solved by determining which party had title to the goods. The Uniform Commercial Code has updated the former rules by taking into consideration the actual practices of modern merchants and their more sophisticated contracts.

The five main rules are:

1. Where the contract requires or authorizes the seller to ship goods by carrier, but does not provide for delivery of the goods at a particular destination, the risk of loss passes to the buyer on the delivery of the goods to the carrier.

The Dexter Card Company contracted to buy 1,000 rolls of paper from the English Paper Company to be used in several of Dexter's plants. The contract required English to ship the paper by carrier but was silent as to the particular destination. A truck load of paper was destroyed by fire en route to one of Dexter's plants. Dexter would have to bear the loss because the goods had been delivered to the carrier.

2. Where the contract requires the seller to deliver the goods at a particular destination, the risk of loss passes to the buyer when the goods reach that destination.

Mr. Wilson purchased a boat from the Hydro Boat Co. with the understanding that Hydro would have to ship the boat to his cottage at Silver Lake, New York. The boat was destroyed in an accident en route. Hydro would bear the loss because the boat had not yet reached its destination.

3. When goods are held by a bailee to be delivered without being moved, the risk of loss passes to the buyer upon his receipt of a negotiable instrument of title or upon an acknowledgment on the part of the bailee of the buyer's right to possession.

Samuels owned 1,000 boxes of bookends that were stored in the Ajax Warehouse. Edwards entered into an agreement with Samuels to purchase the bookends, but Edwards wanted them to remain stored. Samuels, who had a warehouse receipt, indorsed it and gave it to Edwards. A few days later the warehouse was destroyed by fire. The risk of loss would be on Edwards because he had received a negotiable instrument of title, the warehouse receipt.

4. When the seller is a merchant (defined in the statute as a person who in his business normally deals with the type of goods sold) and is in possession of the goods, and the contract does not require or authorize shipment by a carrier, the risk of loss passes to the buyer when the buyer takes physical possession of the goods.

Kearse owns an appliance store specializing in household items, such as stoves, refrigerators and freezers. Bullock decides to buy a stove and negotiates a deal. It is agreed that Bullock will return in three days to pick up the stove and take it home. Later that day there is an explosion in the store which destroys the stove. Bullock will not have to bear the loss because Kearse is a merchant who still had possession of the stove at the time of the loss.

5. When the seller is not a merchant (as defined above) and is in possession of the goods, and the contract does not require or authorize shipment by a carrier, the risk of loss passes to the buyer when the seller tenders delivery of the goods to the buyer.

Everett, a policeman, agrees to sell his used refrigerator to his neighbor Bertram. They agree that Bertram, as part of the deal, must move the refrigerator, which is located in Everett's garage. Everett offers to let Bertram have the refrigerator at the time of the deal, but Bertram wanted to wait a few days. Before Bertram got around to hauling the refrigerator home, it was destroyed by fire. The buyer would have to bear the risk of loss because the seller was not a merchant and had tendered delivery of the goods.

Ineffectual Transfer

When goods are sold by a person not the owner, the buyer ordinarily acquires no better title to the goods than the seller had. Title, like a stream, cannot rise higher than its source.

Professional auto thieves steal an automobile from Preston, substitute new motor and model numbers, and sell the automobile to Miller. Ownership of the automobile remains with Preston, and Miller does not get good title to it.

The question often arises: How does a bona fide purchaser who has no notice of any defect in title acquire ownership of the property? The answer is: When he can prove the owner led him to believe that he was getting good title.

The mere fact that the owner turns possession of goods over to a third person does not mean that he has clothed that third person with authority to sell. For instance, when goods are stored with a warehouseman and the warehouseman wrongfully sells them to a bona fide purchaser, the bona fide purchaser does not acquire good title.

On the other hand, when the owner clothes an agent or other third person with the apparent right to sell, the owner is precluded from asserting his claim against a bona fide purchaser.

Hamilton, residing in California, employed Carmichael as his agent to enter into a contract for and superintend the building of an expensive power boat in New York City and furnished him with funds for that purpose. Hamilton advised Carmichael that he wanted the ownership of the boat kept a secret and suggested to Carmichael that if anyone asked him who was the real owner of the boat that he, Carmichael, could say that he was. Hamilton said to Carmichael, "In any event, don't let people know that I am the real owner of this boat." Carmichael got into a squabble with Hamilton and claimed Hamilton owed him money. Hamilton denied this. Carmichael sold the boat to Forrest, representing himself as the true owner. Under such circumstances, even though Carmichael had no real title to transfer, Forrest as a bona fide purchaser became the owner because Hamilton had clothed Carmichael with apparent title to the boat.

WARRANTIES

A warranty grows out of a contract of sale; there can be no warranty without a sale. A *warranty* is a statement or representation made by the seller (of personal property), promising that certain facts are or shall be as he represents them. There are two kinds of warranties, express and implied. A warranty should not be confused with other independent agreements between sellers and buyers, such as a seller's agreement to do certain things with respect to the goods sold.

If the statements or representations which make up the warranty are false and the buyer is harmed by reason of such falsity, the seller is said to be guilty of a *breach of warranty*, or breach of contract. Then the buyer may sue the seller for his damages. There is a distinction between claims for breach of warranty and claims arising out of misrepresentation, deceit, and fraud. The seller may be innocently liable for a breach of warranty. The goods may not measure up to what he thought they were. However, in the case of misrepresentation or fraud or deceit, there is an element of wrongdoing which does not necessarily exist in the case of a breach of warranty.

Warranty of Title

The Uniform Commercial Code provides that there is in every contract for the sale of goods a warranty by the seller that:

1. the title conveyed shall be good, and its transfer rightful; and
2. the goods shall be free from liens or encumbrances held by other people.

The following examples illustrate warranties of title:

Penny buys an automobile from Crocker, who had purchased the car in good faith from a dealer and did not know that the registration transfer had been forged and that the car was a stolen vehicle. The rightful owner of the car proves it was stolen from him and takes possession from Penny. Penny then sues and recovers judgment against Crocker because, even though Crocker had acted in good faith, he had warranted to Penny that he was the owner and had a right to sell when, in fact, he did not have such right.

Sanborn buys "distress" merchandise consisting of new stoves, refrigerators, and washing machines from a merchant "going out of business." He resells the refrigerators to the McClure Furniture Company. It develops that the original owner had given a chattel mortgage on the refrigerators to the Faithful Trust Company to secure a bank loan. The Faithful Trust Company repossesses the refrigerators from McClure Furniture Company. Sanborn, having warranted that the refrigerators were free from any lien or encumbrance, becomes liable to the McClure Furniture Company for the value of the refrigerators.

Express Warranty

An *express warranty* is a statement of fact or a promise by the seller phrased to induce the buyer to purchase the goods. Examples of express warranties follow:

A claim that a radio could pick up any station in Europe
A statement that seed peas would "pick 4 or 5 days earlier than other seed on the market"
A claim that a derrick would require a load of 250 tons to break it
A statement that a horse was not lame

The law also says that a seller expressly warrants that the bulk of goods shall correspond to any description of the goods given by the seller or to the quality of any sample or model which was used in arriving at the contract. For example:

The Henry Printing Company submitted a sample of printing and by accident used alkali-proof ink, which the purchaser, the Stone Manufacturing Co., required. The same alkali-proof ink was used in the first order but not in the second and third orders. The Henry Printing Company was bound by the sample submitted and was liable to the Stone Manufacturing Company for its failure to print the remaining orders in the same ink.

Mere "puffing" or dealer's talk may be just opinion and does not constitute an express warranty. Such puffing includes:

Claims that an article was "unsurpassed and unsurpassable"
A claim that a suit of clothes "will wear like iron"
A statement that certain books "were very fine reading literature, fit for anybody to read"
A statement that certain roses came from "very fine stock"
A claim that a horse was "well-broken and will fill the bill"

The old rule of *caveat emptor* ("let the buyer beware") has been largely replaced, first, by the Uniform Commercial Code and, second, by the tendency of the courts to enlarge the responsibilities of the seller.

Implied Warranty

In the average case warranty does not have to be spelled out because, even though silent on the subject of warranties, a seller is deemed to have made a statement or promise amounting to an *implied warranty*. According to the Uniform Commercial Code there are two kinds of implied warranties—(1) of merchantability and (2) of fitness for particular purpose.

Implied Warranty of Merchantability Where the seller is a merchant, that is, a person who normally deals with the type of goods sold, there is implied a warranty that the goods shall be merchantable. In order to be merchantable, such goods must meet the following tests:

1. pass without "objection in the trade" under the contract description;
2. be of fair average quality within the description in the case of fungible goods;
3. be fit for the ordinary purposes for which such goods are used;
4. run of even kind, quality, and quantity when goods are purchased in units;
5. be adequately contained, packaged, and labeled as the agreement may require;
6. conform to any promises which may be on the container or label.

The sale of food or drink to be consumed either on the premises or elsewhere gives rise to an implied warranty of merchantability.

Alexander buys a can of crabmeat from the Singer Delicatessen Company. He brings the can home and makes a crabmeat salad that makes him sick. An analysis discloses that the crabmeat was contaminated and unfit for human consumption. He presents to the Singer Delicatessen Company his hospital and doctor bills and claims for lost wages because of his illness. The delicatessen company says, "Sorry, we bought it from one of the country's leading distributors, and we shouldn't be liable." Alexander sues. The court holds that the Singer Delicatessen Company was responsible under its implied warranty that the food was fit for human consumption. The delicatessen company has a remedy: It can file a claim against the distributor that sold it the canned goods. In such case, the distributor could in turn bring a cross-suit against the manufacturer.

Miss Howard was made sick when she ate dessert served to her by the Excelsior Restaurant. The restaurant claimed that it had taken all necessary precautions and disclaimed negligence. Miss Howard, however, was able to prove that there was ground glass in the food and that it made her ill. The court held that negligence is not the test in warranty cases and that when foreign objects get in the food, the food is not fit for human consumption. The court ruled in Miss Howard's favor.

Implied Warranty of Fitness for Particular Purpose Where the seller of goods at the time of making the contract has reason to know any particular purpose for which the goods are required and also has reason to know that the buyer is relying on the seller's skill to select or furnish suitable goods, there arises an implied warranty that the goods shall be fit for such purpose.

Madigan is in the process of refinishing an antique maple table. He goes to the Acme Paint Store and explains to the owner that he needs a sealer, but doesn't know what kind to buy. The owner picks out a can of sealer and sells it to Madigan. If the sealer doesn't work, there would be a breach of an implied warranty of fitness for a particular purpose because the seller knew the particular purpose for which the sealer was to be used and also knew that Madigan was relying on his skill to select the proper sealer.

REMEDIES IN SALES CONTRACTS

The buyer and the seller are parties to a contract and hence have certain contractual obligations toward each other. If either the buyer or the seller fails to live up to the contract of sale, the other party has the ordinary legal remedies which every party to a contract has and, in addition, has certain special remedies which are tailored especially to sales.

Remedies of the Seller

The seller may protect himself in a number of ways. He may (1) part with title and retain possession of goods until paid, (2) part with possession and retain title, or (3) he may part with both title and possession before payment.

In any event, once a seller has elected to pursue one remedy, he may not thereafter resort to another inconsistent remedy. For example, it would be inconsistent for a seller to bring an action for a rescision of the contract of sale and at the same time act as if there had been no rescision and bring an action for the full purchase price.

Seller's Lien   Unless there is a specific contract to extend credit to the buyer, the seller who retains possession of goods has a lien for the purchase price. This simply means that the seller can hold onto the goods until the purchase price is paid.

Stoppage in Transit   If the buyer becomes insolvent and the seller has turned the goods over to a common carrier for transportation to the buyer, the seller may stop the goods in transit. As long as the goods are in transit he may retake possession and may retain them until the purchase price is paid.

Resale   If the original buyer without just cause refuses to receive and pay for the goods, the seller who is in possession of the goods may, as one of his remedies, resell them. When the seller resells on the default of the buyer, he is also entitled to recover his damages for breach of contract, that is, the difference between the contract price and the price realized at the resale.

Action for the Purchase Price When goods have been delivered to the buyer and title has passed to him, the remedy of the unpaid seller is generally limited to bringing an action for the price or value of the goods.

Action for Damages The seller generally has a right of action for damages when the buyer has failed to live up to his obligation under the contract. In order to be entitled to maintain an action for damages for the buyer's breach of contract, the seller must show his performance of the contract or his offer or readiness to perform. Unless it can be shown that the buyer notified the seller in advance that he would not take the goods or similarly indicated that he was going to breach the contract, the seller in order to recover damages either must have delivered the goods or tendered an offer of delivery. The purpose of the law in awarding damages to a seller for the buyer's breach of contract is to put the seller in the same position as he would have been in had the buyer performed his contract.

Broadly speaking, the measure of damage is the loss which the seller sustains by reason of the breach when the buyer refuses to accept and pay for goods which are offered to him. The seller's legal damages generally, when there is an available market for the goods, is the difference between the contract price and the current market price at the time when the goods were to be delivered and paid for. Obviously, under such circumstances, the seller is not entitled to recover the full contract price. For example:

The ABC Company agrees to buy wool and yarn from the Triple Z Yarn Company at a price of thirty cents a pound and then refuses to accept the goods. The Triple Z Yarn Company, in suing for damages for the ABC Company's breach of contract, may if the market price has dropped to twenty-five cents a pound recover the difference between the contract price of thirty cents and the market price of twenty-five cents, namely, five cents a pound.

Rescision When the goods have not been delivered to the buyer and the buyer has repudiated the sale or has indicated or demonstrated his inability to perform his obligations under the sale or has otherwise breached the contract of sale, the seller may totally rescind the contract of sale by giving notice to the buyer. In addition, when there is fraud on the part of the buyer, the seller has the option of rescinding and disaffirming the contract of sale and recovering the property or affirming the contract of sale and suing for the price or for damages.

Remedies of the Buyer

In the breach of an ordinary contract, the buyer, as well as the seller, is given special remedies (in addition to those afforded by law). Under certain circumstances the buyer may keep the goods and sue for damages arising out of the seller's breach of the contract, under other circumstances he may rescind the contract, and in other cases he may recover the purchase price.

Suit for Damages When the seller neglects to or refuses to deliver goods, the buyer may maintain an action against the seller for damages. Damages usually amount to approximately the loss naturally resulting from the seller's breach of contract. When there is an available market for the goods in question, damages are ordinarily the difference between the contract price and the market or current price of the goods at the time when the goods should have been delivered.

The April Department Store entered into a contract with the Georgia Mills to purchase 5,000 yards of cotton goods at 10 cents a yard to be delivered at the department store on June 1. Because the Georgia Mills defaults in the delivery of the cotton, the April Department Store is forced to buy the cotton goods in the open market at 20 cents a yard. The April Department Store may sue the Georgia Mills for breach of contract and recover the difference between the contract price of 10 cents a yard and the market price of 20 cents a yard, or $500 damages.

Under the Uniform Commercial Code a buyer is afforded the option to fix the market value by purchasing substitute goods. His monetary damages will then be measured as the difference between the contract price and the cost of these substitute goods. This is known as "covering."

Specific Performance The Uniform Commercial Code provides that when the seller breaks his contract by refusing to deliver the goods specified a court of equity may, if it thinks fit, direct *specific performance* of the contract; that is, the court may require the seller to deliver the goods. Under the previous law this remedy was rarely granted as a court of equity would require specific performance of a contract only if the goods are so unique or unusual that the simple remedy for damages would be a gross injustice.

Manley, collector of rare jewels, makes a contract with the R. Importing Company to purchase from them a collection of rare emerald stones for $600,000. The contract was formally signed and Manley makes a payment of $50,000. R. Importing Company then discovers that it can sell the stones for $750,000 to another customer and declines to make the sale to Manley. Manley demonstrates to a court of equity that there is no other similar collection of emeralds available and that damages would not be adequate compensation. Thus, the court of equity requires the R. Importing Company to comply with its contract and deliver the jewels to Manley on his payment of the balance of the purchase price.

The remedy of specific performance is substantially modified by the Uniform Commercial Code. Under this law, a buyer is entitled to specific performance if the goods are unique, or in other proper circumstances. The flexibility of this test will probably encourage courts to look beyond the traditional tests and to exercise their discretion under general equitable principles.

Rescission and Other Remedies In the event of the seller's fraud or default, the buyer may elect to rescind the contract (refuse to accept the goods) and sue for damages. When title to the goods has passed to the buyer and the seller wrongfully neglects or refuses to deliver the goods, the buyer may maintain an action against the seller for wrongfully converting or withholding the goods and may even maintain an action for *replevin* (an action to recover possession of the goods).

Breach of Warranty When the seller commits breach of warranty, the buyer may act in *one* of the following three ways:

1. He may accept or may keep the goods and maintain an action against the seller for damages for breach of warranty (or if the purchase price has not been paid, decline to pay it).
2. He may refuse to accept the goods if title therein has not passed and maintain an action against the seller for damages for breach of warranty.
3. He may rescind the contract of sale and may refuse to receive the goods or, if the goods have already been received, return them or offer to return them to the seller and sue to recover the price or any part of it that has been paid.

When the buyer elects to claim one of these remedies, he cannot thereafter change his mind and claim another remedy.

If the buyer knew of the breach of warranty when he accepted the goods or if he failed to notify the seller of it within a reasonable time, he cannot rescind the sale. Furthermore, if he fails to return the goods to the seller in substantially as good condition as the property was in when transferred to the buyer, he cannot rescind the sale. On the other hand, if deterioration or injury to the goods is caused by the breach of warranty, deterioration or injury shall not prevent the buyer from returning or offering to return the goods to the seller and rescinding the sale.

When a buyer of carpeting knew at the time of purchase that carpet dyes were not color fast, he may not thereafter claim a breach of warranty and sue to recover the purchase price or rescind the contract.

In a similar case, when Easter hats were delivered in February and held for thirty-six days after delivery and thereafter were returned to the seller on the ground that the hats were defective, the court held that the retention of Easter hats for thirty-six days constituted a waiver of the right to rescind by reason of breach of warranty.

CONDITIONAL SALES CONTRACTS

A *conditional sale* is a contract for the sale of personal property; under this type of contract the goods are delivered to the buyer (he takes possession of them), but the title is retained by the seller until the payment of the purchase price. Installment sales of merchandise, whether it be clothing or household goods or automobiles, play an important part in our economy today. In an installment plan sale, the seller, by means of a conditional sales contract, receives only a small down payment, but he is protected until the entire balance of the purchase is paid. His property rights in the article sold are protected against others who have no actual personal knowledge of the transaction.

Under the Uniform Commercial Code, all agreements which create or provide for a security interest in personal property are called "security agreements." Where a seller retains a security interest to secure all or part of the purchase price of an article (such as in the case of a conditional sales contract or chattel mortgage), the Code defines such interest as a "purchase-money security interest." Thus, the distinctions between a conditional sales contract and a chattel mortgage are no longer of great importance.

Filing the Conditional Sales Contract

Conditional sales contracts are used most frequently for the purchase of goods that may be classified as consumer goods. Under the Code, consumer goods are defined as those used or bought for use primarily for personal, family, or household purposes. Examples would be stoves, refrigerators, clothing, and automobiles. Except in the case of automobiles, purchase-money security interests in consumer goods do not have to be filed in order to be effective.

The Beauty Furniture Company sells a suite of living room furniture to Slitt on a conditional sales contract whereby Slitt pays $10 down and the balance in 40 installments of $10 a week. The Beauty Furniture Company does not file the contract. Six months thereafter, Slitt is in need of money and sells the furniture to Canyon, who moves it into his house. The Beauty Furniture Company goes to Canyon and says, "Sorry, this furniture is not paid for; it is ours." Canyon takes the matter to court only to learn that the Beauty Furniture Company may repossess the furniture and sell it.

In those circumstances where filing is required, the failure to file the security interest will render it void when any purchaser from or creditor of a buyer acquires the property without notice of the seller's interest in the property.

Adam enters into a conditional sales contract with the Eddy Motor Company for the purchase of a used car. The motor company fails to file the contract. Later, Adam's creditors bear down and he gives the car to one of them in payment for his debt. When Adam defaults in his payments to the motor company, it will no longer have the ability to take back the car, because it failed to file the contract.

The place of filing will vary from state to state and will also depend upon the type of goods purchased, but generally it will be filed in the county clerk's office in the county where the buyer resides. It is important to note that the filing will be ineffective where improperly made and where a subsequent purchaser or creditor does not have knowledge of the existence of the security agreement.

Distinction between Chattel Mortgage and Conditional Sales Contract

In both conditional sales contracts and chattel mortgages, property is held as security for debt. In a chattel mortgage, the property is owned by the debtor, who gives the chattel mortgage. In a conditional sales contract, the debtor is the buyer of the property, but he does not become the owner of the property until the debt (purchase price) is paid.

Meaker buys a refrigerator from the Daily Ice Machine Company. He agrees to pay $350 for the refrigerator in 70 monthly installments of $5 each. The conditional sales contract provides that Meaker does not become the absolute owner of the refrigerator until the last payment is made.

Jennings borrows $500 from Colby. Colby asks for security for the debt. Jennings executes a chattel mortgage on his automobile, which will be discharged as soon as the debt is paid in full.

Repossession of Goods Conditionally Sold

When the buyer is in default in the payment of any sum due under the contract, the seller has the right to take possession of the goods unless otherwise agreed in the security agreement. This may be done without resorting to the courts, if the seller can repossess his property without committing a breach of the peace. If it is provided in the security agreement, the seller may also require the buyer to assemble the property and make it available to him in a reasonably convenient place. The buyer has the right to redeem the goods at any time before disposition of them by the seller. This may be accomplished by paying in full all monetary obligations then due and performance in full of all other obligations then matured.

Resale or Retention by the Seller

If the seller repossesses the goods, he has one of two choices: He may resell the goods or keep them in satisfaction of the debt. The Uniform Commercial Code provides that a seller may resell the goods at either a private or public sale at any time or place and on any terms, provided that it be done in a "commercially reasonable" manner. The buyer must be given notice of the time and place of the sale. Under the Code, there is no set period during which the goods must be held by the seller before resale. Likewise, there is no set time within which the sale must be made, but it must be done within a commercially reasonable time.

As an alternative, the seller may keep the goods in satisfaction of the buyer's obligation if he proceeds as follows: (1) sends written notice to the buyer of his proposal to keep the goods, (2) sends notice to other persons who have a security interest in the goods (except where they are consumer goods), (3) refrains from disposing of the goods for thirty days. If the seller does not receive an objection to his proposal within the thirty-day period, he may keep the goods. The buyer is then discharged of all obligations.

Proceeds of Resale

The proceeds of the resale shall be applied (1) to the payment of the reasonable expenses of retaking, holding and disposing of the property, including restoring the property to its condition at the time of the original sale, and, where the security agreement permits, attorney's fees and other legal expenses permitted by law, (2) to reimbursing the seller for the balance due under the contract, and (3) to the satisfaction of any indebtedness secured by other security interests, provided such other parties submit a written notice before the proceeds are distributed. Any sum remaining shall be paid to the buyer. If the proceeds of the resale are not sufficient to defray the expenses of the sale, the expenses of retaking, keeping, and restoring, and the amount due on the purchase price, the seller may sue the buyer for the deficiency.

Rights of the Buyer and Seller When There Is No Resale or Retention

Under certain circumstances, if the seller does not either resell or retain the goods, the Uniform Commercial Code gives the buyer the right to sue the seller, when the seller does not dispose of the goods within 90 days after obtaining possession. To come under this provision, two requirements must be met: (1) the goods must be consumer goods and (2) the buyer must have paid 60 percent of the cash price. If these requirements are met, the buyer may sue to recover the goods or may elect to recover an amount not less than the credit service charge together with 10 percent of the principal amount of the debt.

21
Patents, Copyrights, and Trademarks

Patents, copyrights, and trademarks seem to be related subjects but are actually separate and distinct entities. Although all three grant certain exclusive rights or privileges, it should be borne in mind that they are based on different principles of law. A patent rests on the principle of protecting original inventions. Originality is not necessary to a valid trademark; it is a question of distinctive identification of goods. A copyright possesses the same qualities of monopoly as a patent or trademark but differs from both of them in that it applies exclusively to works of art. At first the idea of monopolies seems undemocratic because it appears to benefit only the few; however, patents, copyrights, and trademarks do actually encourage invention, techniques, arts, letters, and trade and, thus, benefit the majority.

PATENTS

A *patent* is a contract between the federal government and an inventor whereby, in consideration of the disclosure of a new and useful device to the public, the inventor (and, in certain instances, his heirs and assigns) is granted the exclusive right to manufacture, use, and sell the device for a fixed period (usually seventeen years).

Determining an Invention

Although admitting that the word *invention* is not susceptible of precise definition, the courts have said that an invention is a new, useful, and operative idea. A change merely in form or degree of a device or method ordinarily will not constitute an invention when it involves doing something substantially the same by a new means, nor will the substitution of one material for another constitute a patentable invention unless the substitution went beyond what was intended by the originators of the idea. An invention, however, may result from a substitution of materials when the substitution involves a new method of construction or operation or results in new functions of the art or machine.

A change in the location of parts of a machine without changing the functions performed is not an invention even though the new method brings about better results, but an invention does result when a problem is solved by reason of relocating parts, and new and useful results are obtained. When old elements are combined in one or more inventions, the new combination must produce a new and useful result in order to be an invention.

Is a particular discovery an invention? Each case must be answered after considering its originality and the history of the product or the operation. Among the facts considered as good evidence of an invention are novelty, utility, commercial success, satisfaction of a long-felt want, others' unsuccessful efforts, attempted imitation of others' disclosed methods or apparatus, and the like.

Requirement for a Patent

In order to be *patentable* an idea must (1) relate to new arts, machines, manufactures, compositions of matter, plants, or designs, (2) be useful and novel, and (3) result in an actual invention. By *art* is meant a process or method of producing a new and useful industrial result; by *machine*, an apparatus which will perform a function and produce a definite result; by *manufacture*, any article useful in trade and produced by hand, labor, or machinery; by *composition of matter*, chemical compounds or mixtures of ingredients and so on; by *plant*, a development of a new form of vegetable life; by *design*, only the appearance of an article, not its structure or utilitarian features.

Part of the second basic requirement of patentability is that an invention be new or novel. If the invention has been previously disclosed or is something identical with the art or instrument for which the patent is sought, the inventor is either not granted a patent or the patent which may have been erroneously granted is invalid. In addition, in order to be patentable, an invention must possess a basic utility or be useful. The courts have said that the term *useful* means that the art or machine must be capable of performing a beneficial function and not be just frivolous. Thus, a Rube Goldberg machine, which goes through a lot of motions without accomplishing anything in particular, would not be patentable.

Moreover, the mere existence of something new or something

useful will not suffice. The third requirement is that an actual invention must result from the idea in order for the patent to be valid.

Types and Duration of Patents

The Constitution gives Congress the power to "promote the Progress of Science and the useful Arts, by securing for limited Times to Authors and Inventors the exclusive Right to their Respective Writings and Discoveries." In keeping with this power, Congress has passed legislation which gives the Commissioner of Patents the right to grant to an inventor for a specified period the right to exclude others from making, using, or selling his invention.

Patents may be classified as patents for (1) an art or process, (2) a machine, (3) composition of matter, (4) an improvement on an existing patent, (5) a design, or (6) a plant. A plant patent is granted to one who has invented or discovered and asexually reproduced any distinct and new variety of plant. (Asexually propagated plants are those that are reproduced by means other than from seeds, such as by the rooting of cuttings, by layering, budding, grafting, inarching, and so on.)

Patents (except design patents) are granted for a term of seventeen years. Design patents may be granted for the terms of three years and six months or for seven years or for fourteen years; the applicant for a design patent may specify in his application which of these three periods he elects as the duration of his patent.

ADMISSION TO PRACTICE BEFORE THE PATENT OFFICE

Representation of an inventor before the Patent Office of the United States is permitted only to those registered to practice. Admission to practice before the patent office is by examination. Qualified persons are designated patent attorneys (if they are lawyers) or patent agents if they are not lawyers.

Procedure for Obtaining a Patent

A valid patent can be secured only by the inventor himself or by his guardian or estate. If an inventor is dead, the administrator or executor of his estate may apply for the patent. If the inventor is insane, the application may be made by his guardian or committee.

An inventor should submit his invention to his attorney, who will have a drawing or model of the invention prepared to conform with the requirements of the United States Patent Office. If his attorney is satisfied that his idea may be patentable, he will make a preliminary patent search. Although an inventor may think that he is the pioneer in his discovery area, others may have filed patents or claims covering the same or substantially the same invention.

A patent search must be made in Washington, D.C., because only the patent office there has a complete record of all American patents. The search will include a review of similar patents granted within the past seventeen years. The patent search may cost $250 and in some complex cases considerably more.

In applying for a patent, the inventor must file: (1) a petition requesting the Commissioner of Patents to grant letters patent, (2) a specification containing a description of the invention, the inventor's name, title of the invention, a brief summary of the invention, drawings, and also the respects in which the inventor claims that his invention is patentable, (3) an oath stating that the applicant believes that he is the first inventor, (4) a basic fee of $65 plus certain extras, depending on the classification and the period of time for which protection is sought. The specification for a plant patent should include a complete detailed description of the plant and the characteristics that distinguish it from related known varieties and its antecedents, expressed in botanical terms and in the general form followed in standard botanical textbooks or publications dealing with the varieties of the kind of plant involved.

The application is turned over to an examiner who searches for prior patents both in the United States and foreign countries and prior available literature to determine if the invention is new. As a result of his search, the claim then will be allowed or disallowed. If the examiner rejects some of the claims in the patent application, he must give the applicant the reasons why. If the inventor persists in his application, he may request that the patent office reexamine the application. If it is rejected a second time, he may appeal to the board of appeals in the patent office and, subsequently, to the courts.*

If there are two or more pending applications for the same invention, the patent office initiates a proceeding to determine who is

---

* A more detailed outline of procedure may be found in the pamphlet, "General Information Concerning Patents," which may be obtained from the United States Government Printing Office, Washington, D.C., 20102.

the first inventor and, thus, entitled to the patent. This proceeding, known as an *interference,* occurs in only about 1 percent of patent applications.

Assignment and Licenses

A patent is a property right and may be assigned; that is, licenses to manufacture and sell patented articles with or without royalties may be granted to others by the inventor. In order to be valid against a future purchaser of the patent, the assignment must be recorded in the patent office within three months after the date of the assignment.

Effect of Registration (Letters Patent)

The issuance of a letters patent simply raises the presumption of validity; it does not mean that the patent is valid for all purposes. Anyone may attack the validity of a patent and have the question decided by a federal court.

Among the reasons for holding that a patent is invalid are (1) that there was prior use or knowledge of the alleged invention, that is, the patent was not novel, (2) that the subject matter of the patent was covered by a prior patent in this or a foreign country, or (3) that the patent was not issued to the inventor.

Infringement Suits

One who wrongfully manufactures or sells a patented article or makes any unauthorized use or sale of the invention is guilty of *infringement.* The owner of the infringed patent has two remedies: (1) he may apply to the court for an injunction to restrain the unlawful infringement of the patent or (2) he may bring an action for damages. The infringement suit may consist of either a claim for damages or an application for an injunction or both.

An infringement suit is generally a long-drawn-out affair, and the judge has the difficult task of weighing technical data regarding patents. It has been proposed that the determination of the validity of patents should not be entrusted to federal judges who have limited knowledge in highly technical scientific fields but that these suits should be referred to experts.

COPYRIGHTS

A *copyright* is the registration of the owner's exclusive right to print, to publish, and to sell literary, dramatic, musical, artistic, and similar works for twenty-eight years. The holder of the copyright is protected (by copyright) only in his *form of expression*; that is, his ideas, themes, emotions must be embodied in a form of expression (for example, a book, painting, composition, or letter) in order to be protected by a copyright.

Copyrightable Material

The copyright act classifies copyrightable material into thirteen groups: (1) books, (2) periodicals, (3) lectures, (4) dramatic and dramatico-musical compositions, (5) musical compositions, (6) maps, (7) works of art and models or designs for works of art, (8) reproductions of works of art, (9) drawings or plastic works of scientific or technical character, (10) photographs, (11) prints, pictorial illustrations, and commercial prints or labels, (12) motion picture photoplays, and (13) other motion pictures.

The following matters are *excluded* from copyright protection:

1. Words and short phrases such as names, titles, and slogans; familiar symbols or designs; mere variations of typographic ornamentation, lettering, or coloring; mere listing of ingredients or contents
2. Works designed for recording information that do not in themselves convey information, such as time cards, graph paper, account books, diaries, and the like
3. Works consisting entirely of information that is common property and containing no original authorship, such as standard calendars, height and weight charts, tape measures and rules, schedules of sporting events, and lists or tables taken from public documents or other common sources
4. Sound recordings and the performances recorded on them
5. Government publications. (Material contained in government publications may be gleaned, however, from copyrighted sources.)
6. Seditious, libelous, obscene, or fraudulent works
7. Ideas, plans, methods, systems, or devices as distinguished from the particular manner in which they are expressed or described in a writing

Procedure in Securing a Statutory Copyright

The copyright law provides that the author may secure a copyright by publication of the work containing a notice of the copyright. The notice, which is specifically prescribed by statute, shall be affixed to each copy published and offered for sale in the United States.

Form of the Notice   As a general rule, the copyright notice should consist of three elements:

1. The word "copyright," the abbreviation "copr.," or the symbol ©. Use of the symbol © may result in securing copyright in countries which are members of the Universal Copyright Convention.
2. The name of the copyright owner
3. The year of publication. If the work has previously been registered as unpublished, the year of such registration should be given. These three elements should appear together on the copies in one of the following ways:

Copyright, John Doe, 1975
© John Doe, 1975
© Copyright by John Doe, 1975
© Copyright by Harper & Row, Publishers, Inc., 1975.

Optional Form of Notice   For works registrable in classes *F* through *K*—maps, works of art, models or designs for works of art, reproductions of works of art, drawings or plastic works of a scientific or technical character, photographs, prints and pictorial illustrations, and prints or labels used for articles of merchandise—a special form of notice is permissible. This may consist of the symbol © accompanied by the initials, monogram, mark, or symbol of the copyright owner if the owner's name appears on an accessible portion of the work.

Position of the Notice   For a book or other publication printed in book form, the copyright notice should appear on the title page or page immediately following. The "page immediately following" is normally the reverse side of the page bearing the title; in books, the copyright notice appears much more frequently on this page than on the title page, so much so that this page is called the "copyright page." In a periodical, the notice should appear on the title page, on the first page of text, or under the title heading. In a musical work, the notice may appear either on the title page or on the first page of music.

Rights Granted by a Copyright

The statute gives the owner of a copyright certain exclusive rights for a twenty-eight-year term, renewable for a second term of twenty-eight years; thus copyright protection may be secured for fifty-six years. The rights of a copyright holder are listed below.

The right to print, copy, sell, or distribute. This restriction not only prevents someone from reprinting the copyrighted work, but also prevents the reproduction of the work by any other means of expression. If a book or periodical is printed in English, it must be printed from type or plates made in the United States; if it is produced by another process, the process must be completely performed in the United States and the book or periodical must also be bound here.

The right to translate, transform, or revise the work by means of dramatization, translation, musical arrangement, or the like. The importance of preservation of the right to transform is illustrated frequently by the substantial amounts which are paid authors of stories or novels in return for the right to make motion pictures of stories.

The right to deliver, record, or perform. The right to deliver, record, or perform relates to lectures or sermons prepared primarily for delivery as well as dramatic works and musical compositions.

The right to transfer, mortgage, or bequeath. Copyrights may often be valuable. Thus, their owners may wish to sell them (transfer ownership), use them as collateral for a loan, or bequeath them by will.

Fair Use

The courts have said that "fair use" may be made of every copyrighted production. Sometimes it is difficult to draw the line between fair and unlawful use of copyrighted works.

For example, a teacher may copy portions of a textbook, copyrighted by another, for use in his own lectures. And, a book or dramatic review may actually quote portions of the copyrighted work. But, if the teacher wants to write his own textbook and use in it the material he has copied from the first text, he must obtain the copyright holder's permission and also print notice of the source of the quoted material in his book. Again, if another author wishes to quote a book or dramatic review in his book, he must obtain permission to do so from the newspaper or magazine which first printed the review, and he must cite the periodical and the reviewer (if the review is by-lined) as the source of the review.

One must obtain permission from the copyright holder to reproduce even one line of a poem in a book, but one may quote a small portion of a book in another work. This is fair use.

A person writing a biography of William Faulkner must obtain permission from the copyright holder to quote in his book a total of 3,500 words from Faulkner's works.

Another person writing a textbook on English composition may use an eight-line prose quotation from Faulkner, as an illustration of effective writing, without the copyright holder's permission; he must, however, cite the source of the quotation.

Infringement of Copyrighted Works

Before a suit for infringement is brought in the courts, copies of the copyrighted work must be deposited in the copyright office. The requirement of the statute is that after the copyright has been secured by publication of the work containing a notice of the copyright, "there shall promptly be deposited in the copyright office or in the mail addressed to the registrar of copyrights, two complete copies of the best edition then published," accompanied by a claim of copyright and a six-dollar fee. The courts have been liberal in interpretation of the word, "promptly." In one case the United States Supreme Court held that the right of infringement was not lost even though the deposit in the copyright office was delayed for fourteen months.

In bringing an infringement suit, the owner of a copyright may seek an injunction—to stop the reproduction of the infringing material—against the person improperly using the copyrighted work, and he may also seek damages by reason of the infringement. In some cases, the court may require that the infringing material be delivered up for destruction. The statute also permits the successful party in an infringement suit, unlike most other legal proceedings, to recover a reasonable attorney's fee.

The owner of the copyright may recover from the infringer the actual damages he has sustained plus the profits the infringer has made as a result of his wrongful use of the copyright. Sometimes it is not possible to prove actual damages. The statute sets up certain guides to assist the court in awarding penalties in lieu of damages: $10 for every infringing copy of a painting, statue, or sculpture; $1 for every copy of other works (such as books); $50 for every unauthorized delivery of a lecture, sermon, or address; $100 for the first infringing performance of a dramatic or musical work or choral or orchestral composition and $50 for each subsequent performance; and $10 for each performance of all other musical works. The foregoing amounts are popularly referred to as "in lieu" damages.

Common-Law and Statutory Copyrights

A copyright may be secured for unpublished works by depositing copies or prints with a claim of copyright in the United States Copyright Office, Library of Congress, Washington, D.C. 20540. If the owner of the copyright subsequently decides to publish the work, the copy must bear the usual statutory notice; in this case, the date of copyright is that obtained for the unpublished work, not the date of publication. The filing of copies of unpublished works in the copyright office is only an added precaution because, independent of statutory protection, an author has a common-law copyright under state law (that is, a property right in an intellectual production before it is published) and may obtain legal redress against anyone who pilfers it.

TRADEMARKS

A *trademark* is a distinctive mark or symbol or device which a manufacturer affixes to the goods he produces so that they may be identified in the market. It should not be confused with a *trade name*, which is a name used in the trade to designate as an entity the particular business of certain individuals or sometimes to designate a class of goods. The registered trade name identifies both the goods *and* the persons selling or making them, whereas a registered trademark designates *only* the product. For example, the product "Sunshine Cola Drink" could be the subject of a trademark, and the "Sunshine Soft Drink Company" could be a trade name.

Besides registration of marks and names of manufacture, service, certification, and collective marks may also be registered. A *service mark* is a device used in the sale or advertising of services to distinguish the services of one from the services of others; service marks include without limitation the marks, names, symbols, titles, designations, slogans, character names, and distinctive features of radio or other advertising used in commerce. For example, a fire-insurance agency might use as a service mark a fire engine rushing to the scene of a fire to indicate the type of service rendered by the agency.

A *certification mark* is a mark used in connection with the products or services of one or more persons other than the owner of the mark to certify regional or other origin, material, mode of manufacture, quality, accuracy, or other characteristics of such goods or services or to certify that the work or labor on the goods or services was performed by members of a union or other organization. For example, the ILGWU label indicates that a garment was made by members of the International Ladies Garment Workers Union.

A *collective mark* is a trademark or service mark used by the members of a cooperative association or other collective group or organization. Marks used to indicate membership in a union, an association, or other organization may be registered as collective membership marks. For example, a group of textile manufacturers could join together under the name "Atlantic Ocean Textile Manufacturers Association," devise a trademark "Atlantic Ocean Products," and use the trademark on all products manufactured by members of the association.

Trademarks serve to indicate the manufacturer, producer, and origin of the product. They may also serve to insure uniformity of quality in the goods bearing the mark and, through advertising, to create and maintain a demand for the product. Registration of a trademark in the United States Patent Office does not in itself create or establish any exclusive right but rather indicates recognition by the federal government of the owner's right to use the mark in commerce to distinguish his goods from those of others.

Common-Law Rights in Trademarks

Although Congress and the various states have enacted laws authorizing the registration of trademarks, registration is not necessary for the legal protection of the marks. Rights in a trademark are acquired only by use and use must continue if the rights so acquired are to be preserved. Valid trademarks can be obtained by showing priority of adoption and use.

When the Federal Trademark Law was adopted in 1905, Congress said that nothing should change the rights or remedies which then existed, even if the trademark law had not been passed. Thus, Congress indicated that common-law rights in trademarks will prevail over registered trademarks provided the claimant of the trademark can show from business records that he was the first to adopt and use the trademark.

Registration under Federal Laws

Though trademark rights are acquired without registration, it is generally advisable to register a trademark and preferably advisable to register it under federal law. Registration under the federal law gives the owner the stamp of approval of the federal government and creates a presumption of ownership which would have to be overcome in litigation, by proof that someone else had previously used the mark. Also, registration in the United States Patent Office may make it easier to register the mark in foreign countries, and it would restrict certain imports which bear the registrant's mark. The registration of a mark gives the registered owner the right to sue in federal courts and to recover under the statutory provision for treble damages for unlawful use of the trademark. (When there are complicated problems in connection with the registration of the trademark, a patent attorney should be consulted.)

Marks Subject to Registration   For a trademark to be registered in the patent office, it must be a distinctive design, combination of letters, words, or figures and must be shown to be first adopted and used by the applicant.

Marks Not Subject to Registration   A trademark cannot be registered if it (1) consists of or comprises immoral, deceptive, or scandalous matter or matter that may disparage or falsely suggest a connection with persons living or dead, institutions, beliefs, or national symbols or bring them into contempt or disrepute, (2) consists of or comprises the flag or coat of arms or other insignia of the United States or of any state or municipality or of any foreign nation or any simulation thereof, (3) consists of or comprises a name, portrait, or signature identifying a particular living individual except by his written consent or the name, signature, or portrait of a deceased president of the United States during the life of his widow, if any, except by the written consent of the widow, (4) consists of or comprises a mark which so resembles a mark registered in the patent office or a mark or trade name previously used in the United States by another and not abandoned as to be likely, when applied to the goods of the applicant, to cause confusion or mistake or to deceive purchasers.

Procedure for Registration of Trademarks   Under federal law the application for registration of trademarks must be filed in the name of the owner of the mark and must consist of (1) a written application on a form suggested by the United States Patent Office, (2) a drawing of the mark, and (3) five specimens or facsimiles and payment of the filing fee.

The drawing of the trademark should be an exact representation of the mark as actually used in connection with goods or services. It must be made on pure white durable paper, the surface of which must be calendered and smooth. India ink alone must be used for pen drawings to secure perfectly solid black lines. The use of white pigment to cover lines is not acceptable. The sheet on which the drawing is made must be eight inches wide and eleven to thirteen inches long. The size of the mark must be such as to leave a margin of at least one inch on the sides and bottom of the paper and at least one inch between the mark and the heading. Across the top of the drawing beginning one inch from the top edge and not exceeding one-quarter of the sheet, there should be a heading, listing on separate lines the applicant's name and post office address, the dates the mark was first used, and the goods or services recited in the application.

All drawings must be made by a process which will give them satisfactory reproduction characteristics. Every line and letter, names included, must be blacked. This direction applies to all lines, however fine, and to shading. All lines must be clean, sharp, and solid, and they must not be too fine or crowded. If otherwise suitable, a photolithograph reproduction or printer's proof copy may be used.

If the patent office concludes that the mark is not entitled to registration, after examining the application, the applicant is advised of the reasons for rejection. The applicant has six months from the date of the patent office's notification to respond. If the applicant responds, the application may be reexamined and reconsidered. If after further examination and reconsideration the registration is still refused, an appeal may be made to the Trademark Trial and Appeal Board.

If on examination it appears that an applicant is entitled to have his mark registered, the mark is published in the patent office's official gazette. The mark may then be opposed by any person who believes he would be damaged by registration of the mark. Opposition to the registration should be made within thirty days after publication.

If conflict is found between two co-pending trademark applications, an interference will be instituted, in the same manner as in the case of a patent application, to decide which applicant is entitled to register.

Trademark Registration under State Laws

Federal registration is restricted to marks of goods sold in interstate commerce. In instances where products are sold only within the boundaries of a particular state, it is advisable to register the mark with the state government.

Glossary

Many other legal terms are defined in the text of the book. These are listed in the Index.

Abatement means reduction or decrease; when applied to the payment of claims from a fund which is insufficient to pay claims in full, it means a proportionate reduction of the claims.

Abduction (criminal law) is the offense of taking away a female or child by violence or fraud.

Abeyance is a state of being undetermined or held in suspension.

Ab initio (Latin, "from the beginning") signifies a transaction or document from its inception; thus, a marriage may be held to be unlawful *ab initio* or an insurance policy valid *ab initio*.

Abstract of title is a condensed history of a title to land.

Accord and satisfaction is an agreement between two persons that settles a claim or a lawsuit.

Acknowledgment is the certificate of a notary or another officer having the authority to administer oaths attesting that the person who executed a document declared that the document was his free act and deed.

Acquittal, in the law of contracts, means a release or discharge from an obligation; in the law of crimes, it means the deliverance of a person from a charge of guilt.

Act of God (also known as *force majeure*) is an event caused exclusively by the violence of nature, which people are powerless to prevent.

Ademption is the cancellation of a legacy because an act of the testator is interpreted as an intention to revoke the legacy.

Adjective law refers to rules of procedure or practice (see *substantive law*).

Adjudication ordinarily means the pronouncing of a judgment or decree in a litigated case. When used in bankruptcy proceedings the term refers to the order of a bankruptcy court declaring that the debtor is a bankrupt person.

Adjuster usually refers to a person who is employed to make a settlement; an adjuster is most frequently employed by an insurance company.

Administrative law is that branch of law which governs procedure before various agencies of the government.

Administrator or **administratrix** is the one who administers the estate of a person who dies without leaving a will.

Admiralty designates the branch of law which regulates maritime matters.

Adoption is (1) the act of one who takes another's child into his own family and treats him as his own (assuming all the responsibilties of parenthood and giving the child all the privileges of his own child) and (2) the act of a court which creates between two persons the relationship of parent and child.

Adultery, a crime in most states, is the voluntary sexual intercourse of a married person with a person other than the offender's husband or wife.

Adverse possession is a method of acquiring title to real estate by occupancy for a specified number of years; it is sometimes called "squatters title" (see Chapter 16, "Real Property Law").

Advocate refers to a lawyer who pleads for another person in court.

Affidavit is a written statement sworn to before a notary public or another officer having the authority to administer oaths.

Ambulance chasing refers to the unlawful and unethical conduct of a lawyer in the solicitation of claims arising out of personal injuries.

A mensa et thoro is a kind of divorce by means of which the parties are merely separated; it should be distinguished from a divorce *a vinculo*, which effects a complete dissolution of the marriage. Freely translated "a mensa et thoro" refers to a separation from bed and board; "a vinculo" means the breaking of the bonds or chains (of matrimony).

Amicus curiae (Latin, literally "a friend of the court") generally means a person who is not a party in a court proceeding but who is allowed by the court to introduce argument, authority, or evidence, because he has a corollary or collateral interest in the proceeding.

Arraignment is the bringing of a person accused of a crime before a court to be advised of the charge against him and to state his anwer to the charge.

Arbitration means the submission for determination of a disputed matter to one or more unofficial persons (as distinguished from an official tribunal like a court) who make a decision or award wth respect to the disputed matter. Arbitration is becoming a popular method of settling business disputes; the American Arbitration Association, a private organization, puts at the disposal of businessmen a panel of arbitrators whom the parties to a dispute may use to make an arbitration award or decision.

Arising out of and in the course of employment is a phrase used in connection with Workmen's Compensation Laws to classify an injury incident to employment.

Arrest is the act of depriving a person of his liberty by legal authority.

Arrest of judgment is the act of staying or postponing a judgment.

Arson is the crime of burning a building. In various states this crime is specifically defined as first-, second-, or third-degree arson. For example, in some states arson in the first degree involves setting fire at night to a house or other structure in which there is a human being. Arson in the second degree may be setting fire to a house during the day or setting fire at night to a building in which there is no human being. Arson in the third degree may be setting fire to a vessel, vehicle, or other structure or even setting fire to personal property valued at more than twenty-five dollars.

Articles of agreement consists of a written statement of the terms of an agreement.

Attachment is the act of seizing persons or property by means of legal writ, summons, or other judicial order.

Attestation of a will is the act of witnessing the execution of a will.

Attorney-at-law is an officer of the court and a member of the bar who is authorized to conduct legal proceedings in behalf of others and to give legal advice.

Attorney-in-fact identifies a person, not necessarily a member of the bar, authorized by another to act in his place and stead.

Averment is a statement of facts in legal pleadings.

Bail identifies a person who guarantees the appearance of a defendant in a criminal proceeding at a designated time and place or the security put up for this purpose.

Bail bond is a formal document, executed by an arrested person together with a surety or sureties, providing for the payment of money if the arrested person fails to appear to answer legal process.

Bailee names one to whom property is entrusted; it has nothing to do with criminal bail.

Bailiff usually refers to a sheriff or his deputy or a court attendant who is a representative of the sheriff's office.

Bailment is the delivery of personal property by one person in trust to another (a *bailee*) to carry out a special purpose and with the understanding that the goods will be redelivered when the purpose of the bailment is carried out.

Bench warrant is a process issued by a court in session for the arrest of a person.

Bigamy is the crime of knowingly contracting a second marriage while the first marriage to the knowledge of the offender is undissolved.

Bill is the formal declaration in a complaint or written statement; it is also the draft of a legislative act (before it becomes law).

Bill of attainder is a legislative act in which a person is pronounced guilty of crime, usually treason, without trial or conviction. It is prohibited by the Constitution of the United States.

Bill of costs is an itemized statement of expenses chargeable against the unsuccessful party to an action or suit.

Bill of indictment (same as *indictment*) is a formal written document accusing a person of having committed a crime.

Bill of lading is written evidence of a contract for delivery of goods by freight.

Bill of particulars is a written statement of the details of a claim for which a suit is brought.

Bill of Rights consists of the first ten amendments of the federal Constitution and guarantees rights and privileges to individuals.

Bill of sale is a written instrument by which one person transfers to another his rights in personal property.

Bill payable, in commercial parlance, is an obligation which is owed by the person keeping a ledger account.

Bill receivable, in commercial parlance, is an account owing to the person keeping the ledger account.

Blackmail is a term usually used as the equivalent of the term *extortion;* it is the extraction of money or something else of value in return for silence or for refraining from performing some act.

Bona fide (Latin) means "in good faith," without deceit or fraud.

Bond is a formal certificate or evidence of a debt.

Book value, applied to corporate stock, designates the value shown after deducting the liabilities from the assets.

Breach of the peace is a catchall phrase used in criminal law to describe the offense of disturbing the public peace by any riotous or unlawful act.

Bribery is a crime of offering, giving, or receiving anything of value to influence the action of a public official.

Brief is a written or printed document prepared by counsel and addressed to a court; it is a basis for an argument in support of a litigant's position.

Burden of proof is the duty to establish a fact in dispute in a lawsuit.

Burglary is the crime of breaking and entering the house of another at night with intent to commit a felony in the house. Various states have modified the foregoing common-law definition in order to cover breaking into and entering a house under different circumstances and have labelled burglary in various degrees. Thus, in some instances, the crime of burglary in the first degree is committed by the burglar who enters a house at night armed with a dangerous weapon or assisted by confederates; burglary in the second degree may be committed during the day by a person who simply breaks and enters a house of another; and burglary in the third degree may be committed by a person who commits the crime and then breaks out of the building (that is, he is already in the building and does not break in to commit the burglary, but he does break out of the building).

Bylaws are regulations, ordinances, rules, or laws adopted by an association or corporation for its internal government.

Calendar refers to a list of cases (sometimes called a "trial list") to be tried during a particular term of court.

Capias (Latin) is the general name for a class of writs which require a court officer to take (the body of) the defendant into custody, that is, arrest him.

Capital crime describes a crime for which the maximum penalty is death.

Capital stock describes the amount of stock authorized by a corporate charter.

Carnal knowledge is a phrase used in connection with criminal charges, such as rape, and signifies sexual intercourse.

Carrier, common, is one who undertakes to transport persons or property for hire.

Case law signifies that branch of law established by court decisions, as distinguished from statutes or other sources of law.

Causa mortis (Latin) means "in contemplation of approaching death."

Cause of action is a person's right to bring a lawsuit against another.

Caveat emptor (Latin) means "let the buyer beware."

Caveat venditor (Latin) means "let the seller beware."

Cease and desist is a type of order usually issued by federal regulatory agencies, such as the Federal Trade Commission, to require an individual or a firm to discontinue a practice which is considered objectionable. If the order is not obeyed, the government agency applies to a court for an order requiring the person to cease and desist and the violation of such a court order is punishable as a contempt of court.

Certificate of incorporation is the instrument by which a private corporation is formed. It is sometimes called a "charter," although originally a charter was a direct legislative grant which gave a corporation the right to exist.

Certiorari (Latin, "to be made certain") refers to a legal proceeding by which a court reviews the decision of a lower court or governmental agency.

Cestui que trust (Latin) means "the beneficiary of a trust."

Chambers refers to the private office of a judge.

Charter, see *certificate of incorporation.*

Chattel is an article of personal property.

Check-off system refers to the deduction of union dues by an employer from employees' pay.

Chose in action is the right to personal property which has not been reduced to possession. Most intangible property rights, such as checks, promissory notes, and claims for damage, are choses in action.

Circumstantial evidence is evidence of facts or circumstances from which the existence or nonexistence of a fact may be inferred. For example, if one of the points in issue in a lawsuit was whether John Jones was at a certain house at a certain time, the facts that his car was seen in front of the house and his gloves were found in the house subsequently might be considered circumstances from which the inference could be drawn that he was at the house at the time in question, even though there was no direct proof of his being seen there.

Citation is an order or notice by which a person is directed to appear in a proceeding.

Clean hands is an equitable doctrine that a person is not entitled to relief if he has been guilty of unjust or unfair conduct.

Clerk of court signifies an officer who has charge of the records and proceedings of court.

Client is the person who employs an attorney.

Codicil is a separate document which may modify or supplement a will. It must be executed with the same formalities as the will itself.

Collateral relatives refers to brothers, sisters, cousins, aunts, uncles, nephews, and nieces as distinguished from ancestors, such as parents or grandparents, and descendents, such as children and grandchildren.

Comity of states designates the practice or courtesy by which the courts of one state recognize the laws and judicial decisions of another state.

Commitment, in criminal law, is the act of sending a person to prison. The word may also refer to the warrant or order of the court which directs that a person be taken to a prison or another institution.

Committee of an incompetent person or a lunatic refers to a person who, by order of the court, is given the custody of the person and the estate of one who has been adjudged incompetent.

Common law refers to the ancient, unwritten law which originated in England. It also refers to that body of law in the United States which is derived from judicial decisions based on usage and customs of antiquity and on principles recognized in the English common law.

Common-law marriage is one not solemnized by ecclesiastical or civil ceremony but recognized in some jurisdictions as based on agreement between the parties.

Commutation, in criminal law, means a change from a greater to a lesser punishment.

Condemnation, in property law, is the taking by the government of the property of a private owner for public use.

Confidential communications refer to those which pass between persons who stand in a confidential or fiduciary relationship or who are under a special duty of secrecy, such as husband and wife, attorney and client, guardian and ward, and doctor and patient.

Conjugal rights are those which husband and wife have with respect to each other.

Consignment, broadly speaking, is the act of shipping goods, but in business it has come to mean an arrangement whereby the consignor, who sends goods to the consignee, remains the owner of the property until such time as the consignee sells the property to the ultimate consumer; at that time the consignee holds the proceeds of the sale in trust for the benefit of the consignor.

Conspiracy, in criminal law, refers to a combination or plan between two or more persons for the purpose of committing an unlawful act or an act which might be lawful if committed by one person alone but which becomes unlawful with the joint action of the conspirators.

Construction often refers to a court proceeding the purpose of which is to determine the true and real meaning of a legal document, such as a contract or a will.

Contempt of court is an act which is calculated to obstruct the administration of justice. There are two kinds of contempts of court: (1) those committed in the view and presence of the court and which are often punishable immediately by the court and (2) those which do not occur in the presence of the court, such as when a person fails to obey a court order to perform or refrain from performing certain acts.

Conveyance is a transfer of a right in property and most frequently refers to a transfer of an interest in real estate.

Coram nobis (Latin) is an ancient writ of error, recently revived, by which criminal proceedings are reviewed again by a court to determine whether or not there was an error in the proceedings.

Corpus delicti (Latin, "body of a crime"), as applied in criminal law, is the doctrine that there must be substantial proof of the fact that a crime has been committed.

Counterclaim is a claim presented by a defendant in a lawsuit which tends to defeat or to diminish the plaintiff's demand.

Creditor identifies a person to whom a debt is owing.

Crier signifies an officer of the court who makes announcements for the court.

Damages refers to compensation which may be recovered through the courts by any person who has sustained injury to his person, property, or rights, through the unlawful act of another.

Damnum absque injuria (Latin, "loss without injury"), applies to situations when a person has sustained harm without any breach of legal duty that would be the basis for an action for damages against the person causing the injury. An example is an unavoidable accident in which the person who may have been the immediate cause of the injury was guilty of no legal wrong.

Declaration is the first pleading for the plaintiff at common law and is a formal statement of facts and circumstances constituting the plaintiff's cause of action.

Decree is a final written judgment or determination of a court.

Deed is a conveyance of real estate, a written instrument signed by the owner whereby he transfers title to real estate to another person.

De facto (Latin) is used to characterize an officer, a corporation, a government, or a state of affairs that is accepted for all practical purposes although it may be illegal or illegitimate.

De jure (Latin) means "legitimate or lawful."

De minimis non curat lex (Latin) is a maxim meaning "the law does not take notice of small or trifling matters."

Default, in legal procedure, is a failure of a party to a legal proceeding to take a step or perform an act required by law.

Demise, in real estate law, refers to a lease or a conveyance; in probate law, the word means "death."

Demurrer is the formal common-law method of disputing the sufficiency in law of the written pleading of the opposing party in a lawsuit.

De novo (Latin) means "anew" a second time.

Deponent is one who makes a written statement under oath.

Deposition is the testimony of a witness taken not in open court but pursuant to law and under oath and reduced to writing.

Dicta are the statements of a judge in a particular case that are not essential to the determination of the court.

Disability is the absence of legal capability to perform an act. For example, an infant or a person who is mentally incompetent would be under a disability to perform legal acts.

Dividend, broadly speaking, means a fund to be divided. In corporate law, the term refers to a portion of the corporation's surplus profits set aside to be distributed proportionately to the stockholders. In bankruptcy law, dividends are proportionate payments to creditors out of the insolvent estate.

Docket designates a formal brief record of proceedings in court.

Domicile is the true and permanent home of a person as distinguished from a residence which may be only temporary.

Double jeopardy, prohibited by the federal Constitution, occurs when an accused is prosecuted or tried more than once for the same offense.

Draft, a common term for a bill of exchange, is an order for the payment of money drawn by one person on another.

Due process of law means following law according to prescribed forms through courts of justice; it is guaranteed by the federal Constitution.

Duress is the exercise of unlawful constraint whereby a person is forced to perform an act that he otherwise would not have done.

Easement is the right of the owner of one parcel of real estate, by virtue of his ownership, to use land of another for a special purpose.

Ejectment is the name of a common-law action which may be brought for the recovery of real estate.

Embezzlement is the fraudulent appropriation of property by a person to whom it has been entrusted.

Eminent domain is the power of the state to take private property for public use.

Emolument refers to profit arising from an office or employment.

Encroachment is something which legally intrudes or extends over or on the highway or the land of a neighbor, such as part of a house or building or fence.

Encumbrance is a claim, lien, or other burden on real or personal property which tends to diminish its value and affect its marketability. An encumbrance may be a mortgage, a mechanic's lien, or an easement.

Enjoin means to require a person or organization by a writ of injunction to perform or to desist from an act.

Entrapment refers to a procedure used by police officers in inducing a person to commit a crime so that they may institute a criminal prosecution against him.

Equitable estoppel is the preclusion of a person by his acts or conduct from asserting rights which might otherwise have been his.

Equity of redemption is the right of a landowner to redeem land after the conditions of a mortgage have been broken. Modern laws cut off equity of redemption by foreclosure proceedings.

Escheat is the right of the state to take property or money when there are no heirs surviving.

Escrow is the delivery of property conditionally to a third person, not the owner, who holds it until the happening of an event and then redelivers the same property to the owner.

Estate refers to the kind of interest which a person has in property; it is a broad term with many gradations in meanings. It may also be used to refer to the property of a deceased person.

Et al. (Latin abbreviation of *et alii*) means "and others."

Et ux. (Latin abbreviation of *et uxor*) means "and wife."

Eviction is the act of depriving a person of possession of real property by process of law.

Ex parte means "on one side only." It is generally used in connection with an application to the court by one party to a proceeding.

Ex post facto law is one passed after the occurrence of an act that attempts retroactively to change the legal consequences of that act. Such laws are prohibited by the Constitution of the United States.

Exception, in legal procedure, is a formal objection to the action of a court.

Execution means the performance of all acts necessary to render a written instrument complete, such as signing, sealing, acknowledging, and delivering the instrument. It should be distinguished from the mere signing of an instrument which in and of itself may be *incomplete execution*. In court practice, execution refers to proceedings to enforce a judgment. In the case of a money judgment, it is a direction to the sheriff to take the necessary steps to collect the judgment.

Executory describes that which has yet to be executed or performed.

Exemplary damages, sometimes called "smart money," are punitive in nature and are intended to cover unusual situations in which the loss resulted from violence or wanton or wicked misconduct on the part of the defendant; such damages should be distinguished from ordinary damages which are sometimes called "actual damages," "compensatory damages," or "consequential damages."

Exemption is the right given the debtor to retain a portion of his property free from the claims of creditors.

Exhibit (noun) is a document or other item produced during a trial or a hearing which becomes part of the case.

Extortion involves obtaining property illegally from another by the wrongful use of force or fear.

Extradition is the surrender by one state to a second state of an individual accused or convicted of a criminal offense in the second state.

Falsus in uno, falsus in omnibus (Latin "false in one thing, false in everything") is the doctrine that if any part of the testimony of a witness is willfully false, the jury may disregard all his testimony.

Family car doctrine (also called "family purpose doctrine") is a law in some states that covers the use of the car owned by the head of the family by other family members. Under this doctrine, if the head of the family allows other members of his family to use the automobile for pleasure or convenience, each such member is his agent and the head of the family is, therefore, responsible for their negligence in the operation of the car.

Fee simple is the complete and absolute ownership of real property.

Felony is a crime of a more serious nature than a misdemeanor and is usually punishable by imprisonment or death.

Feme covert refers to a married woman.

Feme sole refers to a single woman.

Fiduciary (noun) is a person holding property for the benefit of another in a trust capacity, such as an executor, guardian, or trustee. As an adjective, "fiduciary" denotes the character of a personal relationship implying great confidence, trust, and good faith.

Fieri facias (Latin) is a writ of execution commanding the sheriff to levy on and to realize the amount of a judgment from the goods of the judgment debtor.

Fixture is something affixed to land or a building that becomes part and parcel of it and is ordinarily the property of the owner of the land.

Force majeure (French) is a superior force, generally an act of God.

Forceable entry is taking possession of land or dwelling place by force, against the will of those entitled to possession.

Forgery is the crime of fraudulently making or altering a writing to prejudice another person's right.

Franchise often refers to a special privilege, generally exclusive, conferred by the government on an individual or corporation to do certain things of a public nature. An example is the privilege (franchise) given by a state or a municipality to a public utility to construct and operate power or telephone lines or public transportation facilities.

Franchise tax is a tax on the right of a corporation to do business in a particular state.

Fraud is a deceitful act with intent to deprive another of his rights or to cause him injury.

Future interests are interests in property, possession or enjoyment of which begins in the future.

Garnishee is a form of execution against the property of a judgment debtor. In many states, a garnishee execution is a direction to an employer or other person who owes money to the judgment debtor to make periodical payments to the sheriff to be applied to and to reduce the money judgment (against the debtor).

Garnishment is a proceeding whereby a person's property is used to pay debts owing to another person.

Gift *causa mortis* describes a gift made in contemplation of death of the donor on the condition that the property shall belong to the donee on the expected death of the donor.

Gift *inter vivos* refers to an absolute gift made between living persons.

Grand jury is the jury of inquiry which is summoned to receive complaints and accusations in criminal cases and to decide if sufficient evidence exists for indictment.

Grand larceny, see *larceny.*

Ground rent originally meant a perpetual rent reserved by the owner of land when he sold the land to another. Today, ground rent is commonly a price paid to the owner, of land for the use of land alone, either when the land is vacant or when the tenant has erected a building on the land owned by the landlord.

Guardian is a person charged by law with the duty of caring for the person of a minor child or the person of an incompetent and/or managing his property and rights.

Guardian *ad litem* is a guardian appointed by a court to prosecute or defend an action in behalf of a minor.

Habeas corpus (literally, "you have the body") is a writ requiring that the officer who has custody of a prisoner bring the prisoner before a court or judge for the purpose of determining whether the prisoner has been unlawfully detained.

Hearsay evidence is that which does not come from the personal knowledge of the witness but rather from what he heard others say.

Heir, at common law, originally was the designation of a person who inherited real or personal property. In some jurisdictions *heir* later became the designation of the person who inherited real estate, and the term *next-of-kin* sometimes designated only those persons who inherited personal property. To avoid confusion, some states adopted the term *distributee* to refer to a person who inherits real and personal property in the absence of a will.

Holding company refers to corporations whose primary business is to buy and hold the stock of other companies.

Holograph is a will written entirely in the handwriting of the person signing it.

Homicide is the killing of a human being. Homicide may be classified as justifiable or felonious. If "justifiable homicide," it is not usually a crime.

Ignorantia legis neminem excusat (Latin) means that "ignorance of the law excuses no one."

Impanel is the act of the clerk of the court in listing jurors for the trial of a case.

Incest is the crime of sexual intercourse between persons who are related to each other within the degrees of consanguinity prohibited by law.

Incompetency is the lack of legal qualification or ability to discharge a required duty; it is also the condition of a person who is mentally unable or unfit to manage his own affairs.

Incumbrance (see *encumbrance*) is a lien or charge against property.

Indemnity is an agreement by which one person promises to protect another from loss or damage.

Indenture designates a formal contract in which two persons obligate themselves to each other.

Indictment is a written accusation in which a grand jury charges a person with having committed a crime (see *bill of indictment*).

Infant describes a person under legal age, in most places, under eighteen years of age.

Information is a formal accusation charging a person with a criminal offense.

Injunction is a writ issued by a court; it forbids or commands a person to perform a particular act.

Inns of court are private educational associations, similar to colleges, founded in the fourteenth century in England and invested with the responsibilty for educating and training barristers.

Inquest is a judicial inquiry. A "coroner's inquest" to determine the legal cause of a person's death is quite common.

Insurance involves a contract whereby a corporation usually called an "insurer" or "underwriter" undertakes to compensate another person usually called the "insured" for an agreed consideration called the "premium." The written contract is usually called a "policy." Such contracts may cover one or more various conditions or occurrences. Insurance may be classified as follows:

Accident insurance whereby the insurer undertakes to indemnify the insured against expense, loss of wages, and so on resulting from accidents which cause injury or death.

Automobile comprehensive insurance whereby the insurer agrees to pay the insured for loss of or damage to a motor vehicle caused by fire, wind, storm, theft, collision, and other similar hazards.

Burglary insurance which protects its owner against loss of property from burglary or theft.

Casualty insurance which protects its owner against one or more kinds of accidents.

Commercial insurance whereby the insurer guarantees parties to business arrangements against loss by breach of contractual obligations.

Fidelity insurance whereby the insurer undertakes to protect employers from the dishonesty (thefts) of officers, agents, or employees of the insured.

Fire insurance where the insurer agrees to reimburse the insured for losses resulting from fire damage to buildings, merchandise, or other forms of personal property.

Fraternal insurance is issued by fraternal organizations to their members as life or accident insurance.

Liability insurance whereby the insurer agrees to protect the insured against liability on account of injuries to the persons or property of another. (This differs from accident or indemnity insurance whereby the insurer pays for losses of the insured.)

Life insurance through which the insurer agrees to pay specified sums to a designated beneficiary on the death of the insured.

Marine insurance whereby the insurer undertakes to indemnify the insured for the perils of the sea or for other risks in connection with marine navigation.

Plate glass insurance through which the insurer agrees to reimburse the insured for loss from accidental breaking of glass.

Title insurance whereby the insurer protects the insured from loss or damage resulting from title defects to real estate.

Workmen's compensation insurance through which the insurer pays in behalf of employers awards to employees or their dependents for injuries sustained on the job.

Intent, an important term in the law of contracts, wills, and other documents, refers to the purpose or design of the person executing an instrument and is often determined by courts in construing the true meaning of an instrument.

International law is a system of rules and principles, founded on treaty, custom, and precedent which civilized nations are expected to recognize as binding upon them in their relationships with others.

Jeopardy is the danger of conviction and punishment which a prisoner faces when he is charged with a crime (see *double jeopardy*).

Judge advocate, in a military court-martial, is an officer who advises the court, but whose main duty is to act as prosecutor.

Judgment describes the official and authentic decision of a court of justice.

Judgment creditor designates one who has obtained a money judgment against his debtor.

Judgment debtor signifies one against whom a money judgment has been recovered.

Judgment lien is the charge of a court judgment against the real estate of a judgment debtor.

Judicial notice refers to the doctrine by which the court in conducting a trial or making its decision recognizes the truth of certain facts without demanding evidence. Facts of which a court may take judicial notice are: the laws of a state, international law, historical events, geography, and so on.

Judiciary refers to the system of courts.

Jurisdiction is the authority by which courts act.

Jurisprudence is the science that treats all the principles of law.

Jury, see *grand jury, petit jury*.

Justice of the peace is a judge of inferior rank whose duties are limited by law in each state.

Kidnapping, a felony, is the forceable abduction or stealing and carrying away of a person against his will. Taking a kidnapped person across state lines makes the crime a federal offense.

King (the) can do no wrong means that the king (and hence the government) is not legally responsible for acts of his representatives (see *sovereign immunity*).

Laches describes an undue delay which results in legal prejudice to another.

Larceny involves the unlawful taking and carrying away of another's personal property. In various jurisdictions, the crime is divided into grand and petit larceny, depending on the value of the property stolen. When the value of the goods stolen is considerable, for example, five hundred dollars, the crime is *grand larceny*. *Petit larceny* is committed when the value of the goods stolen is below that amount.

Last clear chance is a doctrine applied to a situation in which an injured person has been guilty of negligence but his helpless condition was realized by the person causing the injury. The person causing the injury would be held responsible if he could have avoided doing harm after discovering the predicament of the injured person.

Lateral support describes the right to have real property supported by adjoining real property (land or soil).

Leading question is one which suggests to a witness the answer desired by the person asking the question.

Lease is an agreement whereby a landlord rents property to a tenant. It may be written or verbal.

Legal ethics is comprised of the duties which members of the legal profession owe to the public, to the court, to their professional colleagues and to their clients.

Letters of administration is a document issued by a probate court; it gives a person authority to act as administrator of an estate.

Letters of guardianship designates a document, issued by the court, evidencing the authority of the guardian.

Letters rogatory is a request made by one court to another court that a witness be examined on written interrogatories.

Letters testamentary is a document, issued by a probate court, which empowers a person to act as executor of a will.

Levy describes the seizure and sale of property by a court officer to satisfy an execution or garnishment.

Lex fori (Latin) means the "law of the place where the litigation is tried."

Lex loci contractus (Latin) means the "law of the place where the contract was made."

Lex loci delictus (Latin) means the "law of the place where the crime or wrong took place."

Lex loci rei sitae (Latin) means "the law of the place where the subject matter is situated."

Lien is a charge or encumbrance on property.

Life estate is an interest in property that is limited to the lifetime of an individual.

Life tenant designates one who holds an interest in property during the life estate.

Lis pendens (Latin, "pending suit") is commonly used as a notice warning those interested to examine the proceedings.

Magistrate is a public officer, almost everywhere a judge of one of the lower courts.

Majority refers to full legal age; this is the age at which, by law, a person is entitled to manage his own affairs and enjoy all his civil rights.

Malfeasance is performing an act which is wrong and unlawful (see *misfeasance*).

Malicious mischief is the willful destruction of property.

Malicious prosecution involves instituting criminal proceedings without probable cause and for the purpose of injuring a defendant. The term applies only if the criminal proceeding terminates in favor of the person prosecuted.

Malpractice describes any professional misconduct or want of professional skill which results in injury to another. The term may be applied to physicians, surgeons, dentists, lawyers, engineers, and other professional people.

Malum in se refers to a thing that is evil in itself; a thing that is morally wrong.

Malum prohibitum refers to a thing that is wrong because it is prohibited by statute.

Mandamus is the name of a judicial writ, directed to a governmental officer or body and commanding the performance of an act.

Manslaughter is the killing of another without malice or deliberate intention.

Marshal is an officer in the federal judicial system with duties corresponding to those of a sheriff (see *sheriff*).

Marshaling of assets is the arrangement of assets and claims in an estate or in a bankruptcy or insolvency proceeding in order to secure the proper payment of the various claims, taking into consideration which claims have priority over others.

Mayhem is the crime of mutilating a human being or depriving him of a body member.

Mesne assignments are the intermediate assignments by which title to property is transferred.

Minor is a person under the age of legal competence (in most places, eighteen years of age).

Misdemeanor is an act which violates public law, but which is not as serious as a felony. Such acts are generally punishable by fines or short terms of imprisonment.

Misfeasance is the improper performance of an act which a person has a right to do (see *malfeasance*).

Mistrial is a trial brought to a halt because of a procedural mistake.

Moot describes a subject for argument, a topic that is unsettled, undecided.

Motion is an application made to a court for an order.

Municipal law designates that which pertains to towns, cities, villages, and other political subdivisions. It is a highly specialized branch of the law, practiced by village and town attorneys and corporation counsels and certain attorneys in financial circles who approve bonds and other obligations issued by municipalities.

Murder is the killing with malice aforethought of one human being by another.

Mystic testament is in the law of Louisiana a closed or sealed will required by statute to be executed in a particular manner and to be signed on the outside of the envelope containing it by a notary public and seven witnesses.

Ne exeat signifies a decree or writ which forbids a person to leave the jurisdiction of the court.

Next-of-kin means those persons most nearly related to a decedent by blood, but in some jurisdictions it is used in the law of descent and distribution to designate those who inherit personal property only.

Nisi prius designates a court in which a case is tried before a jury; it differs from an appellate court in which a judge or tribunal decides the case.

Nolle pros. (abbreviation of the Latin phrase, *nolle prosequi*) is the plaintiff's declaration in a civil suit or the prosecutor's declaration in a criminal proceeding that he will no longer proceed in the action.

Nolo contendere (Latin, "I will not contest") in a criminal action is a plea that has the consequences of a plea of guilty, but it is not to be used as an admission of guilt or of liability elsewhere.

Non compos mentis means "not of sound mind" or insane.

Nonjoinder is a failure to include a person as a party to a legal proceeding when according to law he ought to have been made a party.

Nonsuit is the name of a judgment given against the plaintiff when he is unable to prove sufficient facts to constitute a cause of action against the defendant.

Notary public is a public officer whose duty it is to administer oaths, to take acknowledgments of deeds and other conveyances, and to perform certain other official acts, such as the protesting of negotiable instruments.

Novation is the substitution of a new debt, contract, or obligation for an existing one.

Nudum pactum (Latin, "a bare pact") is a pact unenforceable by action, that is, it is a voluntary promise or undertaking without legal obligation.

Nuisance is a legal wrong which arises from unreasonable or unlawful use by a person of his own property, or from improper, indecent, or unlawful personal conduct which works an injury to the right or property of another.

Nulla bona (Latin, "no goods") indicates that the judgment debtor has no property on which the sheriff can levy.

Nunc pro tunc (Latin, "now for then") applies to acts allowed to be performed after the time when they should have been, with a retroactive effect.

Oath is a solemn appeal to the Supreme Being in attestation of the truth of a statement.

Obiter dictum (Latin) is a statement in a court's opinion or a remark made by a judge that is incidental or collateral to the point at issue and that does not bear directly on the issue.

Obligee is the person in whose favor an obligation is contracted; for example, the person for whose benefit a bond is given is sometimes called the "obligee."

Obligor designates the person who has agreed to perform an obligation; for example, the person who gives a bond is sometimes called the "obligor."

Office frequently refers in law to a duty and power conferred on an individual by governmental authority and is sometimes used interchangeably for "public office."

Opinion evidence consists of a witness's opinions based on his background or experience. This kind of evidence is not admissible in court except in the testimony of experts such as coroners, ballistic experts, physicians, psychiatrists, and so on.

Option, in the law of contracts, is a privilege given to one person to purchase property from another at a specified price and within a specified time.

Order, in legal practice, is a written direction of a court or judge, other than a judgment.

Ordinance describes a local law passed by a municipality, such as a city, village, or town.

Overt act, in criminal law, is the first open motion or step taken to carry out a criminal plan. It is sometimes necessary to establish that this step has been made to commit a crime in order to justify a right of self-defense.

Oyer and terminer means literally "to hear and to determine"; hence, a judging on oral evidence. (Certain United States superior criminal courts are described as "courts of oyer and terminer.")

Oyez means "hear ye" and is a word used by court criers when about to make a proclamation.

Pardon, in criminal law, is the release of a person charged with crime from the entire punishment prescribed for the offense; it should be distinguished from a "parole," which conditionally releases the prisoner from the balance of his sentence.

Parol evidence rule provides that a contract cannot be modified or changed by oral testimony.

Parole, see *pardon.*

Particeps criminis (Latin) refers to a participant in a crime, an accomplice.

Partition is the division of lands held by joint tenants or tenants in common. When the owners themselves cannot agree, partition is used as a form of a legal action, whereby the court compels the land to be divided between the co-owners or directs that the land be sold and the proceeds of the sale be divided between or among the owners.

Party wall is a wall built partly on the land of one owner and partly on the land of another for the benefit of both.

Patent is both (1) a grant made by the government to an inventor giving him the exclusive right to make, use, and sell his invention for a specified period and (2) an instrument by which the government conveys public lands to an individual.

Pendente lite (Latin) means "pending the suit." It is used in connection with a temporary injunction and other orders issued in the course of a lawsuit.

Per capita (Latin, "by the head"), in the law of wills, denotes the method of dividing property by the number of individuals equally related to the decedent so each individual receives an equal share of the estate (see *per stirpes*).

Per curiam (Latin, "by the court") designates the opinion of the whole court rather than an opinion written by an individual judge.

Per stirpes (Latin, "by the root") is a means, in the law of wills, whereby a class or group takes the share which their ancestor would have taken (see *per capita*).

Perjury, in criminal law, is a willfully false statement given under oath.

Petition, in court practice, is an application in writing for an order of the court.

Petit jury refers to the ordinary jury of twelve (sometimes six) men and women, who serve at the trial of a civil or a criminal action. (The term *petit* [small] is used to distinguish it from the *grand* [large] *jury*.) Members of the petit jury are judges of the facts and make factual determinations, such as the truth or falsity of testimony, whether a contract has been broken, whether a person is guilty of negligence and damages. When a petit jury serves in the trial of a lawsuit the judge or justice presiding makes no determination of the facts, but only rules on the law. Sometimes in the trial of a case without jury, the justice or judge presiding is the judge of not only the law but also of the facts.

Petit larceny, see *larceny*.

Plagiarism is the act of appropriating the literary composition of another. It may constitute a crime in that it is stealing property rights which belong to another.

Pleading generally is the system whereby parties to a lawsuit present written statements of their respective contentions; a formal allegation of what is claimed by one side or denied by the other in a lawsuit. Pleadings in some courts may be oral.

Pledge is a transfer of possession or title to personal property to a creditor as security for a debt.

Power of appointment is a designation by one person in his deed or will of another person (or persons) who is to receive an interest in his property.

Power of attorney is an instrument authorizing another person to act as one's agent.

Preemptive right, in corporation law, is the privilege given to stockholders to purchase new stock issued by the corporation in proportion to their holdings, as stockholders, before the stock is offered to persons other than stockholders.

Presentment is an informal written statement made by the grand jury and representing to the court that a public offense has been committed, that it is triable in the county, and that there is ground for believing a particular individual has committed the crime. It lacks, however, the formality of a bill of indictment.

Presumption of innocence is a fundamental rule, in criminal law, which requires every accused person to be acquitted unless his guilt is established beyond a reasonable doubt.

Presumption of law is a rule requiring courts to draw a particular inference from certain evidence until the truth of such inference is disproved. For example, the courts will presume that an automobile which is registered in the name of a certain man is owned by that man until evidence is brought in to show that the automobile is actually owned by someone else.

Prima facie case is one sufficiently strong to establish a favorable finding for one side until contradicted by other evidence.

Prima facie evidence is that which is sufficient on its face, that is, sufficient to establish a given fact unless rebutted.

Probation, in criminal law, allows a person convicted of an offense to go free with a suspended sentence, during his good behavior, and usually under the supervision of a probation officer.

Process is a legal means, such as a summons, used to subject a defendant in a lawsuit to the jurisdiction of the court; in a broader sense it includes all other writs issued in the course of legal proceedings.

Promoters, in corporation law, are those persons who take the preliminary steps in the organization of a corporation and who issue prospectuses, procure subscriptions to stock, and obtain the certificate of incorporation.

Proof (legal) refers to evidence which is adduced at a trial or evidence that has some probative value in establishing the existence of a fact. Sometimes it signifies evidence which establishes the truth or falsehood of a fact.

Property is something which is of value to the individual who owns it. When a person has a property right in something, he has an interest in it. The word *property* is also used to describe anything which is the subject of ownership whether real or personal, tangible or intangible.

Proximate cause, in legal cases involving accidents and injuries, is that which in the ordinary course of events, unbroken by an intervening cause, produces an injury and without which the injury would not have occurred.

Proxy may be either a person or a written instrument. As a person a *proxy* is one deputized to represent another person at a meeting, such as a stockholders' meeting or a ceremony, such as marriage. When it is a written instrument, a proxy is a document which appoints a person to act at a meeting or similar event.

Publication, in the law of libel, is the act of communicating defamatory matter to one or more persons. In the law of wills, it is the formal declaration at the time of making a will whereby a testator states that the document is his will and testament. In legal procedure, in some states, it is the practice of serving notice or process by newspaper advertisement.

Public law is that branch of the law which is concerned with government in its political or sovereign capacity, including constitutional and administrative law; it should be distinguished from private law which is concerned with only the rights of individuals.

Putative means "commonly reputed": A man who is commonly known as the father of an illegitimate child is said to be the "putative father" of the child.

Quantum meruit (Latin, "as much as he deserved") is a form of pleading in which a plaintiff claims an amount not based on a contract but based on what he reasonably deserves to be paid.

Quash means to vacate or to annul.

Quasi-contract is an obligation which arises not from formal agreement, but from the relationship or the voluntary acts of the parties; it is sometimes referred to as an "implied contract."

Quasi-judicial refers to activities of public administrative officers who are required to investigate facts and draw legal conclusions from them.

Quitclaim deed conveys all interest which one has in a piece of real estate without warranty of title.

Quorum is the number of members of a body, such as a board of directors or stockholders or legislature or other public body, that is required to make the body competent to transact business in the absence of the other members.

Quo warranto (Latin, "by what authority") is a writ or proceeding which allows inquiry into the title of a corporation to a franchise or the right of an individual to hold a public or corporate office.

Rape is the crime committed by a man who has sexual intercourse with a woman (not his wife) without her consent. The crime of *statutory rape* refers to intercourse with a female under a stated age (for example, sixteen or eighteen or twenty-one), either with or without her consent.

Ratification is the confirmation of an act previously done. It either obligates, for the first time, the person doing the act or confirms the act's validity. When an agent performs an act without the authority of his principal, the ratification of the act may make it binding for the first time upon the principal. An infant's act, which is voidable because of his infancy, may be ratified by him after he reaches his majority, making the act binding upon the former infant.

Real estate (or real property) is land and everything growing or built on it.

Real evidence consists of the facts furnished by the things themselves, rather than from verbal testimony.

Recapitalization is the procedure by which stocks, bonds, or other corporation securities are altered in amount, income, or priority.

Receiver is a person appointed by the court to receive and preserve property pending the outcome of a legal proceeding.

Recidivist is a repeater, a habitual criminal.

Recorder is, in some states, a magistrate who has criminal jurisdiction similar to that of a police judge.

Referee is a person to whom the court refers a legal proceeding and who has authority to take testimony or other action, make a decision, or report back to the court.

Reformation is a remedy whereby written instruments may be changed to express the real agreement or intention of the parties.

Relator designates the person at whose instance a legal proceeding is brought but who is not the nominal party.

Release is the surrendering of a right, claim, or privilege by the person who owns the same.

Relevancy describes a quality of evidence which renders it properly applicable to determine the truth or falsity of the matter before the court.

Remainder, in the law of wills, signifies the balance of an estate after the payment of legacies. In property law, *remainder* refers to an interest in land or in a trust estate which takes effect at the termination of an estate for years or an estate for life. For example, Mr. X provides in his will that Mr. A should have the use of a certain piece of land during his lifetime; after Mr. A's death, Mr. B should have the life use of the land, and upon the death of Messrs. A and B the land should go to Mr. C. Mr. C would then have a remainder interest (see *reversion*).

Remand, in legal proceedings, occurs when a high court sends a case back to a lower court in order to have corrective action taken. It also means sending the prisoner back to custody pending a hearing.

Remedy is the means for enforcing a right or redressing an injury.

Remittitur of record is the return of a case record to the trial court by a court of appeal in order that the judgment of the appeal court may be carried out.

Replevin is a legal action brought in court to recover possession of goods unlawfully taken or detained.

Reprieve, in criminal law, is the suspension of execution of sentence for a period of time so a prisoner may carry out an instruction of the court.

Res (Latin, "a thing") refers to the subject matter of the action.

Res gestae (Latin, "things done") designates circumstances which are part of a particular incident. *Res gestae* is important in the law of evidence and procedure; when certain things are said and done as part of the particular transaction, they are considered to be exceptions to the hearsay rule.

Res inter alios acta (Latin, "transactions among others") refers to things done between third persons or strangers and hence not binding on the parties to litigation.

Res ipsa loquitur (Latin, "the thing speaks for itself") is the presumption that a person was responsible through negligence for an accident; it is based on proof that the instrumentality causing the accident was in the defendant's exclusive control and that the accident was one which ordinarily does not happen in the absence of negligence. If the doctrine of *res ipsa loquitur* is applicable, the plaintiff does not have to prove negligence.

Res judicata (Latin) is a controversial matter or dispute that has been settled by the judgment of the court.

Residuary estate is that part of a decedent's property which remains after the payment of his debts, expenses of estate administration, and legacies.

Respondeat superior (Latin, "let the master answer") signifies the doctrine that an employer is liable for the wrongful acts of his employees.

Respondent is the party who answers a petition in a court proceeding; he is also the party against whom an appeal is taken.

Restraint of trade refers to business activity or combinations which tend to eliminate competition or to result in a monopoly.

Retainer is the act of a client or the payment made by a client in employing an attorney.

Reversion is the future interest in land which a person retains for himself or for his heirs after giving possession of land to another for a term of years or for life. It differs from a remainder interest in that the remainder interest vests in someone other than the person who creates the interest, whereas the reversionary interest returns to the person who created it or to his heirs.

Right of way is a legal right to pass over land that belongs to another.

Riparian rights are those possessed by an owner of land on the bank of a body of water; they usually include rights to water for bathing and domestic uses and navigation, but may include rights to the soil and its contents (minerals and so on) under the specified area of water.

Robbery is the crime of taking property from another against his will by means of force or of intimidation.

Rule, in a court procedure, is a court order requiring a person to show why an act should not be performed.

Rule against perpetuities describes the doctrine specifying that no interest in property is valid unless title to the property vests in definite persons who will be alive after the death of certain persons living at the time the property interest is created.

Scienter (Latin, "knowingly," "willfully") refers to the defendant's previous knowledge of the fact which led to a wrongful injury.

Scintilla of evidence signifies the least particle of evidence.

Scire facias (Latin, "do you cause to know") designates a writ requiring a person to show why a record should not be annulled.

Seal is a particular sign or impression made to signify formally the execution of a written instrument.

Sealed instrument is a written instrument to which the party bound has affixed not only his name but also his seal. (The importance of sealed instruments has been gradually done away with by the legislatures in many jurisdictions.)

Search warrant identifies a written order issued by a judge or magistrate and directed to a sheriff, constable, or marshal; it commands one of the latter officers to search specified premises for personal property unlawfully held.

Secondary evidence describes that which is inferior to other evidence. For example, a copy of an instrument or verbal proof of its contents is secondary evidence of the instrument itself.

Seduction is the act of inducing a woman to sexual intercourse.

Seisin is the possession or the right to immediate possession of an interest in real estate.

Self-dealing refers to transactions in which one acting in a fiduciary capacity, such as a trustee, acts at the same time in his own self-interest. This happens when a man individually buys property for himself as trustee. Self-dealing is illegal and sometimes results in the voiding of entire transactions.

Sequestration is a court mandate ordering the sheriff to take over property of a defendant and to hold it until the decision in the suit.

Service of process is the delivery of a summons, subpoena, or other court paper to a person who is thereby officially notified of a court action or proceeding or to appear in court.

Set-off is a counterdemand.

Settlor is one who creates a trust.

Sheriff is an important county officer who is charged with the enforcement of civil and criminal law.

Situs (Latin, "location") is the place where a thing is considered to exist or to have happened.

Social security is a system, enacted by Congress, providing for old-age benefits and unemployment insurance payable by the government from the fund contributed to by both employers and employees.

Sovereign immunity, a doctrine which dates from feudal times, exempts the government from suit at the hands of private individuals unless the government waives such immunity. The federal government has waived this immunity through the federal Tort Claims Act, enacted by Congress. Although many states have waived their sovereign immunity, others still rely on this ancient doctrine.

Spendthrift trust is one created to provide a fund only the income of which will be paid to the beneficiary; the purpose of such a fund is to support the beneficiary and, at the same time, protect him against his own improvidence.

Squatter, in real estate law, refers to one who settles on another's land without legal authority.

Stare decisis (Latin, "to stand by decided matters") refers to the courts' policy of following precedents.

Statute means an act of Congress or a state legislature.

Statute of frauds designates laws which provide that no suit or action shall be based on certain transactions unless there be a note or memorandum thereof in writing signed by the party to be charged with responsibility.

Statute of limitations prescribes that no suit shall be brought on a certain type of claim unless brought within a specified period after the claim accrues.

Stipulation, in court practice, is an agreement made by both parties.

Subordination of perjury, in criminal law, is the offense of procuring another to take a false oath which would constitute perjury.

Subpoena is a legal process commanding a witness to appear and give testimony.

Subpoena duces tecum (Latin) commands a witness to produce a document or property at the trial.

Subrogation acts to put a third person who has paid a debt in the place of the creditor to whom he has paid it, so that he may proceed against the debtor with all rights of the creditor.

Substantive law is the branch of the law that regulates rights; it is the opposite of *adjective law*, which prescribes remedies and procedure for enforcing rights.

Substituted service is the notice or delivery of legal process in a lawful manner other than by personal service (such as by publication or by mail).

Summons notifies a defendant in writing that an action has been commenced against him and that he is required to appear in court and answer it within a stated time.

Supersedeas (Latin) is a court writ that suspends legal proceedings.

Suretyship is the relationship created when one person formally contracts to be responsible for the obligations of another person.

Surrogate is the title of a judicial officer who has jurisdiction over the estates of deceased persons.

Talesman is a person summoned to act as a juror from among bystanders on the street or in the courtroom.

Testament is usually a will; strictly speaking it is a disposition of personal property to take place after a person's death.

Testamentary pertains to a will. It is often used in combination with other words—testamentary trustee, testamentary guardian, testamentary capacity.

Title, in the law of property, is the evidence of a person's right to possession and ownership of property.

Tort is a wrong committed upon the person or property of another, other than the violation of a contract.

Trade name is an appellation by which a person or persons are known in business; it functions as trade protection.

Treason, in criminal law, is the offense of attempting to overthrow the government or to betray the government into the hands of a foreign power.

Trespass is an unlawful injury to another's person or property by force or violence.

Trial is a judicial examination of a controversy.

True bill, in criminal law, is a bill of indictment handed down by a grand jury against an accused person, although technically it may be an endorsement of the bill of indictment by members of a grand jury and state that they are satisfied with the truth of the accusation.

Trust is the holding of property by one person for the benefit of another. The person who holds the property is called the *trustee*; the beneficiary is called the *cestui que trust*. A *constructive trust* is one arising out of operation of law. An *express trust* is usually in writing and definite in terms. An *implied trust* is created by implication of law. A *passive trust* is one in which the trustee has no active duties to perform. A *totten trust* is created by one person when he deposits money in a bank in his own name as trustee for another.

Trust ex maeficio is a type of constructive trust arising out of misconduct or breach of faith by a person entrusted with property.

Trust receipt is a written instrument whereby a lender who has advanced money for the purchase of property delivers possession of the property to the borrower on the agreement that the borrower will hold the property in trust for the lender until he is paid in full.

Ultra vires (Latin) describes the action of a corporation when it oversteps the powers conferred on it by its charter or by the statutes under which it was incorporated.

Undertaking, in legal procedure, generally refers to a bond or other security which must, by law, be furnished before certain legal steps may be taken.

Undue influence is wrongful persuasion which overpowers a person's will and causes him to do something that he would not have done of his own volition.

Unemployment compensation is money paid to unemployed persons by the government from funds created in large part by employers' contributions.

Uniform laws are those which have been approved by the National Conference of Commissioners on Uniform State Laws and which have been adopted by all or some of the states.

Unilateral contract designates a legal agreement in which one party promises to do certain things without receiving in return any promise of performance from the other party. Such a contract differs from a bilateral contract through which both parties enter into mutual promises.

Unjust enrichment designates a situation by which one person profits unequitably at another's expense.

Unmarketable title refers to a substantially defective title to real estate which raises serious doubt that future purchasers would accept the title.

Usury consists of charging an illegal rate of interest.

Vagrancy is a minor criminal offense. It is a manner of living rather than a single act and consists of wandering from place to place without any apparent means of support.

Vendor is a person who sells real estate.

Venireman designates a member of a panel of jurors.

Venue is the place designated for the trial of a legal proceeding.

Verdict is the decision of a jury.

Verification, in legal pleadings, is an affidavit swearing that a writing is true.

Void designates that something is a nullity and has no legal effect; hence it cannot be confirmed or ratified.

Voidable refers to matter which may be declared void but which is valid until judicially found to be void.

Voting trust is an agreement among stockholders of a corporation that control of the stock shall be vested in a trustee.

Waiver is the relinquishing of a right. A waiver may be written or it may be inferred from a course of conduct which indicates that a person intends to abandon or surrender his legal rights.

Ward, in the law of guardianship, means an infant or person of unsound mind whose interest is represented and protected by a guardian.

Warehouse receipt is a written evidence of title given by a warehouseman for goods received by him for storage.

Warrant (verb) means to assure that certain facts are true.

Warrant (noun) is a document directing a public officer to perform certain acts (for example, make an arrest or a search).

Warranty is a promise that a certain statement of fact is true. An *express warranty* is one created by explicit statements. An *implied warranty* is one which the law infers from the nature of the transaction.

Waste is the destructive use of property by one in possession of it.

Witness may refer either to one who is present and observes a transaction (such as a witness to a will) or to one who observes an accident (an eyewitness). It may also refer to an individual who testifies in court.

Writ designates a court order directed to the sheriff or another public officer requiring the performance of a certain act.

Zoning is the division of a municipality into districts for governmental regulation of the use to which buildings or lands may be put.

Index

For definitions of additional terms, see the Glossary, pages 277 to 301.